5,000 GREAT ONE-LINERS

5,000 GREAT ONE-LINERS

COMPILED BY
GRANT TUCKER

The Robson Press

First published in Great Britain in 2012 by
The Robson Press (an imprint of Biteback Publishing Ltd)
Westminster Tower
3 Albert Embankment
London SE1 7SP
Copyright in the foreword and selection © Grant Tucker 2012

ISBN 978-1-84954-403-0

10 9 8 7 6 5 4 3 2

A CIP catalogue record for this book is available from the British Library.

Set in Sabon

Printed and bound in Great Britain by
CPI Group (UK) Ltd, Croydon CR0 4YY

FOREWORD

I have always found one-liners the cleverest form of comedy: the way they can garner a laugh with just a few short words inspires my untold admiration for those who make it an art form. Once a staple of many comedy acts, the one-liner was perfected by two of my personal favourite stand-ups, Bob Monkhouse and Les Dawson. Who can forget Monkhouse's classic "I want to die like my father peacefully in his sleep, not screaming and terrified like his passengers"? Sadly, neither of these comedy legends is still with us today, but their legacy is being continued by a new generation of comedians. I'm sure if Bob or Les were with us now they would look proudly upon modern comics who are helping to introduce young audiences to the beauty of the one-liner. In recent years, the quick-fire gag has enjoyed a resurgence not only among the big-name stars, but also among us ordinary folk, and this is thanks partly to social media. Twitter in particular has given new life to the format, challenging us to condense our jokes to fit the 140-character limit. Some of the funniest one-liners I've ever read have been the creation of the Twitter hive-mind, and have been retweeted and retold around the world, being constantly refined and refreshed along the way.

This book has taken many months to put together, but I hope you will agree it was worth it. It brings together 5,000 of the best one-liners I have ever heard or read, and is designed entirely to make you chuckle. I have picked up these jokes in a huge variety of venues in all parts of the country, from the rugby clubs of Wales to the gentleman's clubs of London, but one thing they all have in common is that they are timelessly funny. I'm sure many of these jokes were told long before I was born, in the corners of pubs up and down the country, so I cannot take credit for them all. What I would rather do is to thank every person who has ever told a joke, every person who has ever made anybody else laugh. Laughter is one of the most beautiful things in the world: it lends colour to our daily life, it helps us get over the most tragic situations, and it can unite people from all different backgrounds, colours and creeds, bringing them together in fits of laughter over a shared experience.

In that spirit, I would like to thank some of the people who have made my life that little bit better through the power of laughter. Namely, my dad, Carl Tucker, who is always the first to crack a joke in any situation; my friend Huw Anslow, who has the ability to turn the most serious moments into a joke; my friend Ryan Bourne, whose impressions will forever keep me entertained; and my work colleague Holly Smith: all I need to do is look at her and she can make me laugh. Jeremy Robson, my publisher, also deserves a special mention. He is one of the best in the publishing business, but despite that he is also one of the nicest people you could ever wish to meet.

Finally, I would like to thank my long-suffering editor Olivia Beattie for her patience during this mammoth project. I can't imagine it was as much fun for her to edit this book as it was for me to write it. But despite several deadline extensions, and numerous changes, she has created a brilliant book out of what was originally a quite incomprehensible manuscript!

I do hope that this book gives you the same entertainment and moments of laugh-out-loud hilarity that it gave me when writing it.

Grant Tucker
London, August 2012

THE JOKES

I just bought an alcoholic ginger beer. He asked for strong lager, but I don't want to encourage him.

A vicar was booking into a hotel, and he asked the receptionist: 'I trust the pornography channel is disabled, young man?' 'No,' replied the receptionist, 'it's just regular porn, you filthy bastard.'

There's a new contraceptive pill for men. Put it in your shoe and it makes you limp.

A teacher at the school for obese children has been sacked for taking cocaine. He was given away by his massive pupils.

My wife's leaving me for two reasons: 1. Premature ejaculation; 2. My terrible memory. I don't know what's come over her.

As a musician, I hate the key of E minor. It gives me the E-B-G-Bs.

I met a French guy on holiday and he forced me to start drinking and smoking. Bloody Pierre Pressure.

My wife texted me after a row to say I was very condescending. To be honest I was surprised she could spell it.

In prison, I dropped the soap in the shower. I was so scared about all the stories, I was shitting myself... Put them right off.

I took the wife bungee jumping. As her body hit and spread out over the rocks below, I thought, 'That'll teach you to lie about your weight.'

If a fat kid falls in the forest, and there's no one around to see it, is it still hilarious?

Last night a hypnotist convinced me I was a soft, malleable metal with an atomic number of eighty-two. I'm easily lead.

I did an exam about marriage today. I answered every question with, 'The Wife' and failed. Turns out she's not always right.

Doctor: 'OK, Mrs A, let's have a look at your results.' Patient: 'My name isn't Mrs A.' Doctor: 'I have some bad news then. It appears you have MRSA.'

My wife has just delivered twin boys and let me name them. From her reaction, I'm guessing 'Pete' and 'Repeat' wasn't the best choice.

I'm sick of all the shit on the TV these days. Although it's probably my fault for putting the birdcage there in the first place.

My girlfriend said that I'm annoying. I was so stunned I stopped poking her.

My missus says she hates the way I narrate every situation, and here she comes now.

I was enjoying a brilliant singalong last night, until I was asked to leave the opera.

Chickens: the only animals you eat before they're born and after they're dead.

My wife says I exaggerate the amount of time I work so that I don't have to spend time with her. I'd like to see her work twelve days a week, 576 days a year.

My wife's got a cracking pair of jugs... So we're taking them back to John Lewis to get a refund.

I love Facebook. It's the only place where I can talk to a wall and not look like an idiot.

Did you hear about the band who were due to play a concert against teenage pregnancies? They pulled out at the last second.

Sky News: 'Whale washes up on beach.' Surely that's Sea News?

If I had a pound for every time I leave something unfinished,

My wife said she's leaving because of my Facebook addiction. I didn't like her comment.

Everybody has an ego. Mine's just bigger... and better.

Bulbs are gay. Just a bit of light humour, there.

I'm not a big fan of shopping centres. Once you've seen one, you've seen the mall.

World's shortest joke: two women were sitting quietly.

Never kiss a newborn baby. You don't want to know where it's been.

Predictive text is for aunts.

My friend's going to attempt a world record for the world's longest wank. I think he might just pull it off.

Some girl asked me, 'Do you believe in coincidences?' I replied, 'Are you kidding? I was about to ask you the same question.'

I've just seen my neighbour sunbathing topless in the garden. I've never seen tits that big in all my life. He really needs to go on a diet.

There's a fine line between hyphenated words.

There's a gang going through our town, systematically shoplifting clothes in size order. The police believe they're still at large.

An elephant says to a naked man, 'You poor creature – how can you possibly drink through that tiny thing?'

A man goes into a library and asks, 'Do you have a book on how to deal with rejection without killing?' 'N... umm, let me check in the back.'

At what age is it appropriate to tell my dogs that they're adopted?

Irony: telling someone to 'get a life' on Facebook.

My wife is a great lover ... of cakes.

At school I was often accused of eavesdropping. I just wish they'd had the guts to say it to my face.

Ivory hunters, tsk tsk.

The average bloke thinks about sex once every six tits.

I don't buy fat-free milk, because I don't want to encourage cows with negative body image issues.

I was looking at smoking pipes online when I realised that my boss could check my history and make me do a drugs test. So I Googled Sherlock Holmes hats.

If I had a penny for every time I heard a bad terrorist joke... You guessed it... That £9.11 would be in my wallet right now.

'For Pete's sake, I'm getting sick and tired of you accusing me of cheating on you,' said my wife. 'Who's Pete?' I replied.

Strangely, my wife wasn't happy at all when I gave her a ring on our wedding day. Perhaps I should have texted her instead.

I thought I'd forgotten how to play Tetris, but once I started all the pieces seemed to fall into place.

My fat wife started crying because the airline made her book two seats. I said, 'Yes, but you'll get two meals.' That cheered her right up.

I've just bought an earthquake detection stone. You place it on the ground and if there is an earthquake it jumps up and down.

'You know why it's called *Jackass*?' complained my girlfriend. 'Because only jackasses like you watch it.' 'That must be why you watch *Loose Women* then.'

I've set up a charity called 'Tourette's Welfare and Treatment'. All we need is an acronym, and we're good to go.

I went on a bus tour yesterday – what a rip-off. £10 just to look round a double-decker.

Eskimos eat whale meat and blubber. I'd blubber too if I had to eat whale meat.

I made my girl's wishes come true when we got married in a castle. Although you wouldn't have thought it from her face as we were bouncing around.

My girlfriend was telling me that obesity is in her genes. I told her that can't be true: she looks fat in a skirt as well.

When I was at school I belonged to a gang called the Secret Seven. We were sworn to secrecy. We were so good that I never found out who the other six were.

I've got the memory of an elephant. I remember one time I went to the zoo and saw an elephant.

National Geographic +1... Where lightning does strike twice.

Last night my wife called me a lazy bastard. I almost fell off my stairlift.

My wife said she's leaving me because I always relate everything to Batman. What a joker.

Local headline: 'Man jailed in fake washing powder scam.' Obviously they are trying to deter gents like him.

Just found out how to grow four inches in four weeks. It really does work! Regards, Pinocchio.

Adam speaks out. Claims eviction from Garden of Eden was because of forbidden apple – iPods aren't allowed on the premises.

I dispute those studies that claim people often die from smoking. My uncle smoked, and he only died once.

Getting hit in the balls is more painful than giving birth. Proof: guys don't want to be hit in the balls, but women want to give birth.

My wife said she's leaving me because I'm 'not an effective communicator'. I'll email her about it tomorrow.

Sex is like music. For every person who pays for it, there are thousands more getting it for free.

My wife got worried when she noticed the M I L and F buttons on my keyboard were wearing off... I just told her I was a film fanatic.

I went to an Italian restaurant, and they had spaghetti on the menu. So I had to call the waiter to wipe it off.

Despite being on the contraceptive pill, my girlfriend keeps getting pregnant. I might as well just not bother taking them.

I want to get a tattoo, but I don't want to get something that's going to look stupid when I'm older. So I'm getting 'World's Sexiest Grandpa'.

My wife won't stop going on at me for spending thirty quid on a fake Rolex. Really, she hasn't stopped nagging me since 1.83 o'clock.

I never question myself. Why should I start now?

I was watching some kids TV earlier. 'Who are you and why are you in my bedroom?' he asked.

I had a wet dream. I fell asleep in the bath.

I got sacked as the tour guide of the Vatican City. As I was talking about the Pope, we turned a corner and I said, 'Ah, speak of the devil.'

I've decided to pimp my car. I'm going to rent it out so people can have sex with it.

I bought a parrot last week because I thought it'd be cool to have a pet that could talk. But it couldn't say 'I'm hungry', so it died.

I just bought a vibrating cock ring. Now my chickens refuse to fight.

My wife asked me if I'd put the cat out. I didn't know it was on fire.

Just given my nan a cream pie... And this proves that porn has damaged your mind forever.

How do you torture a homosexual? Throw him into a bottomless pit.

A man walks into a library and asks for a book about disappointing jokes. The librarian points him towards the book he is looking for.

I don't understand fast food. I've been eating it for years but I seem to be getting slower and slower.

My wife said she's going to leave me. But she is going to make sure that my bank balance is £0. That's nice of her, paying off my overdraft.

What do you call a Mexican with a rubber toe? Roberto.

I surprised my girlfriend during sex the other night with a little move I like to call 'coming home early'.

I can't believe Google is cocky enough to start guessing after one letter.

What is the biggest lie ever? 'I have read and agreed to the terms of use.'

I tried to hang myself the other day, but it was taking ages. The suspense was killing me.

It's annoying when fat people say obesity 'runs' in their family. Clearly nothing runs in their family.

Man to woman: 'Have you ever had sex?' Woman: 'That's my business!' Man: 'Ah, a professional.'

I was only young when I learned to count. It was odd at first, even then.

I've noticed that if you're scared of spiders they always turn up in your bedroom. Using that logic, I'm scared of blonde girls with big boobs.

Self-service checkouts: making shoplifting 'a mistake' since 2008.

I can't wait for my daughter's first birthday. She's getting a PS3 with CoD and the night-vision goggles. Spoilt little bugger.

My colleague just told me, 'If the boss doesn't take back what he said to me, I'm leaving the company.' 'What did he say?' 'Leave the company.'

I was an hour late for work this morning. I apologised to the boss and promised to make up for it by leaving an hour early.

A neutron walks into a bar and says to the barman, 'How much for a pint?' To which the barman replies, 'For you, no charge.'

I thought I found a mass snowman grave the other day. Turns out it's just a field of carrots.

They say the early bird catches the worm. On the other hand, the early worm gets eaten.

Sometimes I watch football holding an Xbox controller just to screw with my mum's head.

I got kicked out of my local record store after enquiring about a Coldplay song. I only went in looking for 'Trouble'.

Behind every fat girl there is a beautiful woman. No, seriously, you're in the way.

My wife told me I was immature and needed to grow up... So guess who's not allowed in my tree house now.

The new version of Pac-Man is so awesome, it comes with a search engine built into it.

They say that one in five friends have difficulty sleeping. Took me all night but I've narrowed it down to Ollie or Steve.

I was out on a double date last night. Although I don't really think he looked much like me.

I'm doing my bit for global warming. I've taken the door off my fridge.

My son told me he was gay. So I bought him a straightjacket.

My wife said she's leaving me because my eyesight is shit and I can't see anything. I nearly dropped my linesman flag.

What do you call a sleepwalking nun? A roaming Catholic.

There are people who think you should drink more and there are people who say you should drink less. They both share a common opinion: you should drink.

I married a girl who said she didn't believe in sex before marriage. With hindsight I should have made sure that she believed in sex after marriage.

My nephew got a lip piercing behind my back today, and I was furious. Ridiculous place for him to stand while I'm casting my fishing rod.

I've changed my Facebook name to 'Nobody Actually'. Just to screw with people's heads when I like their statuses.

What's all this fuss about 3DTV all of a sudden? My TV's always been three-dimensional.

There are two types of people I hate: 1. People who find a way of putting animals into words when they aren't actually there. And 2. Hippocrites.

They say you should find a girl who's 1/1000000. I'd much rather wait for one who's at least 8/10 though.

Star Wars: A very long time ago, but somehow still in the future.

Many people are worrying about the affects of genetically modified crops. 'There is no proof of any adverse affects,' said one carrot.

I don't understand why people are worried about erectile dysfunction... I mean, it can't be that hard.

I hate when I wish on a star only to realise afterward that I just wished on an aeroplane.

I didn't know how to spell 'plagiarised' so I copied and pasted it.

Nine out of ten doctors agree that 10 per cent of people with PhDs love to contradict their colleagues.

I should have known I'd never last as a deep-sea diving instructor. I'm no good under pressure.

My grandfather's a little forgetful, but he likes to give me advice. One day he took me aside and left me there.

My girlfriend said that when she runs her hands over herself, she's got lumps and mounds of fat that really piss her off. I said, 'I know how you feel.'

My wife said I'm an idiot who can't do the simplest of things right. So I packed her bags and left.

Some guy came up to me in a club and said, 'I get twenty times more girls than you do – haha.' I said, 'Twenty times zero equals zero.' That shut him up.

I wanted to propose to my girlfriend over the phone. So I gave her a ring.

Serving time in prison can sometimes be described as 'a stretch on the inside'. I wonder where that phrase originated...?

My wife just told me she wanted to have a baby. I didn't have the balls to tell her I was castrated.

My girlfriend just texted me to say that she has just stuck a whole lemon up her pussy. That might not seem like a big deal but she's dyslexic.

Typical Americans, making a national holiday out of a Will Smith film.

'Doctor! Doctor! I think I'm invisible!' 'Who said that?'

Sky News: 'Pilot grounded after failed breath test.' I'm not really sure his parents should get involved.

I can't believe pretzels are knot bread.

Make it look like you have an iPad by drawing the Internet onto an Etch-a-Sketch.

As I said before, I never repeat myself.

I love social networks that allow people to instantly upload their holiday photos. As a professional burglar, it makes my job a lot easier.

OCD sufferers: their days are numbered.

Do cross eyed teachers have trouble controlling their pupils?

I needed to measure my waist, but I couldn't find the tape measure anywhere. In the end I just shoved a ruler up my arse and multiplied it by pi.

According to Einstein, $E = MC^2$. For me, E = a great night out.

I said to my mate, 'My cat can say her own name!' He said, 'That's amazing! What's she called?' 'Meow.'

The wife said she's sick of me 'always being right'. So I left.

People who confuse the metaphorical and the factual make my head literally explode.

My mate just got sacked from his quality control job at the match factory. He was standing at the production line going, 'This one works ... and this one ... and this one...'

A conspiracy theorist walks into a bar... Or so the government would have us believe.

My wife left me the other day, apparently because I'm 'too formal'. So I sent her a letter of complaint.

My mate S-S-S-Steve has a bit of a stammer. I sent him to the shop to get some Maltesers. He came back with M&Ms.

If it weren't for marriage, men would spend their lives thinking they had no faults at all.

I hate living in the Tetris flats. Someone moved into the empty apartment next door, and the entire floor disappeared.

They should ban semi-colons; no one knows how to use them.

I'm not the jealous type. I wish I was, though.

The bank says this is my final notice. Isn't it fantastic that they're not going to bother me any more?

It must be really hard to judge a wet T-shirt contest: I saw one recently and all the T-shirts looked equally wet.

Nothing induces as much fear as your girlfriend asking to use your laptop.

A girl just told me I've got a huge ego... I think she meant cock.

I hate people who don't keep their mirrors clean. It reflects really badly on them.

One of the most difficult things in the world is convincing a man that shopping isn't just about buying something.

My diabetic uncle used to beat me as a child, and I always swore I would get him back for it. Revenge will be sweet.

British summer: six weeks of warm rain.

The most important thing in a relationship is trust. If you don't trust your girlfriend, how do you know she's not going to tell your wife?

Suicide is never the answer. Unless the question is, 'What rhymes with "muicide"?'

Police were called to a daycare centre today. A two-year-old boy was resisting a rest.

My wife asked me to buy a baby bouncer. I came back with a little fat kid in a suit.

Sky News: 'Darth Vader caught on CCTV robbing New York bank.' Now he's running from the force.

The male penis is the lightest object on earth. Just a thought can lift it.

I was in the gym earlier and I decided to jump on the treadmill. People were giving me weird looks, so I started jogging instead.

I fell in love with my girlfriend at second sight... At first sight I didn't see that she owned an Audi R8.

Past, Present and Future walked into a bar. It was tense.

My wife says I blame other people too easily and never take responsibility for my own actions. It's not my fault though – it runs in my family.

The party was going well at my house until someone smashed the Ouija board. That's when all hell broke loose.

My mate just told me that he's been diagnosed with HIV. I promised I wouldn't tell anyone. In fact, we both pricked our fingers and made a blood oath.

BBC News: 'Pilot walks away from serious crash.' What a bastard. You'd think he would have helped out.

I asked my mate the other day, 'Where's your mum from?' He replied, 'Alaska.' I said, 'Don't worry, I'll ask her myself.'

My dog was just getting used to not getting fed... Then he died.

My maths teacher recently asked me what comes after sixty-nine. Apparently 'I do' is not the correct answer.

...Anything you do say may be given in evidence... 'DON'T HIT ME AGAIN, OFFICER.'

Abortion: it really brings out the child in you.

'My girlfriend has a stalker.' 'Oh wow, that's terrible. I didn't even realise you had a girlfriend.' 'I don't.'

I saw a kid earlier with a hairy face and horrible beady eyes. Saying that, I suppose it's normal for a goat.

My granddad suffers from Alzheimer's. It's his birthday next week, so I've bought him a memory card.

Can anyone tell me what concise means? Please be short, brief and to the point.

Paddy says to Murphy, 'If you can guess how many doughnuts I've got in this bag, I'll give you both of them.'

I have two brothers. Well, three actually, but one has learning difficulties so he can't count.

The police have banned me from driving, but I thought it was perfectly legal to drive after only having six points. Or 'pints' as the police spelt it.

I don't celebrate Father's Day. I'm such a bastard.

Spelling yllistsuj backwards is just silly.

My gran always used to say that, 'No news is good news.' No surprise that she was soon sacked from her job as a journalist.

A survey has shown that smoking is one of the leading causes of statistics.

I kicked the kid from downstairs in the face as I thought he was spying on my wife. Turns out he just got a new trampoline.

I've been working out to impress my girlfriend. But apparently quadratic equations aren't much of a turn on.

In an effort to be a gentleman, I held the door open for my girlfriend. Five minutes later she said, 'Can you please get lost while I'm trying to have a shit.'

I need to make a pencil drawing of Shakespeare for my art exam. 2B or not 2B?

BBC News: 'Man survives fall out of forty-storey building.' Let me guess, he was on the ground floor, right?

I've just seen a kidnapping outside my house. So I threw water over him – that woke the little fucker up.

Sports news: 'Cricket declares war on cheaters.' What a brave little insect, taking on all those big cats single-handedly.

Sometimes life throws you a curve ball and you just don't know enough about baseball to finish the metaphor...

A golfer came home in a bad mood. 'I only hit two good balls today,' he moaned, 'and that was when I stood on a rake.'

A reporter interviewed a millionaire and asked what he was before getting married. He replied, 'A billionaire.'

My wife was getting ready to go out and she said to me, 'Do my tits look square to you?' I said, 'You're supposed to take the tissues out of the box.'

Air freshener: because there's no louder way of telling the whole house that you've just had a shit.

Breaking news: 'Bomb defuser has fingers blown off by friendly explosion.' He's not pressing charges.

My wife is leaving me because apparently I'm not 'man enough'. Well, at least now I can watch Glee without her changing the channel.

The bishop came to our church today, but I think he was an impostor. He never once moved diagonally.

Man, I'm tired... I stayed up all night trying to remember if I have amnesia or insomnia.

Police are looking for a man who robbed an off-licence using scissors. They say the guy could be a real danger... Unless you have a rock.

How did I get out of Iraq? Iran.

Last night I was so drunk that when I walked across the dance floor to get to the bar, I won the dance competition.

Breaking news: 'British Spy Found Murdered Near MI6 HQ.' This is bullshit: according to my satnav that postcode doesn't even exist.

I just drank some WKD with ice in it. It was wicked.

You know your team is shit when the highlight of the game was a bird sitting on the goal.

'Man up': a simple phrase to make your friends do stupid things.

News headline: 'Chocolate Linked to Depression.' Especially for those people that are depressed about their weight.

A teacher beat a pupil around the head while shouting, 'Die, die, die.' That'll teach him for not knowing what the singular of 'dice' is.

'And what's the lady having?' asked the waiter, while my wife was in the toilet. 'I don't know,' I replied. 'Probably a wee.'

My girlfriend complained that I'm a childish geek. So I slapped her and said, 'Biff!' then punched her and said, 'Kapow!'

The new Internet Explorer is out. Which means I can download a new browser even faster now.

Teacher: 'Simon, can you say your name backwards?' Simon: 'No Mis.'

Irony: not having the balls to shave your balls.

People think that I'm a good mind-reader.

Trying to be funny is like trying to force a fart – it never turns out quite as you expect and you'll likely have to leave the room.

Had a serious row with my wife the other day. We never make jokes in the boat.

BBC News: 'Spelling mistakes "cost millions".' Or is that 'billions'? Guess we'll never know.

I've just bought a transparent megaphone. Now everyone can hear me loud and clear.

My boxing instructor can't throw a punch to save his life. But he sure knows his stuff when it comes to cardboard packaging.

I've just bought a load of cheap Harry Potter DVDs, only two Quidditch.

If women ruled the world, a country would get bombed every twenty-eight days.

Two gypsy fortune-tellers meet on the street: 'You're fine, how am I?'

For a cheap laugh when walking through town, it's always funny to bump into someone in a camouflage jacket and say, 'Sorry, didn't see you there.'

If you hit me at thirty, there is a 100 per cent chance I'm shit at blackjack.

I've been trying to teach my dog to dance, but he's kind of useless. He's got two left feet.

My wife said she was leaving me because of my lack of vocabulary. I was lost for words.

I just met this amazing girl, but we couldn't go back to hers because she still lives with her parents. Mine isn't much better though: I still live with my wife.

I was doing some decorating, so I got out my step-ladder. I don't get on with my real ladder.

It's hard to explain how good I am at describing things.

Me and the wife decided to make our own sex tape. She was pissed off when I started holding auditions for her part.

Sex is for people who can't afford Xbox Live membership.

'Man jailed for assaulting a fortune-teller who predicted he'd go to jail...'

The man who invented Chinese Whispers has died. Pass it on.

What happens if you get addicted to rehab?

My wife is a self-harmer. She eats her own cooking.

I love being schizophrenic. I managed to do a Mexican wave all by myself today.

Putting the clocks forward seems like a complete waste of time.

Prison walls are never built to scale.

Long-distance relationships are like fat people: they very rarely work out.

Have you ever found an anagram for the word 'this'? You don't want to, it's shit.

Dear Agony Aunt, My girlfriend says that I never solve my own problems. How do I prove her wrong?

I got into a taxi and started shouting, 'Stop, don't drive, stay here!' 'That type of language won't get you anywhere,' the driver said.

Romeo&Juliet.doc is a play on Word.

I saw a hilarious joke about Alzheimer's by a guy with the same user name as me.

My wife called me a useless druggie today. I almost fell off my unicorn.

I bet the Icelandics were pretty pissed off when Eyjafjallajökull erupted. Well, shift happens.

What do a near-sighted gynaecologist and a puppy have in common? A wet nose.

I'm worried that my addiction to helter-skelters is spiralling out of control.

Some helium floats into a bar and tries to order a drink. The bartender says, 'We don't serve noble gases in here.' The helium doesn't react.

I just lost out in a drag race. My bloody stilettos snapped.

I always take my wife's side no matter what. She is fat enough without eating KFC gravy as well.

I love reunions; they're old school.

I saw someone buying a pair of roller boots today in Aldi. I thought, 'What a cheap skate.'

BBC News: 'Survey shows eight out of ten men have watched porn online.' The other two were too busy to answer.

In-car satnav just said, 'Hold on I had the map upside down.'

Apparently masturbation causes blindness. We'll see about that.

My wife had her period and all I got was this bloody T-shirt.

According to the Guitar Hero loading screen, 'You can look even cooler by using the slider bar!' As if you don't look cool enough already...

I've got no beef with vegetarian food.

My wife's hot... Shame she's fat and sweaty too.

Facebook is a woman. A man would never ask, 'What's on your mind?'

I got in the car with my drug dealer the other day. He drove around slowly for a while, before picking up speed.

I once heard a joke in the toilet. I pissed myself laughing.

My wife said that she was sick of my childish games. As she packed her bags, I told her, 'You can't.' 'Why not?' she asked. 'I didn't say Simon Says.'

My wife claims she's not that fat, but the picture I took of her last Christmas is still printing.

I was recently the subject of a joke. I chickened out of a fight and crossed the road to get away.

In the news today: 'Man arrested over 1982 murders.' You would have thought the police would have caught him after just a few.

Listerine kills 99 per cent of bacteria. Sadly the other 1 per cent of bacteria is the shit that really does the damage.

If a prostitute gets pregnant by a client can she call the National Accident Helpline?

I found a rock yesterday which measured 1,760 yards in length. Must be some kind of milestone.

The car of the year, as voted for by the readers of Woman's Own magazine, is... A blue one.

I was going through airport customs and they asked me, 'Do you have any firearms?' Apparently, 'What do you need?' wasn't the right answer.

My wife said I'm a useless lazy slob and she deserves much better. I said, 'You've woken me at 3 p.m. just to tell me that?'

Breaking news: 'Constipated woman can't poo.' No shit.

I sometimes use phrases that I don't understand, and vice versa.

Don't talk to me about lie detectors. I married one.

Exercise bikes get you nowhere.

What a pregnant teen thinks: my mum is gonna kill me. What the foetus thinks: my mum is gonna kill me.

Golden shower? I'm in if urine.

Studies have shown that smoking cannabis causes short-term memory loss... Next they'll be saying that smoking cannabis causes short-term memory loss.

If anybody steals my identity at least I'll know who to look for.

I popped into the bank to set up a new 'Transvestite Account'. They asked me to provide proof of a dress.

A librarian walks into a bar and asks for a book on irony.

Breaking news: 'Facebook is more popular than porn.' Three words: beach holiday albums.

Just saw the 3D screening of *Harry Potter*. The cinema was completely full of nerds in those Harry Potter glasses.

If women are so obsessed with big cocks, why are they so happy when they make a smaller tampon?

Next time I'm in a lift with four or more strangers I'm going to turn around and say, 'I'm sure you're wondering why I've gathered you all here.'

Breaking news: 'Shark swims ashore in New Jersey.' What? Where the hell did he buy that from?

Two men walk into a bar, and the third one ducks.

Junk: something you keep for years and throw away two weeks before you need it.

The best measure of someone's honesty is the zero adjust on their bathroom scales.

Underwear is for pussies.

Today I took a class on castration. It was all neuter me.

A little girl asked her father, 'Do all fairy tales begin with "once upon a time?"' Her father replied, 'No, some begin with "if elected I promise..."'

Scientists today confirmed today that they are adding a new square to the periodic table. Bu: the element of surprise.

I was going to buy a book on phobias, but I was afraid it wouldn't help me.

What do you call a Chinese man with a video camera? Phil Ming.

My wife was always complaining that nobody phoned her, so I put a 'How's my driving?' sticker on her car. The phone hasn't stopped ringing since.

I was having a row with my girlfriend last night and she accused me of being childish. What does she know? She's just a stinky poo face.

Time to get a new fitness plan. The old one wasn't working out.

As a child I enjoyed reading the *Spot the Dog* books. They were a lot easier than *Where's Wally?*

My wife is always saying that my muscles affect our sex life. I get a lot of ab use.

I have an image of Jesus that pops up on my PC monitor if I leave it idle for ten minutes. It's my screen saviour.

My doctor knew that I was married. When I went for a check-up, he said, 'Have you had sex in the last seven days?' I replied, 'No, my birthday is in July.'

I always try to pull feminists. That way I know they'll pay for half of the meal when we go to dinner.

My wife said that whatever I get her for her birthday, she will wear. So I'm buying her nothing. It's a win-win situation.

When leaving the pub I decided that I was in no condition to drive home. But then I realised I couldn't trust my judgement: I was drunk.

I wonder what Cambridge University Netball Team abbreviate their name to.

How many psychiatrists does it take to change a light bulb? Only one, but the light bulb has really got to want to change.

I asked on Yahoo Questions, 'My font colour is white, how do I change it?' I can't understand why I've had no answers.

My doctor said I have ADD. So he prescribed me SUBTRACT.

I have a fantastic memory. In fact, I can't remember the last time I forgot something.

I keep getting mice in my wheelie bin. Does anyone know how I can get rid of them?

If I had a pound for every time my wife accused me of being unfaithful, I could've bought my girlfriend that necklace she's always wanted.

'All's well that ends well.' Except perhaps for, 'I'm trapped down a...'

My girlfriend's nose is pointed like a triangle. The first time I met her I told her she had acute nose.

What's got wings and sucks blood? Always Ultra.

I hate petty people. I keep a list of who they are.

Things not to say in a taxi: 'I call shotgun.'

Dim light bulbs or bright light bulbs? Watts the difference.

When I was a kid people used to cover me in cream and put a cherry on my head. It was tough being brought up in the gateau.

My wife said she was leaving me because of my obsession with Kit Kats. I tried to calm her down by suggesting we have a break.

A Prius tried to race me from a red light earlier. I totally had it for the first 100 metres, but I can only walk so fast.

How can women can take boiling hot wax, pour it onto their upper thigh, rip the hair out by the root, and yet still be afraid of a spider?

My wife told me she's leaving because of my obsession with health and safety. I said, 'Don't let the door hit you on the way out.'

Statistics show that men prefer to go without intercourse with their wives for five days straight at least once a month. That's bleeding obvious.

I hate the old tramp who lives under the railway bridge. He's my arch enemy.

Child photography. If you misread that, you're a paedophile.

What happened just before the big bang? The big foreplay.

I'm bored of the 'Never had sex with a goat' group. But it's suspicious to quit.

My Chinese mate always tells the truth. Believe Yu-Mi, he never lies.

Why are there no casinos in China? Because the Chinese hate Tibet.

Whenever I say something to my mates, they always expect it to be a joke and wait for the punch line... I hate that.

It's been exactly a year since I stopped smoking. And 364 days since I started again.

Why should I pay for 3D at the cinema when I can get it for free by looking at stuff?

Rats are under rated. Just check your dictionary.

If you have a stutter, don't ask for a Peroni in an Italian restaurant. You'll get a pizza.

Sometimes I enjoy my steak undercooked, but that's rare.

Fourteen per cent of children have ADHD. It used to just be called AD but they decided to upgrade.

My mum said, 'If there was a record for being clumsy, you should have it.' I said, 'Yeah, I broke it.'

Dear Confused Teen Girls: Someone who sparkles and won't have sex with you isn't a vampire, it's a gay guy.

Why do fat chance and slim chance mean the same thing?

Do you want to hear a joke about constipation and dementia? Well, tough shit, I forgot it.

I can play piano with my eyes closed. It sounds really awful though.

I was eating my tea last night when I suddenly thought to myself, 'This milk must be seriously out of date.'

Fat paedophile caught with child pornography images... I guess he just couldn't handle getting rid of his cookies.

My girlfriend dumped me because I 'take things too far'. So I called the police.

I was thinking about robbing this French city. But then I remembered they have nothing Toulouse.

'Politician resigns over secret gay lover.' So he's finally come out of the cabinet, eh?

I'll act my age when I'm sixty-nine.

I just pissed so hard a little bit of laugh came out.

Now they're saying cigarettes can cause rectal cancer. I'll be OK though, I'm always very careful to put them in my mouth.

I've just watched my dyslexic cousin searching for 'Horn Pub' on Google. He's not even old enough to drink.

Knock knock... Who's there? ... The Internet Browsing Authorities ... Knock knock ... knock knock ... knock knock knock.

I accidentally locked my coat hanger in my car today. Luckily for me, I had my keys.

I'm so happy – I think I've found the one. It's right beside the two on my keyboard.

My mum cooked alphabetti spaghetti again. In an act of defiance, I spelt out: 'I won't eat this – learn to cook.' Needless to say, she made me eat my words.

When I masturbate in front of a mirror, I always wear a wig and lipstick... So it doesn't get weird.

Curry: the only food that comes out looking the same as it went in.

How come Mario can smash through bricks, yet he dies when he touches a turtle?

My mate's never had much of an appetite. Yet today he ate a dozen Kinder Eggs whole. He's full of surprises.

Seeing London is easy on the Eye.

Your mum's so fat, when she had a threesome the two guys never even saw each other.

After putting on weight, I lost my job as a Disneyland Donald Duck. I didn't fit the bill.

So I was working in a library and this bloke comes up to me and says, 'Do you have a bookmark?' I said, 'Yes, we have hundreds... But my name's Sean.'

I was named after my father... I don't really like the name 'Dad', though.

I was dancing in a nightclub the other night when my friend called me a wanker. At least I think it was him – I had my sunglasses on at the time.

I've just been robbed by a Teenage Mutant Ninja Turtle. Though ironically, he wasn't wearing a mask so I don't know which one it was.

What's the height of laziness? Sleeping and then dreaming about sleeping.

A friend of mine said that he wanted to improve his golf. I suggested that he should go on a course.

My girlfriend just texted me, saying, 'I want you to get me wet when I get home.' I've got fifteen water balloons ready... I can't wait.

I was attacked by some little ginger boy doing martial arts. It turned out to be the carroty kid.

My friend asked me if I was bulimic the other day. I nearly choked on my finger.

Breaking news: 'UK flights to remain grounded.' The pilots must have really strict parents.

I'm getting sick of all those penis enlargement emails clogging up my inbox. I've told my girlfriend to bloody stop it.

If I had a billion pounds for every time I underestimated, I'd be a millionaire.

All men like to think they are marrying nymphomaniacs. The problem is that after a few years, the nympho leaves but the maniac doesn't.

A detective I know dropped his iPhone today. He cracked the case.

Women find me extremely attractive. The fatter I am, the better. They'll do anything for me and they love me more than they do you. I'm your wallet.

My wife kissed me this morning, so I kissed her back. There was no way I was kissing her face.

Tip for out-of-work actors: pretend you have some work, and hey presto, you're working.

I pay £4,000 for the wife to have a nose job and she's delighted. I treat myself to a £30 hand job and she goes mad.

My missus put on a real XXX show in front of the kids and some mates last night. That's the last time I take her bowling.

Gold: worth its weight in gold.

Just because I'm unemployed doesn't mean that I'm not busy. These mines aren't going to sweep themselves.

My fear of insomnia keeps me awake at night.

My niece isn't obese, she's kidnap-resistant.

I just saw *Toy Story* in 3D... The guy in 4D asked me to take off my hat.

After winning a race, a jockey was found to have given his animal drugs and was disqualified. I bet that took him off his high horse.

When people ask me 'plz' just because it's shorter than 'please', I feel perfectly justified answering 'no' just because its shorter then 'yes'.

It wasn't a bad idea to do trigonometry in the sun. I got a tan.

I told everyone that I won the 'Bullshitter of the Year' award. But no one believed me.

When I'm sad I like to cut myself ... a nice slice of chocolate cake.

I used to be quite good at wordplay. Once a pun a time.

I'm planning a remake of *The Never-Ending Story*. It starts with me asking my wife, 'How was work?'

Did you know 'emas eht yltcaxe' is exactly the same spelt backwards?

I've decided I want to know you a whole lot better. Let's start with your bank details.

Breaking news: 'Disability cheat caught skydiving.' Wouldn't it have been easier to make the arrest on the ground?

My wife sent me shopping today. She told me to go and buy something that'll make her look sexy. I came back with two litres of vodka and a keg.

You think seven years is bad for breaking a mirror? Try breaking a condom.

When I was young my mother said I could be anything I wanted to and that the sky was the limit. Which was a bit shit, because I wanted to be an astronaut.

Before I go home from work, I always make sure that I turn everything off. Which is probably why I lost my job as a doctor.

If you live to be one hundred, you've got it made. Very few people die past that age.

My electrician mate accidentally blew the power to the ice-cube factory next door. The company has gone into liquidation.

I told my wife not to turn her head away after giving me a blowjob, but she didn't listen. It went in one ear and out the other.

If you're using public transport, never give up your seat to an old lady. That's how my uncle lost his job as a bus driver.

The other day I went to the toilet. Or was it... Oh yeah, the other day I had diarrhoea... Sorry, I can't remember the joke. It had a shit ending anyway.

My mum always said, 'Never do anything that you'll regret later in life.' I thought it was great advice. So I got it tattooed on my forehead.

I texted my mate the other day to ask who his favourite composer is. Surprisingly, he didn't text Bach.

Breaking news: 'Rare Picasso sells for £106 million.' Who the hell would pay that for a Citroën?

Not impressed by these so-called long-life light bulbs. We kitted out Granddad's whole house with them and he still died.

Me and the wife tried swinging. But she just sat on her fat arse and I ended up doing all the pushing.

I hate the fact that I'm not allowed to celebrate St George's Day. Since magic mushrooms have been illegal I can never find any dragons to kill.

Hey kids, why don't you try a new social networking tool? It's called 'outside'.

My nephew just called me to say that he got over 100 per cent in seventeen of his GCSEs. The only one he failed was maths.

As my late father always said, get a decent watch.

My password is MickeyMinnieGoofyPluto. Because it has to be at least four characters.

I'm so hot even my dad calls me sun.

Fox is so twentieth century.

If you stand by the sea, it sounds like putting a shell to your ear.

I want to be able to edit some of the most watched porn videos to add the sound of a car door closing randomly in the middle.

I miss my umbilical cord. I grew attached to it.

Golf: the only sport where foursomes are encouraged, you can show off your wood, you can polish your balls and it's OK to have a short shaft.

I've recently got a job as a shepherd and it's so tiring. I can't even count my flock without falling asleep.

I just read that iPhone users have more sex than Blackberry users. Should I worry that my girlfriend has an iPhone and I have a Blackberry?

Dear Student Loan, Thank you for saving my life. I can't think how I can ever repay you.

How can it be considered stealing when the Wi-Fi signal is trespassing in my house?

I wonder how many mime artists have died because nobody believed they were choking?

How do you stop a child wetting the bed? Electric blanket.

My mates call me gay because I can't stay on a skateboard for longer than a minute. I'd like to see them try it with high heels on.

I went to this new French restaurant on a blind date. She had frog's legs and chicken breasts but her personality was absolutely fantastic.

My older brother just called me a moron. I'm going kick his arse when I'm older than him.

I'm fed up with my boss forcing me to stand on one leg every single day. Tomorrow I'm putting my foot down.

I'm about to have a cup of dangerous coffee. Safe tea first though.

Reasons I don't feel bad about illegally downloading music: 1. MTV Cribs.

To protect yourself from identity theft, steal someone else's identity. Lightning doesn't strike twice.

My mate asked if I wanted to play electric shock Monopoly. I jumped at the Chance.

I'm not paranoid, but I'm sure people think I am.

Some guy knocked on my door and asked me if I've ever considered an alternative energy supplier. I said, 'No, I'm quite happy with food.'

Kids can be so irresponsible. In fact, that applies to all goats.

This angry looking copper just came up to me and said, 'Give me your name.' I said, 'Why, what's wrong with yours?'

Please tell your boobs to stop looking at my eyes.

Windmills: big fan; big, big fan.

People say I'm a sex addict. Well, they can suck my dick.

My wife laughed at me earlier when I slipped on a banana skin. In my defence, I didn't have any condoms on me.

Dear Cash for Gold, Here is a ring. Please save me from myself. Yours gratefully, Frodo Baggins.

My friends say I'm too easy to please. I was delighted when they told me.

I just read a list of '100 things to do before you die'. I'm pretty surprised 'yell for help' wasn't one of them.

I walked into HMV and the assistant said, 'Good morning.' I said, 'You too.' He said, 'Second aisle, first shelf on the left.' Funny guy.

In a cave I found pictures of women's breasts, but when I picked them up, a giant net fell on me. Damn booby trap.

I get nervous whenever people talk about sex, so I always change the topic of conversation to maths. Standard deviation really.

Today, my boss told me to 'take a note'. So I flicked through his wallet and grabbed a fifty.

Someone once told me that the camera adds 10lb. Which is why I didn't pack it in my suitcase.

Some people have a portrait gallery. The Queen has a stamp collection.

One of the most difficult things in the world is to convince a woman that even a bargain costs money.

You know that look you get from women when they want you? Nah, me neither.

So Apple are making an announcement tonight. Maybe they're going to merge with Blackberry and launch their new 'Crumble'.

I think the highlight of my life was climbing Mount Everest. It was all downhill from there.

Women bake cookies. Men delete them.

I asked my girlfriend to record something for me on ITV2+1. She recorded ITV3.

I went to see the doctor to see if he had anything I could take for my kleptomania.

Maybe it's Maybelline... Or maybe it's Photoshop.

I hear the gay channel have dropped the soap awards tonight.

My wife just said she left me four weeks ago because of how unobservant I am.

All my life I've wanted to be somebody. It is now clear that I should have been more specific.

While driving yesterday I saw a banner over the road saying 'The Influence'. Then the police pulled me over for driving under it.

I've had to start drug testing all of my employees. Just so I know who I can buy stuff off in the future.

I have a friend who's half Indian. Ian.

I cheated on my blonde girlfriend and she found out. Which made her unsure if the baby was hers.

My doctor told me that I had to give up drinking. It's been three days now and I feel really dehydrated.

Statistically, three in one people have schizophrenia.

People call me Mr Compromise. It wasn't my first choice for a nickname, but I can live with it.

A postman came to my door and said, 'Is this letter for you? The name is smudged.' I said, 'No, my name is Bob.'

Another morning dawns and once again I've woken up with the woman of my dreams. I'm a lucky man. Best get home before the wife wakes up.

Regular naps prevent ageing. Especially if you take them while driving.

The supermarket has stopped selling tropical fruit! It's enough to make a mango crazy.

People learn from history. Which is why you should always delete it before your girlfriend uses the computer.

Whenever I see a virgin I think, 'Wow!' Or World of Warcraft, to give it its full name.

My friends say I'll believe anything. Damn, I suppose they're right.

My wife's leaving me because she's apparently fed up of me 'quoting her all the time'.

When the shit hits the fan ... your fetishes have gone too far.

They say a picture paints a thousand words. That's my dissertation finished.

My mate told me that I just don't understand irony. Which was ironic because we were at a bus stop at the time.

How long a minute is depends on what side of the bathroom door you're on.

My wife kicked me out so I've been living in a telephone box. I just wanted somewhere to call home.

I saved loads of cash on the new iPhone yesterday. I didn't buy one.

When people ask me what my best qualities are, I always tell them my second-best quality is being mysterious.

I turned up at a fancy dress party dressed as a football. I was immediately kicked out.

If you quit rehab, does that mean it worked?

I just saw a beautiful girl with a massive gut. What a waist.

Hey Timex, if I end up 660ft under water, I'm pretty sure I won't need a watch.

My girlfriend said I was awful in bed so, as a treat for her, some very nice women have been helping me train to get better.

Note to vegetarians: plants are living things too, they're just easier to catch.

My wife found loads of animal porn on our computer, but I think I got away with it. I blamed the dog.

My friend is sick to death of people always taking the piss out of him for having brittle bone disease. One day he's going to snap.

Is there anything more terrifying than that moment when you're watching porn with headphones in and they come unplugged?

I completely agree with sex before marriage. How else would I know that my brother's future wife is good enough for him?

I think it's time for me to start making my own decisions. Or maybe not. What do you think I should do?

My wife said she was going to leave me if I didn't stop being so sarcastic. I really I should have thought of a better response than 'Oooooh, I'm soooo scared.'

I should have known getting married was a mistake. After I said 'I do', the vicar looked at her and then asked me if that was my final answer.

Me: 'If only the man upstairs could have blessed you with brains as well as beauty...' My girlfriend: 'Why the hell is there a man upstairs?'

The judge has got a stutter, so it doesn't look like I'm getting a sentence.

I'm so good at sleep, I can do it with my eyes closed.

I was thinking of writing a book, *A Guide to Better Shoplifting* – but who the hell is going to buy it?

My wife said I'm full of my own self-importance. Anyway that's enough about her...

I've just bought some ghost-shaped laxative tablets. They scare the shit out of me.

Breaking news: '*Saw* most successful horror film.' Are they going to tell us which film they saw?

I heard rumours about my wife having sex behind an Italian restaurant. I wouldn't put it pasta.

A dog's bark may be worse than his bite, but everyone prefers his bark.

Bored shopping with the wife? Then get a tub of ketchup and leave a trail from the entrance to the tampon section.

My car's so crap that the resale value goes up and down depending on how much petrol is in it.

Today I was conned into buying two fake entry tickets to Alton Towers. I thought I was going to be taken for a ride.

Do you know how annoying it is when people answer their own questions? Very.

Why don't autobiographies ever end with the person writing a book?

I told a volcano joke down the pub last night. The whole place erupted.

Little Jimmy says to his mum, 'When I grow up I want to be a man.' Mum says, 'Don't be silly, you can't do both.'

A Chinese couple are in bed. The husband says, 'I want a sixty-nine.' His wife says, 'You want beef and broccoli now?'

Some people say it's hard being a hostage. Pfft... I could do it with my hands tied behind my back.

I have a stalker. Everywhere I go, she's always there, ten paces ahead of me.

'Coming soon to a cinema near you' ... How do they know where I live?

Your mum's so stupid she went to DFS and bought a full-price sofa.

The easiest time to add insult to injury is when you're signing somebody's plaster cast.

I was arrested today over a slight misunderstanding at work. Apparently taking your work home is classed as theft when you work in a bank.

What do you get when you ask a politician to tell 'the truth, the whole truth and nothing but the truth'? Three different answers.

There are two types of people: those with Alzheimer's.

Last week the candle factory burned down. Everyone just stood around and sang, 'Happy Birthday'.

The problem with the gene pool is that there's no life guard.

I was awarded a medal last week for my modesty. The bastards took it off me today because I wore it.

Rape: small word, but long sentence.

Breaking news: 'Nearly 500 million eggs recalled.' I'd hate to be the guy who has to put them back in the hens.

Summer: the only thing that can come early and not disappoint women.

I don't know why I just bought some new coconut shampoo... I haven't even got any coconuts.

The wife says I don't open up to her. She can try all she likes, that strap-on is going nowhere near my arsehole.

What a load of bollocks those '24-hour' petrol stations are. I only filled up four hours ago and it's already run out.

My mate went to bed a boy, woke up a man. Bloody coma.

Why oh why don't people poof read stuff before posting?

During a geography test, our teacher told us to write down two capitals. 'That's too easy,' I thought, as I wrote 'I I'.

Are you interested in making ££££ fast? Just follow this simple procedure: 1. Open a Word document. 2. Hold down the shift key. 3. Hit the '3' key four times.

For just £10 a month you can reduce your annual salary by £120.

Advert for The Braille Superstore: 'Thousands of Braille products, many of which you've never seen before.'

I played poker last night with an origami expert. Waste of time – he kept folding.

What have the films *The Sixth Sense* and *Titanic* got in common? Icy dead people.

Period pain is for pussies.

I've got gay friends but I'd never let one in my inner circle.

Avalanche: what Italians do every day at about half past twelve.

Just had an awkward time with a prostitute who expected me to take her on a date. She must have misunderstood when I asked if she was free in the morning.

I gave my sister away at her wedding. I stood up and shouted, 'She used to be a man.'

Father to son after exam: 'Let me see your report card.' Son: 'My friend's borrowed it. He wants to scare his parents.'

Did you know? It's impossible to say 'good eye might' without sounding Australian.

How come all the girls on Facebook take so many photos of their mirrors?

I used to go to AA meetings. We would meet up in the pub, get absolutely wasted and not tell each other our names. Anonymous Alcoholics was great.

And that, Romeo, is why we usually try to take a pulse first.

I blew the opportunity of a lifetime last night. No idea why he called his cock that.

After several karate lessons, I can now break a five-inch board with my cast.

All you get when you pick my pocket is practice.

My wife is always accusing me of making stuff up. I wouldn't mind but I'm not even married.

For sale: ten used condoms. No weirdos please.

I can't believe no one has come up with a cure for anorexia yet. Surely it must be a piece of cake.

'Smoking causes lung cancer.' So does having lungs.

I just want to congratulate the Viagra pharmaceutical company for selling over 1 million tablets last month. Keep it up, lads!

My parents have gone to India with some friends. Mumbai? No, she's straight, but I don't think it's that kind of trip anyway.

I've been voted employee of the month for the last fifteen months. Being self-employed has its advantages.

Unwritten rule of the day: don't make eye contact while eating a banana.

I remember the first time I attempted suicide: my whole life flashed before my eyes. But that just reminded me why I needed to try again.

A fly meets another fly on the collar of an American golfer and says, 'What brings you to this neck of the Woods?'

My wife is fed up of my wordplay jokes. I asked, 'What can I do to stop my addiction?' She said, 'Whatever means necessary.' 'No it doesn't,' I said.

I entered a swimming contest at the weekend. I won the 100m butterfly. What the hell am I going to do with an insect that big?

I love my satnav. I don't know where I'd be without it.

I took a Fonzie impersonation class at university. I got straight Eyyyyyyys.

Can you believe it? This guy wins £181 million in the lottery on a Wednesday and then finds the love of his life just two days later. Talk about luck.

I'm a pretty good ventriloquist, even though I say so myself.

My dad told me that a leader is someone who has followers, and the more followers, the greater the leader. Twitter messed that theory up.

I didn't help myself in court yesterday. I was facing child porn charges and the judge said, 'How does five to six years sound?' I said, 'Sexy.'

I just got a notice about an 'outstanding payment' of mine. I don't remember making it, but I'm glad they liked it so much.

There are two words that scare almost every male: Internet history.

I met a hooker last night called Ggetlfoapfoerr. Easier done than said.

Two dragons walk into a bar. One dragon says, 'It's warm in here.' The other says, 'Shut your mouth.'

Snakes: they're like bits of rope, only angrier.

It pains me to say it, but I have a sore throat.

Crystal balls: I don't know what people see in them.

'Dad, can you do my maths homework for me?' 'No son, it wouldn't be right.' 'Well, at least you could try.'

I couldn't believe it when I walked in on my best mate shagging my wife. Finally, I get to take the piss out of him for shagging a fat bird.

My girlfriend came home and said, 'I've got a surprise for you: I'm three months pregnant.' 'I've got a surprise for you,' I said. 'Pack your bags... I'm impotent.'

How do you get a fat policewoman into bed? PC cake.

Just for once I'd like to see a realistic tampon ad. One with a woman sobbing herself to sleep with a half-chewed Mars Bar hanging out of her mouth.

Breaking news: 'Man lucky to be alive after being hit by train.' I think I'm luckier: I've never been hit by a train.

If you're trying to improve your memory, lend someone money.

All we ever do is ask questions... Why?

Everybody says stealing is wrong. Personally I don't buy it.

I'm officially changing my TV remote's name to Wally.

I was arrested yesterday for robbing a boyband CD from a shop, but it was all my mate's fault. He pointed to it and said, 'Take that.'

I am going to make some felt pens. Does anyone have any tips?

I used to date a paedophile. But I was young and naive back then.

There are three things I want to do in my lifetime: 2. Learn to count.

I've just built a working catapult. It's disguised as a chair, so it tends to throw a lot of people.

'Is your husband in?' my neighbour asked my wife. That's the last time we invite her for a threesome.

My wife's leaving me because I spend too much time online. Or at least that's what she just tweeted.

My dad used to say that honesty was the best policy. Bit rich coming from the man who told me about Santa, the Easter Bunny and the Tooth Fairy.

What's the French for dentures? Aperitif.

Next time you eat an egg, just keep in mind... You're eating a chicken's period.

I like making a move on my girlfriend first thing in the morning to help wake her up. I usually start with the suplex.

It's never too late to start. Which is why I'm putting it off till tomorrow.

I have got a bit of a reputation as a ladies' man in my local. All I can say is, they smell so much cleaner than the gents.

A train driver's job is very straight forward.

My girlfriend says I treat her like an object. Don't blame me, love, you're the one who says we're an item.

I procrastinate a lot. I was meant to skip work today but I postponed it till tomorrow.

An old lady was driving at sixty in a thirty zone. When asked why she was going so fast, she replied, 'I had to get there, before I forgot where I was going.'

My wife is so bloody immature. There I was having a bath and she walked in and sank all my boats.

When I walked into the shop, the sign on the door said 'Open'. Now I can't leave, because it says 'Closed'.

Welcome back to the World Masturbation Championship... Still to come...

Apparently, three and a half out of seven people overcomplicate things.

My wife left me because I 'never stand up for myself'. Fair enough.

When I was young my mum told me I could be anybody I wanted to be. It turns out the police call it identity theft.

The only thing the doctor found encouraging about my test results was they weren't his.

I tried to buy my dad a World's Greatest Dad mug for his birthday. The cashier told me that I was too late. Somebody else's dad has already won it.

Did you hear about the ship carrying a consignment of yo-yos? It sank fifty-eight times.

My wife has just told me she wants to get pregnant... But only so she has an excuse for being so fat.

My doctor has advised me to start running. I'm not ill or anything: he's just found out I've been shagging his wife.

All through school I tried to work out what made my teacher tick. Turns out it was correct answers.

My mum found my porn collection in my dad's drawer. Hopefully next time he'll let me use his car.

My mate told me that I should really try out Sky Sports. But I hate Quidditch.

It used to get so heavy carrying matches around. I was over the moon when they invented a lighter option.

I was attacked by a tobacconist. I've still got the cigars to prove it.

How many teenage girls does it take to change a light bulb? Eleven: one to change the light bulb and ten to take photos to put on Facebook.

I watched a documentary about pigs last night. I thought they were pretty boring animals, but it turns out there's a twist in the tail.

It might be the wine talking... But more likely it's Dave, the guy I have locked in my wine cellar.

I've been sent to jail for procrastinating. I'll finish my sentence next month.

I was in a nightclub last night and my mate called me gay. I almost choked on my whistle.

I rate myself 9.84520137453850162 out of 10 for precision.

I wrote a 403-page essay about the Internet. There was another page but I can't find it.

'Best of' albums: for people who are big fans but have never bothered to buy a single album.

Mario condoms: they come in Peach.

My wife said I had to give up drinking, so I joined the AA. It turned out to be the Automobile Association, but either way I'm on the road to recovery.

You know you spend too much time on the PlayStation when the letter 'o' is pronounced 'circle'.

It's never polite to lean over to the next table and ask, 'Are you finished with that?' Especially to a guy breaking up with his girlfriend.

I bought a book called *Beating Addiction* yesterday. I haven't been able to put it down.

I said to my girlfriend, 'Everybody thinks I'm too sarcastic.' She said, 'What makes you say that?' I said, 'My mouth.'

I keep one of Peter Pan's turds with me at all times... That shit never gets old.

I'm not an alcoholic; I just like having an attractive wife.

Who is by far the smartest man in the army? General Knowledge.

Drugs are never the answer. Unless the clue is: 'Narcotics, five letters.'

I'm not fat, I'm just easy to see.

At school I was perfect. I don't know why they made me one; I can't even spell.

I went into the toilet and there was a huge shit in it. I knew right away that it was my dad's: I never forget faeces.

I met this amazing telepathic prostitute the other day. She blew my mind.

Two cows are in a field. One cow says to the other, 'Moo.' The other cow replies, 'Shut the hell up, you uneducated twat.'

Fight fire with fire, that's my motto. That's probably why I got thrown out of the fire brigade.

I lost my dog, and I don't even have collar ID.

My dad never loved me as a child. I can't blame him really. I wasn't born until he was an adult.

The only bad thing about my five-figure salary is the decimal point.

Having fake teeth – that'll denture confidence.

My wife is an absolute animal in bed... She somewhat resembles an elephant.

My wife accused me of being a terrible lawyer. I couldn't defend myself.

I hate conformists. I'm going to join a group of people who feel just the same way.

My wife accused me of overcomplicating things. I suffered a mechanical obstruction of the flow of air from the environment into the lungs.

Man: 'I tried to commit suicide yesterday.' Blonde: 'Did it work?'

I don't care how much it costs, I'm getting laser eye surgery. I can't wait to zap all those people who've pissed me off.

I think animal testing is a terrible idea; they get all nervous and give the wrong answers.

I'm always poking my nose in my mate's business. He's a coke dealer.

I'm sick of being bulimic.

What do you call a bear with no ear? 'B.'

Sometimes I like to find a couple in the supermarket and drop a bottle of anal lube in their trolley. The resulting arguments are priceless.

I know how women feel: I've had some breasts tattooed on my forehead and now it's like, 'Hello, my eyes are down here.'

A gay friend asked me if I liked to blow people. I told him I'm not a fan.

Halloumi – the only cheese that greets itself in the third person.

Being calm is not something I rate.

I don't like giving fat people a lift, because fat people are heavy and I don't have a car.

Tip: if you've forgotten your bluetooth headset, wearing sunglasses indoors is an equally effective twat indicator.

My wife said she had no sleep last night because my snoring kept waking her up. If my snoring was waking her up then she obviously had some sleep.

Major car collision at Spaghetti Junction: twelve injured, four pasta way.

Is it just me, or does hot weather always seem to bring out the breast in women?

Few people know I was an extra in one of the *Harry Potter* movies. I stood up and got into the bloke behind me's pirate copy.

Last night I walked up to a prostitute and asked, 'How much for sex?' She replied, '£250.' I just stood there laughing at her expense.

Tips for a happy marriage: Tools, Internet Options, Delete Cookies, Delete Temporary Internet Files, Delete History.

My wife said she wanted more excitement in the bedroom. So I bought one of those beds that look like a racing car.

Am I right in thinking *The Vagina Monologues* is a period drama?

I think my wife said I'm never certain about anything.

'Hiya' is the worst way you can possibly greet a karate instructor.

How to make Easter easier: replace the 't' with an 'i'.

I'm scared of what the future may bring. That's why I never drive faster than 87mph.

I was shocked when I walked in and saw my son's head between my wife's legs... Luckily, I didn't miss the whole birth.

My wife walked out on me after I blew our life savings on a penis extension. She said she just couldn't take it any longer.

The Prime Minister held a meeting with the Cabinet today. He also spoke to the bookcase and the chest of drawers.

People ask who you'd most like to be stuck in a lift with. Probably the lift engineer.

I sure buy a lot of alcohol. Hope I'm not a shopaholic.

Last night I shot an elephant in my pyjamas. How he got in my pyjamas, I'll never know.

Does Satan get a lot of letters from dyslexic kids at Christmas?

I asked my Welsh mate how many sexual partners he's had. He started counting then fell asleep.

I got an email saying 'At Google Earth we can read maps backwards!' I thought, 'That's just spam.'

You know you take Championship Manager too seriously when you put a suit on to play it.

I've just seen a woman with cigarettes poking out of the front of her stilettos. Worst case of Camel toe I've ever seen.

A minute's silence for a recently deceased deaf person: fitting tribute or more of a piss take?

My wife's wake was a tearful occasion. Somebody had put raw onions in the sandwiches.

Not a single person is in a relationship.

I've just written 'You have no new messages' on a piece of paper, put it in a bottle and thrown it far out to sea.

I've been comforting my wife lately because one of our kids died. She really loved that goat.

There's nothing I like more than smoking a nice bit of Iranian ganja. It gets me completely stoned.

I thought it was cute to name my dog 'trouble', but I keep getting beaten up whenever I lose him.

On a scale of 7 to 1.2, how much do you not hate being confused?

What's worse than finding a fly in your soup? A vein in your hot dog.

Parallel lines have got so much in common. It's a shame they'll never meet.

I like to sleep with the bedside lamp on, even though my wife reckons it's weird. I don't see why – I think it makes a great hat.

My wife couldn't afford to pay the rent so I sent her out on the game to raise some cash. I probably take Monopoly too seriously.

I tried looking up 'opaque' in the dictionary today. The definition was not very clear.

To keep in shape, I jump queues. It reduces my wait.

Timing. What's the most important thing in comedy?

People often ask me why I wanted to be a film editor. Well, to cut a long story short.

Vodka, whisky, tequila. I'm calling the shots.

My girlfriend has warned me that if I don't stop talking in similes she's going to leave me. I was as confused as a blind lesbian at a fish market.

Convince your wife that you work night shifts at a brewery by leaving at 8 p.m. and coming home at 6 a.m. smelling of beer.

I'll never forget what my granddad said to me just before he kicked the bucket. He said, 'Grandson, how far do you think I can kick this bucket?'

Did you hear about that new film, *Constipated*? It hasn't come out yet.

My wife complained that I never lift a finger around the house. So I did: the middle one.

My hot neighbour confronted me at my front door this morning in her underwear. She wanted to know why I was wearing it.

Lesson in life: always proofread carefully to see if you any words out.

Never have a motto. That's my motto.

I love watching videos of lakes and rivers on the Internet. I'm viewing a live stream right now.

Me and my recliner go way back.

Never trust a man in a wheelchair with dirty shoes.

Some woman at my hotel told me I speak 'too posh'. Upon which, I ravaged the filly.

I was just about to nail some shelves to the wall. Then I thought, screw it.

I feel empty inside, like part of my soul has been torn out. I still feel the pain every time I think of you. That was one hell of a shit.

I fell down a really deep dark hole today. I couldn't see that well.

Where does it say that Humpty Dumpty is an egg?

My wife called me insensitive today. I almost gave a shit.

I was looking through the dictionary when I saw a nasty-looking word. When I looked closer though, I realised it was hasty.

I struggled to lift a bottle of water earlier. It was an Evian.

Local news: 'Hapless burglar trapped by window.' He's obviously been framed.

'You wouldn't have believed it! There was a blinding light and I flew towards it!' 'Big deal.' Near-death experiences must be pretty shit for moths.

I met a gay guy last night. He had a better arse than me, but that's fine. He clearly puts a lot into it.

What do Alexander the Great, Attila the Hun, and Krusty the Clown have in common? They all share the same middle name.

I enjoy exams so much I usually take them twice.

Dr Pepper: Doesn't have a PhD. Doesn't taste like pepper. LIES! ALL LIES!

I went to Boots and said, 'Can I have a bottle of shampoo please?' The woman said, 'Extra volume?' I said, 'CAN I HAVE A BOTTLE OF SHAMPOO PLEASE?'

Exaggeration is a billion times worse than understatement.

I bought some extra-sensitive condoms today. I put one on and I felt really emotional.

Local news: 'Man's body found by tree.' It's been promoted to Chief Detective Tree.

Urinals take the piss.

I'm fed up with the amount of crap there is on the telly every evening. From now on, the bloody cat can live outside.

When the missus refuses me sex I just take matters into my own hand.

The grass may be greener on the other side but I imagine their water bill is higher.

World news: 'Air strike planned.' Well, I hope it doesn't last long – I can't hold my breath for more than twenty seconds.

My new girlfriend told me I was the best thing that ever happened to her. Doesn't she know she's got tits?

I've just started a band called 999 Megabytes. We haven't done a gig yet.

Be a team player: it diffuses the blame.

I've made a product that increases the size of your basement. I hope it'll be a big cellar.

The mop: a useful tool for spreading dirt from one place to the rest of the floor...

I try to be modest at all times, and that's what makes me better than everyone else.

I've put in so many shifts where I work recently that they've decided to fire me. Keyboard manufacturing isn't as easy as it looks.

I said to the pharmacist, 'I need some condoms.' She said, 'Just a minute.' I said, 'Yes, they're the ones.'

Each year, more people are killed by donkeys than in plane crashes. So to summarise, if you ever see a donkey on an aeroplane, you're in trouble.

Don't you just hate it when people think there clever but use the wrong grammar?

Coffee is not my cup of tea.

Dear Maths, Grow up and solve your own problems. Hate, Me.

I don't think my wife likes me very much. When I had a heart attack she wrote for an ambulance.

A man walks into a pet shop and says, 'I'll have a wasp, please.' The shopkeeper says, 'We don't sell wasps.' The man replies, 'There's one in the window.'

My wife had a go at me last night. She said, 'You'll drive me to my grave.' I had the car out in thirty seconds.

I can still enjoy sex at seventy-five. I live at No. 74, so it's no problem.

You know it's time to start using mouthwash when the dentist leaves the room and sends in a canary.

When I was kidnapped my parents immediately leapt into action. They rented out my room.

I've often wanted to drown my troubles, but I can't get my wife to go swimming.

Some people say that age is just a number. In China, 'Too Young' is just a name.

My brother just updated his status to 'I love my girlfriend <3'. I always knew he liked them young, but that's ridiculous.

Knowledge is power if you know it about the right person.

I never could figure out why my career as tpyist came to a sudden ned.

My wife left me because of my obsession with Africa. Kenya believe that?

I told my gran a knock knock joke, but she wouldn't answer it until I'd shown her three forms of ID.

My wife's so fat she speaks in surround sound.

'If you wanna be my lover, you gotta get with my friends.' If only all girls thought like the Spice Girls.

My wife is leaving me because I always go off-topic in the middle of the Mediterranean, and we had a lovely time.

I bought a litre of Tipp-Ex today. Big mistake.

A man walks into a library and asks for a book on confusing endings. But she did.

I was an accountant from the age of twenty to the age of thirty before I was sacked for no apparent reason. What a waste of fourteen years

A man walks into a bakery and asks for a book on wrong places.

I told a girl she'd drawn her eyebrows on too high. She looked pretty surprised.

Plagiarism: getting in trouble for something you didn't do.

I learn from the mistakes of others who have taken my advice.

I've just bought a rusty second-hand car and the only gear that works is reverse. Oh well, it gets me from B to A.

I think the hardest part of solving a Rubik's Cube is not getting all the little stickers stuck to your fingers.

I've always wanted to be a comedian, but I'm scared of being laughed at.

I remember when I was diagnosed with Alzheimer's, which makes me think that doctor wasn't properly qualified.

If at first you don't sucseed ... succeedd ... suxeedd ... sucks... Fuck it, I give up.

Holocaust jokes aren't funny, Anne. Frankly, I won't stand for it.

A man walks into a library and asks for a book on suffocation. The librarian says, 'Would you like a bag with that?'

As a kid my ambition was to be a detective, but now I haven't got a clue.

Giraffes look down on people like you

Don't use foreign words in an attempt to sound intelligent. It will backfire and make you look like a twat. Comprende?

I impress cool people by telling them I'm involved with drugs and have different people in my bed daily. I don't tell them I'm a doctor though.

I just walked into my Sarcastics Anonymous club five minutes late. They said, 'Oh, nice of you to join us.'

The Valentine's Day present I got my wife will really take her breath away. I've got the fatty a treadmill.

The Internet: where men are men, women are men, and children are FBI agents.

I live every day like it's my last ... day of Xbox Live membership.

I've just published a book on preserving the rainforest and what we can do as a human race to help protect it. It's over 2,000 pages long.

I cheered myself up earlier by putting a 'no U-turn' sign in a dead-end street.

Nothing says 'I'm guilty' like a completely clear Internet history.

A man stole a case of soap from the corner store. The police said he made a clean getaway.

Save money this Christmas by simply buying your kids an Easter egg each and telling them they overslept.

I got a slap yesterday for calling my missus by the wrong name. I said, 'Happy New Year, Claire!' What made it worse is, her name's Eve.

My father worked in a steel fabrication plant. They didn't produce anything, they just said they did.

Maths problems: the only place where someone can buy eighty watermelons and no one wonders why.

My wife says that I should use our recycle bin more. Little does she know that I've been deleting porn for years into the recycle bin.

I got woken up today with some guy banging on my window. I was raging. There were two other tellers who could have cashed his pension.

My hamster died from lack of exercise. He just didn't have the wheel to live.

It really bugs me when people make insect puns.

I only go out with fat women. I do it so I can tell people I've been with tonnes of women.

Ignorant? I don't know the meaning of the word.

My wife said she's going to leave me if I don't stop treating her like a child. And for that comment, she is now sat on the naughty step.

I'm so lonely I bought a plane ticket just for the airport pat-down.

I had to shut down my brothel. The customers just stopped coming.

Breaking news: 'Prison rioters "must be punished".' If only there was a place they could be sent where they couldn't do this sort of thing.

Borrow money from pessimists; they don't expect it back.

Local news: 'Mother high on drugs puts baby girl in washing machine.' She's now clean.

It really pisses me off when people abbreviate their words. 'Nuff said.

I had an ice-cube fight last night. It didn't last long; things got a bit heated.

Are babies natural or man-made?

I met a woman on a dating site who said, I want a man that can make me laugh. She'll love me – wait until she sees my cock.

I was checking this girl out when she said, 'Stop looking at my tits, you pervert.' I said, 'This is your first night working in a strip club, isn't it?'

STDs: allowing morons to pass tests too.

'Why are you talking during my lesson?' 'Why are you teaching during my conversation?'

When I was eighteen I used to have sex almost every day. Almost on a Monday, almost on a Tuesday...

What should be in a book to make it a bestseller? A girl on the cover and no cover on the girl.

Oral exam tomorrow... Hope I don't blow it.

I bought a Christmas tree that was too big to get in the car, so we had to cut the top off. I didn't really mind – I've always wanted a convertible.

Sign language: it's very handy.

If women say men only think with their penis ... will she be offended if I ask her to blow my mind?

Humans: zero to sixty in sixty years.

What did the worm say when he fell in a plate of spaghetti? 'Orgy!'

When you catch a fish and put it back, do you reckon it goes back to its mates and says it was abducted by aliens?

My friends say I'm too condescending. It means that I talk down to people.

My boss said to me, 'Why is it that when things go wrong you always blame somebody else?' I said, 'No, you're thinking of Steve: he's the one always blaming others.'

Just had a look at the statistics on female obesity. Awful figures.

Bad news: rioting has broken out in Ireland. Poor Paddy has just smashed his laptop screen, after trying to loot eBay.

If at first you don't succeed, destroy all evidence that you tried.

I just threw some salt over my shoulder for good luck. Ended up smashing a mirror with the salt shaker.

I was surprised when my psychic friend complimented me on the way I had cooked his steak. 'Well done' is rare from a medium.

I have a mental disorder than means I have to make everything I say sound mysterious. Or do I?

Suspect you have schizophrenia? Don't worry, you're not alone.

My husband is dark and handsome. When it's dark, he's handsome.

Does an optimist still think positive when he's going for an HIV test?

My obese friend died last night. In her memory I am just about to eat a chocolate gateau. It's what she would've wanted.

I have to exaggerate or I'll die.

A woman stopped me in the street and asked why I was wearing sunglasses when it was cloudy. 'I'm blind,' I replied.' 'Oh, I see,' she said. There was no need to rub it in.

My wife said she was absolutely fed up with the world. 'Why?' I asked. 'Arrogant people like you!' she screamed back. I said, 'Yeah, they do, don't they?'

Newsreader: 'Melted snow could freeze and turn to ice.' Looks like someone has a degree in chemistry.

Christmas shopping is a pain in the cash.

My mate walked into a mirror shop and said, 'I want a mirror, you fat ugly bastard.' 'I'm over here, sir,' said the shopkeeper.

Apparently in a past life I was really gullible.

I was clinging on for dear life. As the rescue team approached one of the guys shouted: 'Whatever you do, don't look down.' So I started smiling.

Today's generation: six-year-old boy to four-year-old boy: 'Dude, I found a condom on the balcony.' Four-year-old boy: 'What's a balcony?'

I just took some pills and now my pupils look massive! I really shouldn't take hallucinogenic drugs while teaching.

It's going to be a lonely Valentine's Day, so I've stocked up on tissues and Vaseline. My girlfriend is away on a business trip, and I've got a cold and chapped lips.

I for one... But that's Roman numerals for you.

Twice: so good they named it twice.

Every time I pour a round of drinks, it goes all over the place. I think I need glasses.

So I lay on my death bed with my wife Tina and my sister Marge. When I saw them getting upset, I said: 'Don't cry for me, Marge and Tina...'

It's coming to that day again when I make a resolution not to cheat on my wife for the rest of the year. 30 December.

I was walking through town today and saw a group of fat goths. They were morbidly obese.

My doctor said to me, 'Do you know your sperm count?' I said I didn't know they were that clever.

My girlfriend got fed up of all the bullying and finally took a razor to end it all. It worked. The name-calling has stopped since she got rid of the moustache.

It came as a massive shock when I was fired today. Being a human cannonball with Alzheimer's is not easy.

This girl I was seeing stopped me taking mushrooms... I'm not seeing her any more.

I was involved in sexual activity today, and I even got paid for it. Does having a wank at work make me a prostitute then?

My spam folder is full of emails offering cheap Viagra. They must think I'm a soft target.

After ten pints of beer, my wife becomes very attractive. I have to tell her that: she's a violent drunk.

My wife has just left me for Arnold Schwarzenegger... She'll be back.

I like the fact that my penis gives me a standing ovation just for waking up in the morning.

I've decided not to be pessimistic. It wouldn't work anyway.

Musical chairs: because kids don't have a hard enough time feeling left out.

Interviewer: 'Now, could you describe yourself in three words for me?' Me: 'Lazy.'

What do ninjas drink? WATAH!

Did you know that iPads and iPhones float in water? Go on, try it, I promise it's true!

Baby, you're lucky to be born beautiful... Unlike me, who was born a big liar.

I've just finished building Rome with my nephew's Lego. Took me a day.

If a man sleeps with a lot of women he gets called a stud. If a woman sleeps with a lot of men she gets called a lot.

I got my heavy goods licence today. My wife prefers to call it a marriage certificate.

Reincarnation is making a comeback.

I was standing in the queue at the supermarket today and a voice announced, 'Checkout number forty-five.' I've seen better.

I thought I'd found the perfect website to help me overcome my fear of flying – until it crashed.

A man gets the words 'I love you' tattooed on his penis. His wife tells him, 'Stop putting words in my mouth.'

I believe in the hereafter; so hereafter, don't bother me.

A touching story: A little boy saw a puppy. He went near it and touched it. Again he touched it. Again he touched it. Oh! What a touching story.

Sunglasses: because you can't see my eyes, but I can see your tits.

A recent test showed that the average man burns 125 calories after having sex for an hour... But if he had sex for an hour, he's not an average man.

I'm a terrible psychic – I don't know about you.

Girl: 'What colour are my eyes?' Guy: '34C.'

My granddad doesn't like fried chicken, but my Nandos.

People who hate hand gestures: I salute you.

Two rights don't make a wrong. They make a U-turn.

A pessimist is always alone. An optimist is always two people away from a threesome.

Life must be sick of people grabbing him by the balls.

Menstrual jokes are not funny. Period.

I asked my boss if I could leave half an hour early today. He said, 'Only if you make up the time.' I said, 'OK. It's thirty-five past fifty.'

My girlfriend ended up with two black eyes last night. I can't believe she fell for the old boot polish on the binoculars trick.

There are three sizes of condoms: small, medium and liar.

Smartphones: the best thing to happen to shitting since the newspaper.

I work for a genetic engineering firm in Italy. Yeah, that's the one: Genitalia.

There's a girl I really fancy at my Alcoholics Anonymous meeting. I'm getting up the courage to ask if she fancies going for a drink.

Dear Film Viewer, Your parents are about to walk in. Yours sincerely, The Only Sex Scene in the Film.

I work as a waiter and I love it when people ask, 'How do you prepare the chicken?' I always reply, 'We tell it straight: "You're gonna die."'

Breaking news: 'Nuclear submarine on the rocks in Scotland.' Those Scots really will drink anything.

My chemistry teacher asked me what my favourite element is so I replied, 'The element of surprise', before karate-chopping her to the floor.

I ordered a whole duck at a Chinese restaurant last night. It was great until I got to the bill.

I've reached the age where I can't function without glasses. Especially if they're empty.

Women say that men have it easy because we never experience childbirth. How the hell do they think we got here?

There's no need for women to behave the way they do on their period. It's an ovary action.

I kept wondering why people describe certain dates as blind dates, until I realised they must mean those dates where you wish you were blind.

Every time I hear a joke, I throw up. It must be my gag reflex.

My wife's against sex on TV... She keeps falling off.

My dad said to me, 'Any chance you can help me write my will?' 'No problem, Dad,' I said. 'Just leave everything to me.'

To cut a long story short... The End.

Even doctors make mistakes. Mine asked me to undress.

The definition of irony: not knowing the difference between a definition and an example.

Did you hear the joke about the deaf guy who walked into a bar? No, neither did he.

A husband and wife meet in heaven. The wife says: 'We're finally together again.' Her husband replies, 'Girl, I'm free: the deal was 'til death do us part.'

I worry about germs on money. So I try to spend it before it makes me sick.

Nothing says 'I forgot to bring you something back from my holiday' like a bar of Toblerone.

I had myself declared sane by three separate psychiatrists. All of whom were me.

I tried grilling a chicken at lunchtime. 'Right, I'll ask you one more time. Why did you cross the road?'

My girlfriend said to me this morning, 'Man U were shit last night.' I left the room in tears: four minutes is a personal best for me.

A man walks into a library and asks for a book on paranoia. The assistant beckons him closer, looks to the left and to the right, then whispers, 'They're behind you.'

Eye. Watch. Cape. Horn. Now repeat the four words faster and faster.

I have a recurring dream where I divide ten by three.

I saw an advert for an art competition where the grand prize was a year's supply of calendars. Isn't that just one calendar?

My boss said he's going to fire the employee with the worst posture. I've got a hunch it might be me.

Don't name your dog 'Curiosity' unless you're sure the neighbours aren't missing any cats.

A horse walks into a bar. The bartender asks, 'Why the long face?' The horse doesn't respond because it's a horse.

My wife's leaving me because I never take her seriously. It's OK though, she'll be back tomorrow.

I've just finished my research into the effect alcohol has on physical movement. The results were staggering.

My sister wanted to know if it would be OK to give her baby a two-letter name. I told her to go for It.

My career as a professional rock climber is going really well. I'm also taking a course in mattress-making, just so I've got something to fall back on.

My wife told me I need to get a better understanding of human genitalia... So I punched her in the scrotum.

What's the difference between a musician and a large cheese pizza? A large cheese pizza can feed a family of four.

3D home entertainment isn't all it's cracked up to be. Once you get it all set up, you realise you forgot to steal the glasses.

Dating tip for men: when your new girlfriend asks for your view on porn, the correct answer is not 'widescreen HD'.

I said to my girlfriend, 'If I asked you if I could give you anal, would you take it the wrong way?'

Sitting with my pals, one asks: 'Why do you look so sad?' I said, 'I just found out my wife has AIDS... I'm just kidding, why do you all look so frightened?'

Doing the moonwalk is the only way to look cool while wiping dog shit off your shoe.

Whenever I have a problem, I just sing. Then I realise my voice is worse than my problem.

I was having a terrible day at work, so I went for a walk to clear my head. The passenger in my cab was fuming.

If you haven't got anything interesting to say ... join Facebook and tell everyone on there.

Deaf people are lip-reading as we speak.

I warn you, don't mess with me: I know karate, kung fu, judo, tae kwon do, jujitsu and twenty-eight other dangerous words.

I see nothing but continued growth and expansion for the foreseeable future... But enough about my diet.

My mate accused me of cheating at poker last night. I wasn't. I mean, everyone knows five kings beats a royal flush.

Since passing my art exam, I've become very patronising. If you don't know what that means, let me draw you a picture.

If you try to fail, and succeed, which have you done?

Why did the monkey fall out of the tree? Because he was dead.

The other day I was having a long argument with a man, trying to explain to him that burglary is OK. Sadly, he disagreed and sentenced me to two years.

The worst thing about getting hit in the face with pi is that it never ends.

Did you hear the one about the streaker who ran naked through a church? The priest caught him by the organ.

Superglue and non-stick pan... One of you is lying.

A fat kid comes home from school and says to his mum, 'I got the highest score in PE today.' 'Well done,' says his mother. 'By the way, Mum, what is a BMI?'

My mates say my geology jokes are lame, but I think they rock.

I've just changed my relationship status on Facebook to, 'it's complicated'. It took me three hours.

I just won't stand for people who try to take my seat.

My wife reckons I'm just a gullible fool who will never amount to anything. Well, according to my daily horoscope, she's wrong.

My doctor told me to start my exercise programme very gradually. Today I drove past a sports shop.

We don't need a dinner bell in our house: we've got a smoke alarm.

At my last job interview, I told my interviewer that I plan to give 110 per cent. Unfortunately I was applying to be a statistician.

I was waiting for the number 69 bus this morning. Who would have thought it, two came together.

A girl flashed her tits at me today. I giggled like a little boy. Then she said, 'Will you stop fooling around and just check the lump, Doctor?'

Thieving bastard! I wrote that time traveller joke next month.

I've recently been reading a book on reverse psychology. Or have I?

I have a contact lens problem. I have no contact lens solution.

I have a superiority complex. I'll just wait here while you look up what that means.

I'm a massive seaweed enthusiast. I seaweed, I smoke it.

I own a shop selling 'Closed' signs. We haven't had a single customer.

I never let my children watch big-band performances on TV. Too much sax and violins.

I've just made some origami Teenage Mutant Ninja Turtles. Now watch them as they face their greatest foe: Shredder.

I just got home from work early and found my wife on a porn site. I'm going to speak to her about it when she gets home.

Breaking news: 'Man holds up bank with bomb strapped to his chest.' Gives a new meaning to the phrase 'strapped for cash'.

I asked Santa for something to wear and something to play with. I got a pair of trousers with holes in the pockets.

The next person to tell me I'm overreacting is going to get stabbed.

I love watching women's heavyweight boxing. It's hilarious to see them fight back tears when the announcer tells everyone their weight.

What's worse than biting into an apple and seeing a worm? Biting into an apple and seeing half a worm.

What did the nose say to the finger? 'Stop picking on me!'

My mate asked me the other day if you can catch AIDS from a toilet seat. I said, 'Only if you sit down before the other fella gets up.'

My dad always lived by the motto 'work hard, play hard'. Until my mum made him seek help for his Viagra addiction.

I was shopping online and saw a horse that I rather liked. So I clicked 'add to cart'.

I'm considering becoming a mind-reader. What are your thoughts?

I got Way Too drunk last night... I left him sleeping it off in the Chinese Embassy.

I'm more confused than a chameleon in a bag of skittles.

I don't mind going to work. It's the eight-hour wait to go home that annoys me.

I lost five pounds going to Weight Watchers last week. It's OK though, I found it on the way home.

I have a claim to fame, you know: I used to be the world's youngest person.

Do I agree that education is getting too expensive? To a degree, yes.

It's not the same without me. It's just sa.

My wife left me because of my obsession with Scrabble. Obsession: eleven points.

I was sitting in school when my English teacher walked past and said, 'Your grammar is terrible.' I replied, 'Well, your granddad is a twat.'

I hope some day I'm the last guy on earth. I want to see if all those women were lying to me.

Do impotent men watch soft porn?

I have a spider on my keyboard. It's OK though, I have it under Ctrl.

There's only one surefire way to make your penis a few inches bigger: push the ruler into your stomach harder.

I realised my hearing was going bad... So I thought, 'Screw this' and called the judge a twat.

Do I know the molecular formula for sodium hydride? NaH.

I have an amazing ability! I find objects just before people lose them. The police, however, call it theft.

I broke my leg and the doctor said he's going to have to put me in a cast. How does he expect me to sing and dance in this condition?

The life of a snail is taken with a pinch of salt.

I was planning to take a flu shot until I found out it isn't a kind of drink.

My wife thinks I'm too drunk to take the goldfish for a walk. I'll show her.

What is it with women and periods? Everything is your fault when she's having one, and it's your fault if she doesn't.

My teacher said to our class the other day that she hates suck-ups. I couldn't agree more.

The beauty of vodka is that it looks like water. The beauty of the office is that water bottles are allowed.

After many years of coke abuse, I decided to draw the line. Unfortunately I snorted that as well.

Multiple split personality disorder sufferers can't use Twitter: it has a character limit.

My wife knows about the secret mind-reading classes I've been attending. Well, she never actually said it but...

My wife can speak two languages: English and body.

Local news: 'M25 closed by accident.' Proof that the police are getting stupider and stupider.

I was at Wimbledon the other day and was talking to this guy who said he was a ball boy. I told him I'm more of a breast man myself.

Schizophrenia – together I can beat it.

If you throw a cat out of the car window does it become kitty litter?

Learn to spell, kids. Autocorrect isn't always write.

I'll tell you a couple of things that make me jump. My legs.

I was at this party and everyone was queuing for this mixed fruity beverage. Punch line.

What's pink and smells like fish? Salmon.

'May contain traces of nut': for the daredevils among nut allergists.

Alcohol doesn't agree with me... It thinks my wife is attractive.

I've just seen an ad that claimed it could 'teach me to have sex without coming'. I'm not paying for that when I could just ask my girlfriend how she does it.

'Do you have sex with strangers?' 'No.' 'Well then, allow me to introduce myself.'

I tried to order some tennis balls on the Internet last night but the site kept crashing. Must be having problems with their server.

If smoking kills, why does it cure salmon?

Sex with a fat person is just like fractions: its improper for the larger one to be on top.

Everything is easier said than done. Except for talking, that's about the same.

Gran's always up for a laugh, so for a bit of a practical joke I put her walking stick out of her reach. I just can't believe she fell for it.

I could really do with a crowbar. The birds in my garden look like they want somewhere to socialise.

Don't you hate it when Wikipedia copies your homework?

You offer someone a sincere compliment on their moustache, and suddenly she's not your friend any more.

My girlfriend and I are having a communication problem. Every time I ring, her husband answers the phone.

You know you're drunk when mosquitoes get a buzz after attacking you.

I love bookmarks. They're my favourites.

Trying to find an anagram for 'mobile piss' is impossible.

My sister loves reptiles so for her birthday, as money was tight, I told her I had bought her a chameleon. She's been looking for it for three days.

My wife said she's had it with my 'Mr Know-it-all' attitude. I had a feeling she would say that.

I can't stand being paralysed.

I was in the middle of writing a brilliant joke about an anti-climax when all of a sudden nothing remotely interesting happened.

As I pointed the gun at the baby, I decided to add to the dramatic atmosphere. I said, 'Any first words?'

Want to hear a joke about pizza? Never mind, it's too cheesy.

What did the buffalo say to its kid when it went to school? Bison.

I really admire people who keep going even though they're in huge amounts of debt. They deserve a lot of credit.

My girlfriend said to me, 'I want something that goes round my finger that's sparkly and that I can show off to my friends.' I think she'll love the LED yoyo I got her.

My wife's leaving me as I'm too controlling. It's OK though, I'm not letting her.

What do you get the man who has everything? Antibiotics.

I'm not a competitive person... I'll be the first to admit it.

We all know the phrase 'winners don't use drugs'. Which is true, unless of course you're having a game of 'first person to take drugs wins'.

You think you've got problems? I dropped my cocaine in the snow this morning.

A guy walked into a bar. He got a light concussion.

My ex-girlfriend texted to say that she's made a voodoo doll of me. I think she's pulling my leg.

My wife and I just told our son, 'We're going to Disneyland!' He was so excited. I don't know why, we never said he was coming.

My wife's so lazy our smoke alarm has a snooze button.

I can't say I've ever seen anyone wear camouflage before.

They're not blueberries. They're peas holding their breath.

I read somewhere that we only use 10 per cent of our brains. I wonder what the other half is for.

In a Catholic boarding school, how do you know when to go to bed? When the big hand touches the little hand.

What's the difference between a woman on her period and a terrorist? You can negotiate with a terrorist.

I must say, looking back over the last decade, this year would definitely be in my top ten.

I hate having to brush my teeth every morning. I must be the only person in the world with hairy teeth.

I just got a new aftershave that smells like breadcrumbs. The birds love it.

The local council have just told me I can't sell lemonade in my own home. I'm planning to make a stand.

I don't like grudges. My father kept grudges. I always hated him for it.

With great power, comes a great electric bill.

What if I never learn how to use rhetorical questions?

Which artist had the dirtiest hands? Picasso.

Do I really need to tell you the first rule of Rhetorical Question Club?

To be fair, I dye my hair blonde.

One in three suffer from some sort of STD. What kind of syphilisation are we living in?

I phoned the paranoia helpline, but I hung up after fifty-nine seconds. I'm sure they were trying to trace my call.

My girlfriend said I never believe a word that she says. What a lying bitch.

I was taking a bath last night when I suddenly thought to myself... I'm a rubbish burglar.

Russian roulette: you win some, you lose one.

You can look at some people and instantly know they're only going to get two awards in life: a birth certificate and a death certificate.

I went on holiday to China and bought a pair of shoes. I looked on the sole and it said, 'Made around the corner'.

I was quite drunk last night, so I ended up taking a bus home. That may not be a big deal to you, but I've never driven a bus before.

The wife was looking very pleased with herself this morning. She's found something that still fits from her schooldays: a pair of earrings.

'Have sex tonight for only $1.' So who's going to pay for my flight to America?

Officer, I swear to drunk I'm not God.

When we married, she treated me like a god. As time went by, the letters got reversed.

Taxi driver: 'Where to?' Jilted lover: 'Drive off a cliff. I'm committing suicide.'

My girlfriend thinks I have a gambling addiction. She hasn't said anything, but I bet that's what she's thinking.

Piracy is killing the music industry. You try playing the guitar with a hook.

I'm going to change my name to 'none'. Then everyone will claim to be second to me.

Some people call Yoda 'green'. Not once have I seen him recycle.

A dwarf got pickpocketed the other day. How could they stoop so low?

I read something the other day that made me piss myself. It was a sign that said 'Toilets closed'.

I hate it when people steal quotes from films. It makes me angry, and you wouldn't like me when I'm angry.

The lengths people go to win swimming races.

A good essay is like a miniskirt: long enough to cover the subject but short enough to keep things interesting.

It's funny how people change. Although apparently that's not a valid excuse for lurking around changing rooms.

Dear Facebook, Just wait: one day they'll abandon you, too. Sincerely, MySpace.

My wife called me a 'smug bastard' yesterday. I just got out of the house and drove away ... in my new Mercedes ... nineteen-inch rims.

My wife left me because I'm not very approachable. It was the harshest email I ever got.

Judge: 'I thought I told you I never wanted to see you again.' Criminal: 'That's what I told the police, but they wouldn't listen.'

I got caught stealing full stops. I'm looking at a lengthy sentence.

I've made a New Year's resolution to give up masturbating. I might need a helping hand though.

I wonder how things worked out for that guy who grabbed the bull by the horns.

I've just bought myself a hyena. Finally my jokes will be appreciated.

I was alone in the house last night when I heard someone fart. I didn't know whether to laugh or be scared.

My wife's schizophrenia has become very bad lately. Last night she walked in on me having sex with her.

Violence is never the answer. Unless the question is: 'What's an anagram of Noel vice?'

What did O say to Q? 'Is that a gun or are you just pleased to see me?'

I have just worked out that I have no life ... is an anagram of 'alone hi five'.

I said to my wife, 'It smells like Upsexy in here.' She said, 'What's Upsexy?' I said, 'Nothing much.'

'This is shit,' I said. Then I stormed out of Anagrams Anonymous.

I was on my driving lesson when the instructor said, 'You need to change gear.' I said, 'Sorry, I just feel comfortable dressed as a scuba diver.'

Kleptomaniacs always take things literally.

My mate is a virgin by choice. Just not his choice.

I am a recovering alcoholic. I'm not giving up alcohol, I just have a bad hangover.

Someone told me I was very fastidious. I didn't know what that meant. So I spent a few weeks researching it.

Two in one people are Siamese twins.

I know the secret to eternal life. But if I told you, I'd have to kill you.

'Dad, how do you feel about abortion?' 'Well, why don't you ask your sister?' 'But I don't have a...'

I think I'm going to order a load of bubble wrap, just to see what it's delivered in.

There's a monster under my bed. It plays loud music and dances around late at night. That damn boogieman.

I've deleted so much history on my computer it doesn't even know who the Romans were.

I've just had a tattoo done on my arse which says, 'If you're reading this, we're in prison.'

Testicles, balls, scrotum, nuts... My missus hates it when I talk bollocks.

Rubbish: the stuff you throw away. Stuff: the rubbish you keep.

I wish there was a place I could go to collect all the wonderful things people are giving up for Lent.

I can't believe I got sacked from the calendar factory. All I did was take a day off.

Bungee jumping: suicide with strings attached.

A world without bears would be unbearable.

The barman says, 'We don't serve time travellers in here.' A time traveller walks into a bar.

I have a dog called Karma. It's a bitch.

I saw a chameleon today. So I guess it's safe to say it was a pretty shit chameleon.

My New Year's resolution is to save enough money to buy a Velcro wall. And I plan on sticking to it.

Somebody threw some cheese at me the other day. I thought to myself: 'How dairy.'

I wrapped batteries as a Christmas gift for my little cousin and wrote a note saying, 'Toy not included.'

Procrastinators: the leaders of tomorrow.

I've finally got a date for my wedding. Hope my bride is up for a threesome.

There's a fine line between a numerator and a denominator.

American firefighters must have the easiest job in the world. I hear that the fire is always friendly over there.

I just found a carrot, a puddle, two lumps of coal and a suicide note next to our fire. Hope everything's OK.

I used to be in a band called 'Missing Cat'. You probably saw our posters.

I hate jokes that rely on visual imagery. I've had it right up to here with them.

Sports news: 'Golfer playing while on disability benefits.' Obviously not got a very good handicap.

Just past my English exam.

Never, never, never, under any circumstances, should you check your Granddad's browsing history.

I tried a new OCD-themed restaurant today. It wasn't bad, but you do have to order everything on the menu.

It is a little known fact that the Bermuda Triangle used to be called the Bermuda Rectangle. Then one side mysteriously disappeared.

I'm the kind of guy who stops the microwave with one second to go, just to feel like a bomb defuser.

I'm one of those guys who shouts their own name during an orgasm just to see the reaction of their partner.

Mirrors should come with Photoshop pre-installed.

My boss sat me down in his office and said he was going to have to let me go. It took police and hostage negotiators, but we got there in the end.

My lab assistant invented a device that allows you to steal other people's ideas and permanently delete their memory. Why didn't I think of that?

The whole birthing process came as such a shock to me, I couldn't speak for two years.

My mate hung himself in a modern art gallery. It was three weeks before anyone noticed.

Wife: 'Are you having an affair?' Me: 'I'm not going to stand here and lie to you.' So we sat down and I lied to her from there instead.

Twitter: the only place you can legally follow women.

I love make-up sex with my girlfriend. I don't really agree with the eyeliner she makes me put on though.

After I'd been single for ages, my best mate said, 'Can I set you up?' I said, 'Go on then.' Now I'm doing twelve years for a crime I didn't commit.

I'm not a poser. I just pretend to be one.

My wife's a magician. She can turn anything into an argument.

I got on the bus, pissed and stoned out of my mind. An old lady said to me, 'You're going to hell, young man.' So I got off the bus.

If crime doesn't pay, how come the police get wages?

My wife once appeared in a porno DVD. I saw her reflection looking at me angrily in the disc.

I had a good job when I left school, working in a bank. I was bringing home £500 a week until they caught me.

Needles to say, I don't like syringes.

I've devoted my life to breaking records. Which is why I lost my job as a DJ.

I fondly recall the time I discovered a cure for dementia. Ahhh... It certainly brings back memories.

If time is money, aren't all ATMs time machines?

Breaking news: 'The UK army has lost over £6 million worth of equipment.' That's the problem when you cover everything with camouflage.

I saw the trailer for the film *The Social Network* today. I liked it.

I think I speak for everyone when I say I have multiple personality disorder.

I was sorting out loose change when a 5p coin dropped and rolled into a drain. Everyone thought that was hilarious. I'm sick of them laughing at my ex-pence.

The postman left me a card today to let me know my package was too large: that was nice of him.

Who Wants to Be a Millionaire? Everyone except billionaires.

I invented gloves. OK, I'm lying, but I did have a hand in it.

If an indoor shooting range is burning, what does one scream to raise the alarm?

'So, do you come here often?' 'Get lost!' she replied. That's the last time I try and pick someone up in the VD clinic waiting room.

I've discovered the reason women ask so many questions: they have an extra why chromosome.

I wake up with wood, she wakes up with wouldn't.

Do deaf mathematicians speak in sine language?

Some people have a way with words, others not have way.

I tried everything last night to get the baby to sleep. Finally, after five bottles, he went down. He's going to have a terrible hangover when he wakes up.

Roses are blue, violets are red... Bloody hell, my 3D glasses are on the wrong way round.

My mate asked me what my best pick-up line was. I said, 'Cocaine.'

News headline: 'Man in court after sudden death.' Should he not be in the morgue?

My wife said we needed to communicate more. So I gave her my email address.

My wife told me to get on the Internet and buy something that makes me last longer in bed. I've ordered sleeping pills.

I could beat insomnia with my eyes closed.

People who say they sleep like a baby usually don't have one.

My physics teacher told me I had a lot of potential. Then he pushed me off a roof.

I like to call myself a follower of women's fashion. The police like to call it stalking.

Why did the clock phone the ruler? Because desperate times call for desperate measures.

What's a mathematician's favourite place in New York City? Times Square.

I said to my girlfriend, 'Do you want to see me pull a really ugly face?' She laughed and said, 'Go on then.' So I grabbed hers.

Treat each day as your last; one day you will be right.

Don't abuse alcohol, just drink it.

Sometimes my secretary reminds me of my wife. I was unbuttoning her shirt during our lunch break today when she said, 'Remember, you have a wife.'

I must admit I've got a thing for fat women. It's called a gastric band.

My Chinese friend gets really annoyed at me when I spell his name Wrong.

My maths teacher asked me, 'Do you understand inequalities?' I replied, 'More or less.'

I tried to steal a length of railing last night, but some bastard had locked it to a mountain bike.

Life (noun): a sexually transmitted disease that results in death. There is currently no known cure.

A man walks into a library and says, 'I hope you don't have a book on reverse psychology.'

I invested some money in a birth-control company today, but I'm having second thoughts now. I might just pull out.

Be patient. The longer you wait for me, the sooner I will arrive.

'I don't care if you are an usher at the cinema. You can't just tear up every ticket you're given,' said the policeman.

Christmas comes early... Poor Christmas.

I love a good meal. So I don't cook.

I like it when I open a document and my monitor says 'Word'. And I'm like, YO.

What do you call someone who's scared of KFC? A chicken.

Whoever said that laughter is the best medicine has obviously never had broken ribs.

If snow is made of water and water has no calories, how come snowmen are fat?

Scientists claim that coffee is more addictive than heroin. Bollocks – I'm not addicted to coffee, and I drink it all the time.

The only honest people in this world are small children and drunk people.

Say what you like about prostitution, but at least the customer always comes first.

My wife said we should try some role reversal in bed last night... So I said I had a headache.

Fat people: good food gone to waist.

Dear Noah, We could have sworn you said the ark wasn't leaving till five. Sincerely, the Unicorns.

When I was buying condoms, the checkout girl asked me 'Would you like a bag, sir?' I replied, 'No thanks, she's not that ugly.'

What do we want? Procrastination! When do we want it?... Next week.

I love a girl with a trimmed bush. It makes it easier to see into her window at night.

Has anyone pointed out to Americans that the 'gas' they're putting in their cars is a liquid?

Return flights. They take me back.

Don't you hate it when your mum and Santa have the same wrapping paper?

I was looking through the microscope at my wife's DNA and I thought, 'Those genes make her look fat.'

Sometimes I question my sanity. Occasionally it replies.

I don't believe in democracy. Neither do you.

What do you call a black man who fixes your toilet? You call him a plumber, you racist!

Our Brazilian housekeeper is rubbish at making the beds. She's very tidy downstairs though.

Just spent half an hour trying to take the wife's bra off – I wish I'd never tried it on.

I don't see the point in testing cosmetics on rabbits. I mean, aren't they cute enough as it is?

My short attention span really irritates me. But luckily not for too long.

Post-natal depression is a serious condition. I'm twenty-six years old and my mum still bursts into tears every time she sees me.

As a normal man, I just need to get my eight hours sleep a day and my ten at night.

There are ten kinds of people in this world: those who understand binary and those who don't.

'Are there any films or TV shows you want for Christmas?' my wife asked. Unfortunately she misunderstood me telling her to 'get lost'.

My New Year's resolution is to stop procrastinating – in 2015, that is.

It must be awkward for gay people when their satnav tells them to go straight.

My girlfriend is still mad at me because I called her fat last month. Well, you know what they say – elephants never forget.

I had a recurring dream once.

What do you call a pig with three eyes? Piiig.

I appreciate all the fan mail you sexy ladies have written to me. You can go ahead and send it any time now.

Liven up your local library by hiding all the books on anger management.

People often accuse me of lying... They don't really, I made that up.

I asked my friend what antivirus he uses. He said, 'Dettol.'

Better late than pregnant.

I was going to wake up early and go jogging, but my toes voted against me ten to one.

If I ever get taken in for questioning I hope there's no algebra.

My wife said to me, 'I wish I had a pound for every time you've called me fat.' I said, 'You have.'

Two soldiers are in a tank. One looks at the other and goes, 'Blublublub!'

I saw a sign in a car park saying, 'Thieves want your satnav!' I thought, 'Well, they can get lost.'

Ballerinas always dance on their tip-toes, which makes me wonder: why not just hire taller girls?

Programmers do it beta.

What's all the hype about a one-night stand? I've been stood here for six hours now and quite frankly, my legs are killing me.

I was in a spelling bee once. But I lost because the other students cheeted.

I love my new job fixing blinds. Or 'laser eye surgeon', as some people insist on calling it.

My six-year-old daughter attempted suicide this morning. She didn't succeed, but her spelling is definitely improving.

Me and my mate were queuing up to get into a club. As we stood at the back of the line he said, 'I can't wait to get in there.' So he went home.

I work as a waiter. The pay isn't great but I put food on the table.

Terrorists are now planting bombs in tins of alphabetti spaghetti. If one of them explodes it could spell disaster.

Anti-gravity... It never lets you down.

Buying a parachute: the one time that keeping the receipt in case the product's faulty is probably unnecessary.

I've just put my clock backwards. It didn't help at all, I can't see the time now.

I just bought my first Michael Jackson album. It's not *Bad*.

I do all my addition in my head. It's the thought that counts.

I've just published a book on DIY. It's blank and comes with a free pen.

I keep getting homophobia and claustrophobia mixed up. Which is the one about being in a closet?

There are two fish in a tank. One turns to the other and says, 'Do you know how to drive this thing?'

My mate was kidnapped two months ago, and then the same happened to his daughter just a few days later. She's always taken after her dad.

The future is much like the present, only longer.

Seriously, the jokes about pensioners are getting old.

I don't like jokes about pointlessly small memory sticks one bit.

11:59:59 a.m. is my favourite time of day. It's second to noon.

Spiderman's only fear: Rolled-up Newspaper Man.

Finally, the inventor of the clock has released his autobiography. It's about time.

If it's your birthday in November, you know your parents really enjoyed Valentine's Day.

Walking down the road I just saw a man with a multi-coloured turban on. What an attention Sikher.

My friend often goes into the Gents, takes pictures of everyone's poo and then puts them on Twitter. He tweets some random shit.

I suppose when asked by an employer if I have a criminal record, 'Highest number of robberies in an hour' isn't an appropriate answer.

Today I feel like a tampon: in a good place at the wrong time.

A guy broke into my house last week. He didn't take the TV, just the remote. Now he drives by and changes the channels. Sick fuck.

My wife is a famous porn star. She'd be really pissed off if she found out.

Old MacDonald had OCD, E E I I O.

Is the Isle of Dogs the Isle of Man's best friend?

I hate people that take things literally. They should leave them where they are.

Bipolar.com seems to be down. Oh, no, sorry, it's back up again.

I said to my wife, 'I've found this amazing new lipstick that helps you lose weight!' It's called superglue.

I felt quite smug when the iPad came out. I'd been saying for years that the iPhone would be really big one day.

Unfortunately, I have one pair of running shoes and sixteen pairs of eating shoes.

Someone left a bottle of vodka on my doorstep today. Not to worry, I managed to get to the bottom of it.

Waitress: 'Do you have any questions about the menu?' Me: 'Yes. What kind of font is this?'

I went to the game and saw a Mexican wave, so I waved back at him.

I gave blood today. I know it's not the best gift to give my wife for Valentine's Day, but it came from the heart.

As the plane hurtled towards the ground at 600mph, everyone around me was screaming – but me? I wasn't worried. You see, I was wearing my seat belt.

The optician asked me to read the bottom line. 'Made in China,' I replied. I passed the eye examination.

I'm fairly sure my next-door neighbour thinks I'm a stalker. She wrote it on Facebook, Twitter, and even in both of her diaries.

'Now, how's he going to read that magazine all rolled up like that?' thought the spider.

Stereo, stereo, stereo... I love stereotyping.

I once had a girlfriend who couldn't count. We had such great threesomes.

I'm fed up with 'eat as much as you can' deals.

My girlfriend rang to break up with me because I don't understand the simplest of concepts. 'Hang on,' I said. 'How did you get inside my phone?'

Here's a joke for all you mind-readers out there:

'Excuse me, aren't you the guy who's always being mistaken for someone else?' 'No.'

Why did I divide sin by tan? Just cos.

My wife's fanny tastes like tropical fruit. She'll let any mango in there.

I walked past some joggers in the park today. They weren't very fast.

I have a button on my microwave that says 'stop time'. I assume it means the timer, but I don't touch it, just in case.

You can't spell 'prostitution' without 'STI'.

I'd like to thank the person who looked at a buzzing beehive and thought, 'Those bastards are hiding something delicious in there, I just know it.'

One day, my girlfriend sent me a text: 'Let's break up.' I didn't even have time to be sad, because then she sent me another text: 'Sorry, wrong person.'

My gran lives in the past. But in the present she's dead.

Did you blow bubbles as a kid? Well, he's back in town and he wants his money back.

My girlfriend just left me because I'm so lazy. Insert your own punch line here.

My mate asked if he could borrow a bin bag. When I asked for it back he told me he'd thrown it away. That's the last time I lend anyone anything.

Can you imagine what would happen if I got caught up in a hypothetical situation?

My wife said she's leaving me because our sex life is non-existent... I don't see what she means; my sex life is great.

My new girlfriend won't let me spank her ass cheeks during foreplay, so in revenge I glued them together. Well, if you can't beat 'em, join 'em.

Vandals destroyed all road signs in our town last night. They really pulled out all the stops.

What did the egg say to the boiling water? 'It might take me a while to get hard; I just got laid by this chick.'

I parked my car sideways over two disabled spaces. 'What's wrong? You look in perfect health to me,' said the guard. 'Schizophrenia,' we replied.

I fell on my arm and had to have an operation on my funny bone. I was in stitches for two weeks.

Glow-in-the-dark condoms. Now you see it... Now you don't.

I phoned up the Weak Bladder helpline today. The lady said, 'Can you hold for a minute?' I said, 'No.'

I used to think I was great in bed until I discovered that all my girlfriends suffered from asthma.

There are only three things I'm good at: maths.

When he was at school, my friend was always made to stay behind and do lines. They do things a little differently in Colombia.

The term 'ring leader' has a completely different meaning when you're part of a homosexual gang.

It's times like these, when I'm sitting in bed with my computer on my knee, that I really wish I'd bought a laptop.

My mate said to me, 'I love Eminem.' I said, 'I prefer Minstrels.' He said, 'No, you idiot. The rapper.' I said, 'What's so good about an M&M wrapper?'

Dear Maths Students, Please don't try to find us: we owe your teacher money Sincerely, X and Y.

I went for a job interview today and the boss asked me, 'Why did you leave your last job?' I said, 'The company relocated and didn't tell me where.'

I can leap off tall buildings in a single bound, but only once.

I'm ready for work at five every morning. All I need now is a job.

A man goes into a library and asks for a book on chlamydia. The librarian says, 'Your wife already has it. She said that she gave it to you.'

A wise man once said: 'Get lost and stop stealing all my quotes.'

I just got sacked from the night shift at air traffic control because I couldn't sleep with the landing light on.

Mental note: actual notes work better.

Fool people into thinking you have a social life by not tweeting for a few hours.

The Theory of Relativity: time moves more slowly when you are with your relatives.

My girlfriend told me that I'm really crap at thinking of comebacks. To which I replied, 'Ha ha, nice one.'

I eat an apple every day. The wife's a doctor.

I'm setting up a search engine called Askyourdad.com. You type in your query and it sends you straight to Askyourmum.com.

I made a chicken salad last night. Apparently they prefer to eat grain.

Hippopotamus said to Crocodile, 'I'm big and sexy.' Which must be true, because hips don't lie.

A man walks into a library and asks for a book on time travel. The librarian looks at him and says, 'Didn't you just bring it back?'

Time is money. And it's the only kind that can't be counterfeited.

My ex-wife says it was my obsession with horoscopes that Taurus apart.

I needed some extra cash, so I robbed a bank. Now I just need to figure out what to do with all this blood.

My girlfriend said, 'The hot water's cold.' So it's cold water then?

Denial. Anger. Bargaining. Depression. Acceptance. The five stages of dating me.

My wife wants to leave me because apparently I think everything belongs to me. Welcome to my world.

The biggest troublemakers in this country are the police. Have you seen how many protests they attend?

Listen to me carefully, I will say this only once... This.

My uncle was so stubborn, when he died he left a won't.

Yoga class is great. You can close your eyes and imagine yourself in a relaxing place. Like on your sofa, not doing yoga.

Inside every fat person there's a small person trying to get out. It's called pregnancy.

If tomatoes are classed as a fruit, then doesn't that mean that ketchup is technically a smoothie?

What goes from zero to sixty in a minute? A clock.

One of my resolutions is to take more risks. I just had a Quality Street without looking at the flavour.

I saw a sign in a shop: 'Mosquito nets £10.' I didn't even know bugs could play the lottery.

Fool me once, shame on you. Fool me twice, and I should probably stop holidaying in Bangkok.

I spent five minutes fixing a broken clock yesterday. At least, I think it was five minutes.

Beware, Calvin Klein has a cunning plan to make us buy more underwear. I saw the price of boxers and shit myself.

On my tombstone I want it to say: 'Failed to forward chain letter to five friends.'

I got chatting to a lumberjack in a pub. He seemed like a decent feller.

A little birdie told me my golf skills are improving.

Someone asked me today, 'How long have you actually worked here?' I replied, 'Since they threatened to sack me...'

On a scale of Voldemort to Pinocchio, how nosy are you?

If I had a pound for every time someone called my ex-wife ugly... I would have stayed with her for the money.

I stole money from a Dutch holy woman. She was Nun Der Weiser.

I am not fat! I'm just so sexy it's overflowing.

I've never gone to bed with an ugly woman, but I've woken up with a few.

It was my anniversary last week. My girlfriend asked me if I wanted oral sex or a new pair of shoes. I went head over heels.

The obituary pages: Facebook for the over-seventies.

If vegetarians love animals so much, why do they eat all their food?

These Black and Mexican jokes have gone too far. Once you know Juan, you know Jamal.

Siamese triplets: don't pay a surgical consultant, just do it yourself and cut out the middle man.

Smoke detectors need to be tested from time to time. So sometimes I cook something.

Friends today are so violent. One just headbutted my fist for no reason.

My wife will buy anything. Just this afternoon I came home to find a naked man in her wardrobe.

My wife says that I should be more romantic and festive. So I attached some mistletoe to my belt buckle.

My mum says you are what you eat. That's funny, because I haven't eaten any sexy beasts recently.

There are two types of people in the world. Those who like cliffhangers...

The spell czech on my computer has never failed me yet.

I've got a hot tub. Well, I think it's sexy.

There was a piece of cake in the fridge and a note on it: 'Don't eat me.' Now there's an empty plate and a note: 'I don't take orders from a cake.'

My wife is going to leave me in three weeks because my psychic abilities scare her.

If you would like to help with the restoration of our local jeweller's shop, please give us a ring.

'Knock knock.' 'Come in.' 'Oh, thanks for ruining the joke.'

I don't know who Pete is, but he must be pretty important for everyone to worry about his sake.

My girlfriend says she loves me and thinks that I'm 'The One'. I said, 'I think you're confusing me with Neo.'

My wife's leg was badly crushed last night. She crossed it with the other one...

My mother never saw the irony in calling me a son-of-a-bitch.

My niece miscarried last night. She really needs to brush up on her long division skills.

Some things are better left unsaid ... like those times you criticise me.

My wife says I'm too lazy to even think for myself. What does she mean?

The teacher says to his teenage pupil, 'What's the hottest part of the sun?' 'Page three, I think, sir.'

There's a race war going on in my kitchen. It all started when the pot called the kettle black.

My driving instructor always said, 'Never brake if there's an animal in the road.' You should have seen the look on the policeman's face as I knocked him off his horse.

I've joined Alcoholics Anonymous... I still drink, but I use a false name.

Experts say caffeine is bad for you, fat is bad for you, sugar is bad for you. But don't worry, because that's bad for you too.

I don't agree with women when they say a nice dress can make anyone feel sexy. I just felt a bit gay.

I remember when all the other kids would bully me because of the wild exaggerations I'd make. Those were the hardest 400 years of my life.

My first session with the Impatience Support Group is tonight. I can't wait.

I can't remember the last time I heard a good Alzheimer's joke.

I just bought a new 120-inch 3DTV. Or a window, as most people call it.

Looking back, I really hurt my neck.

Why did Gateway computers go out of business? Because they led to stronger and more addictive computers.

The judge to the dentist: 'Pull the tooth, the whole tooth and nothing but the tooth.'

Today, I shall rewrite hostiry.

Try braking: it gives your driving a bit of 00mph.

My girlfriend dumped me because she reckons I'm always one step ahead of her. I said, 'Your bags are in the car.'

Local news: 'Christmas drivers offered free soft drink.' Great news! That gives me something to mix my vodka with.

My wife caught me in a strip club last night. She said, 'What the hell are you doing in here?' I said, 'I'm not paying you to talk.'

What's ten years old and locked in my cellar? My wine, you paedophiles.

Why was the cold tap turned on? Because the other tap was so hot.

What's big, grey and makes you jump? The elephant of surprise.

My eyelids are so sexy I can't keep my eyes off them.

My girlfriend warned me that if I got her one more stupid gift then she would burn it. So I got her a candle. That showed her.

You know you watch too much porn when you go to a hospital expecting a blowjob.

I was absolutely disgusted when I accidentally clicked on some gay porn today. Worst three hours of my life.

I've just deflowered a virgin. I mugged a ginger kid coming out of a florist's.

A few weeks ago, two cartoonists entered a contest. The result was a draw.

I get really irritating when people call me gay because I go to an all-boys school. I tell them that according to their logic, that makes them bi.

Last night I tried to go out for an Italian meal, but there was a huge fat woman standing in the doorway. I couldn't get pasta.

I went to the Missing Persons Bureau to make a report. No one was there.

Autocorrect can kiss my ask.

I needed a bone marrow transplant and I found a perfect match in Argentina. The operation was a great success. My thanks go out to Diego, Marrow Donor.

Chaos: what erupts when he-who-lives-in-a-glass-house invites he-who-is-without-sin for dinner.

I just warned my niece that boys will only want one thing from her. So she hid her PlayStation 3.

Some may call it a 'snowy winter wonderland'. I call it a 'dog shit minefield'.

Do gun manuals have a 'trouble shooting?' section?

I'll stop at nothing to avoid using negative numbers.

My father brought me up single-handedly. It's not easy being the son of a pirate.

Teacher: 'In this box, I have a ten-foot snake.' Pupil: 'You can't fool me, snakes don't have feet.'

I can't wait 'til I find the person that said patience is a virtue.

Yes, I do specialist maths: ladies, please form a $y = mx + c$.

Jail: the government's way of sending you to your room.

A lad at work asked me, 'Please can you lend me two grand? I'll owe you one.' I said, 'You bloody won't, you idiot, you'll owe me two.'

I do not have an obsession with tidiness. I just wanted to clear that up.

Exaggeration: without it the world would end.

When I found out I had one hour to live, it was hard to decide what to do. Eventually I decided I would forward the email to twenty-five of my friends.

Recreate your favourite scenes of *Harry Potter* wearing his invisible cloak by walking around a busy high street with a charity collection tin.

I'm not flying a kite. The kite is walking me on a leash.

I was having dinner with Mr T and he said, 'Don't talk with your mouth full.' I said, 'How else would I talk? And I ain't no fool.'

My new band is called 'Deaf'... We've just been signed.

I tried to fail, and failed... Damn, I'm such an achiever.

I need to find my aim in life before I run out of ammunition.

A cloud just stole away the sunshine. Bloody daylight robbery.

Nobody can say that I'm useless or that I've achieved nothing in life... I have followers.

Nothing says 'Facebook stalker' like updating your status with a girl's name when you meant to put it in the search box.

An onion just told me a joke. I don't know whether to laugh or cry.

Do women shake the petrol pump after filling up, or is it just a man thing?

Him: 'I'd go through anything for you.' Her: 'Just the door would be nice.'

Some guy just gave me half of a peace sign.

As of today, I'm giving up women. Of course, it looks like they've pretty much beaten me to it.

What do you call a girl with one leg? Eileen.

I've managed to lose eight kilos in two weeks. Bloody sniffer dogs.

Your head is so big your ears are in different time zones.

I've installed a skylight in my apartment. The people who live above me are furious.

I'm in big trouble: my girlfriend just found out about my fiancée. Now they're both on their way to my house to tell my wife.

My wife said, 'I've noticed that your new secretary is very pretty and wears a short skirt.' I said, 'Oh, sorry, love... She's not into women.'

I'm at a point in life where enjoying lots of bars just means good phone signal.

A priest, a rabbi and a blind man walk into a bar and the bartender says, 'What is this, some kind of joke?

What's the difference between two dicks and a joke? You can't take a joke.

Tired apostrophes risk falling into a comma.

A man goes into a library and asks for a book on probability. The librarian says, 'It might be on one of those shelves over there.'

I threatened a man with a knife today. It was a bit silly, really – he could have stabbed me.

I have hypochondria. I've no idea what it is, but I know I've got it.

Last night my girlfriend told me I was one in a million. Then she told me about her ex-boyfriends. Turns out I really was one in a million.

Did you hear about the new pirate movie? It's rated ARRRR.

I was arrested at football match for shouting 'Oxidisation! Combustion! Ignition! Friction!' The police said my remarks were inflammatory.

My uncle has been a personal driver for over ten years, and what does he have to chauffeur it?

How do trespassers get in your house? Intruder window.

Don't worry about your diet, just eat around the calories.

I put a wooden desk and a blackboard in my bedroom. You know, to make it classy.

'What do we want?' 'Compromise!' 'When do we want it?' 'What time is good for you?'

What's red and bad for your teeth? A brick.

I got in a load of trouble at the farm recently with my German boss. Turned out he wanted me to order thirty sows and pigs, not 30,000 pigs.

Do not underestimate me. That's my family's job.

My brother's still confused after I asked him if he'd heard that new thing they're not telling gay people.

My uncle choked to death on a piece of cheese. Now I can't have my picture taken without bursting into tears.

I've discovered the cure for insomnia: sleep.

Not many people knew that Albert Einstein had a brother who was experimented on by an evil scientist. His name was Frank Einstein.

I asked Oprah what annoyed her the most. She said, 'It's all the libellous things that are written about me.' And then she asked me to marry her.

My girlfriend told me she was seeing someone else behind my back. I don't know how, I was sitting against the wall.

I haven't been to work in four days. I've almost forgotten how to play solitaire and minesweeper.

Live a life of service to others. You can start by refilling this cup of coffee.

My girlfriend said we each needed to make sacrifices to make our relationship work. She was less than impressed by the dead goat I left in our kitchen.

I've done 100 pull-ups today. This new belt is terrible.

I hate it when the clocks change – I was half an hour early for work this morning.

My wife found a lump in her breast earlier. According to the KFC helpline, it was probably just a breadcrumb.

I think that my assumptions are starting to annoy people.

I got a sixty-nine off the wife last night ... with this new decibel counter I've bought to measure her snoring.

My girlfriend said she thinks I'm a virgin because we have never had sex. I was so shocked I had to pause Call of Duty.

I can't take it any more. The local shop has installed CCTV.

I climbed the ladder of success, but I think the others were smart enough to take the lift.

When my girlfriend told her friends she was going to grab a box of tissues and head to bed, she got sympathy. When I said the same thing, I got disgust.

Has anyone else noticed that mirrors look really sexy?

Since I was fourteen, I've been dating girls in alphabetical order. My newest girlfriend Yvonne is convinced I'll go back to my X.

Last Valentine's Day, my fiancée of five years bought me a lottery ticket and I won £6.2 million. I wonder what she's doing nowadays.

I like really dark cinemas. That way I don't have to buy my own popcorn.

I knew I was going bald when it kept taking longer and longer to wash my face.

My girlfriend is shit at cooking, cleaning and driving, but surprisingly good in numbers and letters. 42DD to be precise.

I'm looking forward to getting a takeaway and some ice cream tomorrow. Some things are worth the weight.

A barman walks into a stable. The horse says, 'Why the small penis?'

My football team is sponsored by Apple. So now there is an 'I' in team.

Hey you! Did you lose your nose? I just found it in my business.

Just got the results of my MRI scan back and I've been diagnosed with Brian. It's a brain disorder.

I got my own back for Christmas shopping. I took my girlfriend into eight different pubs without having a drink, then went back into the first one and bought a pint.

As a male biologist, I refuse to work with women. They keep faking organisms.

I'm very suspicious about joggers. They're always the ones who find the bodies.

Why is it that a woman only believes what a man says when it's a compliment?

A light year: just like a regular year, but with fewer calories.

If you want your spouse to listen and pay strict attention to every word you say, talk in your sleep.

I failed my Geography GCSE. I could never find the class.

If I were to ask you for sex, would your answer be the same as the answer to this question?

Why can't I sleep? This is the question that keeps me awake at night.

Today I did that thing where you walk into a room and totally forget what you went in for. It was only when the shit started going down my leg that I remembered.

I think I must look similar to Richard Branson: everyone keeps calling me 'that Virgin Guy'.

I tried to teach my dog how to fetch. He just doesn't get it.

You know you're going to be unemployed for life when you can't get a job volunteering at a charity shop.

A man complains to his wife, saying: 'We're so poor we can't even afford punch lines to our jokes!' And she says...

The doctor just told me that I suffer from compulsive lying syndrome... So I committed suicide yesterday.

I saw a girl in the distance. She had horizon me.

A man walks into a bar. There goes his dream of winning the limbo competition.

I went to the toilet about four o'clock this morning, and as I was sitting on the bowl I thought to myself, 'I'm getting too cold for this shit.'

My wife's going on holiday to get a break from my constant jealousy. I wish I was going on holiday.

What a top bloke my uncle was. Everywhere he went, he lit up the room. He's doing eight years for arson now.

I miss my wife's cooking ... every chance I get.

My wife announced that she'd been sleeping with another man for the past five years. 'Another man?' I asked. 'Who's the first guy?'

My teacher said I was average. I told him that's just mean.

News headline: 'Hospitals may be forced to make even bigger cuts.' So, no more keyhole surgery then?

'Boob' is the perfect word. The 'B' looks like an aerial view of them, the double 'o' looks like a front view, and the b looks like the side view.

Boss: 'Why aren't you working?' Me: 'There's nothing to do.' Boss: 'Well, pretend you're working.' Me: 'Wouldn't it be easier if YOU pretended I was working?'

It's tough to lose weight when you're older. By then, your body and your fat have grown to be really close friends.

After being escorted out of King's Cross station with concussion, I'm beginning to think my Hogwarts acceptance letter was a hoax.

I think my smartphone is broken. I pressed the home button but I'm still at work.

Isn't it strange how, every time you rub your cock, your hand starts to get smaller?

Every once in a while I stop and think, 'I know you can read my thoughts.' Just in case.

A wanker. What do you call someone who reads the punch line first and then the rest of the joke?

Are you Jewish? Because you Israeli hot.

I just got fired from my job at the Psychic Hotline. Didn't see that coming.

I can beat anybody in a fight with only one hand. It's the two-handed blokes who beat the shit out of me.

I've always been into collecting things. As a kid, it was football cards. As a teen, it was comic books. As an adult, it's debt.

I got stuck in traffic today, wedged in between a couple of cars. I really should lose some weight.

A midget waddles into the library and asks, 'Have you got a book on irony?' The librarian says, 'Yeah, it's on the top shelf.'

Have you ever been in a car accident? Yes I have, and don't call me 'accident'. It was bad enough when my mother used to do it.

I thought my arson habit was keeping me from meeting girls but then I discovered Match.com.

Written on top of a cubicle wall: 'If you can aim this high you should be in the fire brigade.'

I got sent out of class once at school. The teacher yelled at me, 'What would your parents say if I called them?' I replied, 'Hello?'

Whenever I go near a bank I get withdrawal symptoms.

After all those years in school, I finally know what the semi-colon is for. It's to make the winking emotion.

The homeless population is a problem that needs to be addressed.

'Have you ever read *The Hunchback of Notre Dame*?' my nephew asked. I said, 'I can't remember, but it rings a bell.'

What's the difference between ignorance and apathy? I don't know and I don't care.

I've got a friend who's half British and half Indian. Brian.

A policeman pulled me over as I drove through the red-light district. He said, 'Looking for a good time, were we, sir?' I said, 'Why, how much do you charge?'

Now I lay me down to sleep, I pray the Lord my soul to keep. If I die before I wake, will someone please delete my Internet browser history.

My nan has found a lump in each of her breasts. Turns out it was just her knees.

I'm trying to take some drugs through Customs and I'm getting nervous about it. I have weed in my pants.

Gents: buy something that will make your wife look lovely. A pint.

Some girls call me a 'five times a night' man. But hey, I've always had a weak bladder.

My friend just phoned me and said he's got six testicles. I said, 'That's a load of bollocks.'

As a paranoid schizophrenic I take the lift alone to my penthouse apartment... I can't handle the stares.

Cashier: 'Is that £20 note real?' Me: 'I should hope so, it cost me a fiver.'

My granddad has the heart of a lion and a lifetime ban from the zoo.

My wife said she'd kill me if I ever said my ex-girlfriend's name during sex. I did it last night and nothing happened. Then again, I was with my ex-girlfriend.

My girlfriend left me because she thinks I have no respect for women. I'm not sure what she meant exactly but I'm going to miss her tits.

Facebook is like jail: you sit around and waste time, write on walls and get poked by people you don't know.

I hate being bipolar. It's amazing.

I call a spade a spade. Why do the police insist on calling it 'exhibit A'?

You know you're ugly when you're always the one who gets asked to take the photo.

They say the funniest jokes are the shortest. Probably explains why women laugh at my penis.

I went to my first Arsonist Support Group meeting last night. They gave me a warm welcome.

I just don't know why my stunning girlfriend left me. I have the body of a level seventy-eight barbarian and the wit of a level eighty-nine battle mage.

The kids will be mad when they discover there really isn't a law that prohibits them from talking while I drive.

I always refuse to cut corners. Which is why I lost my job as a carpenter.

I have a theory that it's impossible to prove anything. But I can't prove it.

My wife said, 'You get on my tits.' Apparently, it wasn't a command.

Just put my ear plugs in and had a near-deaf experience.

The speed with which a woman says, 'Nothing' when asked, 'What's wrong?' is inversely proportional to the severity of the coming storm.

People who copy and paste jokes from Facebook are idiots... A few seconds ago – Comment – Like.

Last night I settled down to eat some Ben & Jerry's with a DVD. I couldn't be arsed to wash a spoon.

I just got in a car accident while reading a sign telling me to keep my eyes on the road.

My favourite pick-up line: 'Pick that up.'

I don't want to sound like a badass, but I eject my USB without removing it safely.

The healthiest part of the doughnut is the hole. Unfortunately you have to eat the rest of the doughnut to get there.

My girlfriend just told me she thinks my brother is really ugly. I wouldn't mind, but he's my identical twin.

Interviewer: 'We want to hire responsible people.' 'Great! When things go wrong people always say I'm responsible.'

First rule of Procrastination Club: I'll tell you later...

Did you hear about the scarecrow who won a Nobel Prize? He was outstanding in his field.

If at first you don't succeed, destroy all evidence you tried.

If you can't be part of the solution, insist on being most of the problem.

Amish dancers do the Acoustic Slide.

What's big, grey and unimportant? An irrelephant.

Ever notice how people who believe in creationism look really un-evolved?

My therapist says I am socially awkward because I always misunderstand what people mean. I'm pretty sure she wants me.

In my house, I'm the boss. My wife is just the decision-maker.

I hate being strapped for cash – but you've got to make a living somehow.

Honking the whole time isn't going to make everyone in front of you go any faster. Stupid geese.

The therapist told my wife to put some magic in our marriage. So she disappeared.

They say men can never experience the pain of childbirth. They can if you hit them in the goolies with a cricket bat for fourteen hours.

Leadership is about making bold decisions even when you have no idea what anyone in the meeting is talking about.

If there's one thing that having kids will teach you, it's home repair.

Women – can't live with them. But thanks to modern science and my hand, I can live without them.

When your eyes deceive you, that's fibber optics.

Impotence: nature's way of saying 'no hard feelings'.

I was so poor growing up, I didn't build sandcastles – I built sand mobile homes.

If your doctor warns that you have to watch your drinking, find a bar with a mirror.

Man is rated the highest animal, at least among those animals who returned the survey.

Maths and alcohol don't mix. Don't drink and derive.

See, the problem is that men have a brain and a penis, but only enough blood to run one at a time.

If sex with three people is a threesome and sex with two people is a twosome, now I understand why they call you handsome.

If you don't have a sense of humour, you might not have any sense at all.

We live in a society where pizza gets to your house before the police.

Money talks... But all mine ever says is 'goodbye'.

Rap is to music as Etch-A-Sketch is to art.

It's a shame that stupidity can't be converted into a usable energy source.

My bedroom is also known as Never Ever Land.

If people were meant to pop out of bed first thing in the morning, we'd all sleep in toasters.

I think my doctor really likes my choice of sensible footwear. I overheard him telling his colleague that I had 'serious healthy shoes'.

Save money on a bigger TV: move your sofa closer to your existing one.

Mud. Dirt. Gravel. I love all that dirty talk.

I find the most time-consuming part of taking my dogs for a walk is having to clean the shit off the treadmill.

A baby seal walks into a club...

I went to a therapy group to help me cope with loneliness, but no one else turned up.

It's always slightly awkward when you point out how good someone's Hallowe'en costume is, only to be informed that they're not wearing one.

I've tried joining the Procrastinator's Support Group but they keep postponing the meetings.

Sadly, 50 per cent of marriages in this country end in divorce. But hey, the other half end in death. You could be one of the lucky ones.

My family are really poor. On my twelfth birthday they put half a cake with six candles up against a mirror.

A real problem drinker is a guy who never buys.

I always cry at the same spot in the movies. Right at the ticket window.

I love warm summer nights when you can open all the windows and fall asleep naked. Not sure my taxi driver appreciates it though.

I used to know this guy that hung around on the corners of maps. He was a legend.

Standing in the park, I was wondering why a frisbee looks larger the closer it gets... Then it hit me.

My wife said, 'Can my mother come down for the weekend?' So I said, 'Why?' and she said, 'Well, she's been up on the roof two weeks already.'

Dogs and men always look guilty of something. This explains the friendship.

All I asked was if the building had a lift. You should have seen the stairs I got.

My indicator signal has stopped working... No, it hasn't... Yes, it has... No, it hasn't... Yes, it has... No, it hasn't... Yes, it has... No, it hasn't...

I'm a man trapped outside a woman's body.

I live like I type, fast and with lots of mistakes.

Instead of saying 'someone's life was saved', shouldn't it be 'someone's death was postponed'?

They say couples should never go to bed angry. That's why married people always look so tired.

Because of Spain's current financial situation they've had to downgrade Tenerife to Fiverife.

Guillotine: a French chopping centre.

I wish I could figure out which tooth is the sweet tooth, so I could extract it.

I'm having a small, quiet family dinner for Christmas. Small quiet families are easier to eat than large loud ones.

If we aren't supposed to eat animals, then why are they made out of meat?

A friend of mine has a trophy wife, but apparently it's not first place.

How can you tell when a lawyer is lying? His lips are moving.

I never understood the full power of willpower until my grandfather threatened to cut people out of his.

I saw man in graveyard crouching behind a tombstone. 'Morning,' I said. 'No,' he said, 'just having a poo.'

Always remember you're unique – just like everyone else.

I woke up in the police station this morning with no memory of the previous night. I really need to stop drinking on duty.

They call our language the mother tongue because the father seldom gets to speak.

As a dyslexic plumber, can I just say how disappointed I was by the Chelsea Shower Flow.

I don't drink to forget, I ... what was I saying?

My family coat of arms ties at the back. Is that normal?

Prostitution is the only industry where freshers are paid more than the experienced.

I would feel better about going to the dentist if he would just anaesthetise my wallet.

When I was in a supermarket I saw a man and a woman wrapped in a barcode. I asked, 'Are you two an item?'

It's all about perspective. The sinking of the *Titanic* was a miracle to the lobsters in the ship's kitchen.

Though many think the letter 'M' is quite common, it actually only occurs once in a blue moon.

Never hit a man with glasses. Hit him with a baseball bat.

I hate people who mix up 'there', 'their' and 'they're'. It's worse than not knowing the difference between your left and write.

My favourite punch line is 'OW!'

I waited an hour for my starter so I complained: 'It's not rocket salad.'

A bank is a place that will lend you money, if you can prove that you don't need it.

My wife left me last week and I've suddenly realised the truth of the phrase 'you don't know what you've got 'til it's gone'. She took my Game Boy.

I never knew true happiness until I got married. By then, it was too late.

My wife ran off with my best friend last week. I miss him.

I gave a pint of blood yesterday. I hate mosquito season.

I go with the flow. Unfortunately the flow is usually in the direction of Class VI rapids.

If at first you don't succeed, redefine success.

I think hitchhikers are really friendly. I've gone past three in the last hour and they all gave me the thumbs up.

Health insurance and homeowner's insurance are the same thing to a turtle.

The only imaginative fiction being written today is income tax returns.

How many light bulbs does it take to change a tired old cliché?

Hedgehogs – why can't they just share the hedge?

Everything is easier said than done. Except procrastination.

If guns kill people, then spoons make people fat.

Being sick can really affect your grades in school. The kid my son cheats off was off all last week.

If you want to be a leader with a large following, just obey the speed limit on a winding, two-lane road.

If life gives you lemons, teach a man to fish, and make ceviche.

When the automatic petrol pumps ask me to select a grade, I usually give a B for quality and an F for pricing.

Let's see how smug Opportunity will be when he finally knocks at Death's door.

I like your approach. Now, I'd like to see your departure.

It seems like I can't go anywhere in my house without somebody recognising me.

Why don't we take this relationship to the next level and you lend me some money?

Whenever I'm sad, I try to imagine a T-rex trying to put on a hat.

The Insomnia Olympics – you snooze, you lose.

Politics: poli, a Latin word meaning 'many'; and tics, meaning 'blood-sucking creatures'.

If it was the other way around, I doubt one cat would take in twenty-three old ladies.

The bigger my wife gets, the more exciting I find her. She keeps me on the edge of my bed.

I used to be in a relationship which ended because I made too many drugs puns. At least, that's what my ex, Stacey, says.

My wife of ten years told me she has been faking her orgasms every time we've had sex. I can't believe she lied to me, not once but twice.

My wife said to me, 'I wish you'd play with me like you do with computer games.' So I did: I cheated on her.

I'm really easy to get along with once you people learn to worship me.

They finally invented a computer as smart as a person. When it makes a mistake, it blames another computer.

I ran into my ex the other day. Then I hit reverse and ran into him again.

If you were 3.14 inches taller, you might get a pi-in-the-face joke.

Of all the different blood groups, type Os make the most spelling mistakes.

Proof computers are female: even your smallest mistakes are immediately committed to memory for future reference.

I got praised for my parking yesterday. Someone left a piece of paper on my car saying 'parking fine'.

If I were half man, half horse, I would try to be the centaur of attention.

I just bought an adult DVD which had 'Warning: Contains Sexual Content' written on the front. When I opened the box, a used condom fell out.

A good friend is worth pursuing. But why would a good friend be running away?

I may not be the only egomaniac in the world, but I am the only one who matters.

I'm not awake until I've had two cups of coffee and a nap.

Couples who have been married for a long time start finishing off each other's sentences. Usually with 'shut up'.

Birthdays are good for you. Statistics show that the people who have the most live the longest.

How do you stop a fish from smelling? Cut its nose off.

A bird in the hand is the best way to eat chicken.

'Doctor, Doctor! Whenever I look in the mirror I feel violently ill. What's wrong with me?' 'I don't know but your eyesight is perfect.'

I met a Dutch girl with inflatable shoes last week. I phoned her up to arrange a date, but unfortunately she'd popped her clogs.

I don't make mistakes, I date them.

I lost a lot of wait at the doctor's surgery.

If you are what you eat, then my dog is a calculator.

Morris-dancing convention? I'll be there with bells on.

Did you hear about the short-sighted circumciser? He got the sack.

What do you call a boomerang that doesn't come back? A stick.

When it comes to charity, most people stop at nothing.

When I was a kid we were so poor that, when the wolf came to the door, he brought his own sandwiches.

I love the concept of altruism, but what's in it for me?

'How come you're so lucky at cards yet so unlucky at the horses?' 'I don't get to shuffle the horses.'

Every man reaps what he sows, except the amateur gardener.

Fifty per cent of analyst is anal.

So I met this prostitute and she said, 'I'll do anything for money.' Guess who got their homework done!

It never ceases to amaze me how many words are required for politicians to say nothing.

The last thing I want to do is hurt you. But it's still on the list.

Ten times out of nine, you'll find me exaggerating about something.

Children: you spend the first two years of their lives teaching them to walk and talk. Then you spend the next sixteen years telling them to sit down and shut up.

Worry causes hair loss. When the going gets tough, the tufts get going.

You know you're getting old when the bank sends your free calendar one month at a time.

The only member of my family with a personal trainer is the dog.

For you men who think a woman's place is in the kitchen, remember: that's where the knives are kept.

Pain is my body's way of reminding me that I'm a wimp.

Worrying works! Ninety per cent of the things I worry about never happen.

My friend asked me to come up with eleven jokes about Wimbledon. I think tennis enough.

The best thing to have printed on the back of your car: 'If you can read this, I can slam on my brakes and sue you!'

Do you know what's coming back? Boomerangs.

I borrowed my wife's satnav. All it's doing is yelling at me to slow down.

I'm always astounded by the things my wife thinks I want to hear about.

I used go out with an anaesthetist. She was a local girl.

My workmates have been bullying me for the last week, calling me immature. I can't wait till my mum comes in and sorts them out.

I asked God for a bike, but I know God doesn't work that way. So I stole a bike and asked for forgiveness.

I used to work at an orange-juice factory, but I was fired because I couldn't concentrate.

My doctor said I need to quit my helium addiction before I get carried away.

The first step is admitting you're a problem.

'Do you think the betting shop's still open?' I asked my mate. 'It's ten to one,' he said, looking at his watch. 'OK, fiver says it is,' I said.

If I ever got the chance to name a road, I'd call it Skin Road, just so I could laugh at the people at No. 4.

Sure, the lion is the king of the jungle, but airdrop him into Antarctica and he's just a penguin's bitch.

Moths are really butterflies after they've removed their make-up.

I was going to give you a nasty look, but I see you already have one.

The definition of old age is doing the same thing four or five times and... Where was I going with this?

The most terrifying thing a woman can say to me is, 'Notice anything different?'

Police have recovered my stolen sofa – very kind of them. It was looking a bit tatty.

In order to catch a bus, first one must think like a bus.

My wife left me with my six-year-old and my three-year-old ... and as if that's not bad enough, she left the six-year old in charge.

My girlfriend said I make her feel invisible. I didn't even know I had a girlfriend.

These are my principles. If you don't like them, I have others.

At least a stalker is there for you.

So I said to this train driver, 'I want to go to Paris.' He said, 'Eurostar?' I said, 'I've been on telly but I'm no Dean Martin.'

Little did he know, but that never stopped him.

Common sense is so rare these days, it should be classified as a superpower.

Stress is when you wake up screaming and you realise you haven't fallen asleep yet.

Laugh at your problems, everybody else does.

I want to go into a balloon store and threaten to blow the whole place up!

Honesty is the best policy, as long as you agree with the boss.

My kids will be highly intelligent. I find it unpossible to believe otherwise.

Humble and proud of it.

An autobiography without punctuation is a life sentence.

If you believe everything you read it's time to stop reading.

My idea of a high-stress job is one where you work with other people.

To steal ideas from one person is plagiarism; to steal from many is research.

My dad is Irish and my mum is Iranian, which meant that we spent most of our family holidays in Customs.

I'll tell you what makes my blood boil – crematoriums.

You know what I call people who let a smile be their umbrella? Wet.

The worst thing about having ADD and OCD is that I forget to wash my hands fifty times a day.

Yesterday I saw a magician take 12 pence worth of ripped denim and charge my girlfriend £149 for it.

The only thing Google can't tell you is what you forgot that you wanted to look up.

I met the girl of my dreams last night. Then I woke up.

The average power nap is twenty minutes. This works out well because I can fit three of them evenly into one hour.

I didn't fight my way to the top of the food chain to be a vegetarian.

The boss put a 'Conserve Energy' sign in the staff room. Guess I'd better put my feet up and nap for awhile.

I've been carb-loading for the last thirty years in case I ever need to go on a 5,000 mile run.

Sometimes I make a mental note and then forget where I put it.

The best way to have a friend is to be a friend. This is why I have no friends.

Some people are like Slinkies. Not really good for anything, but you can't help smiling when you see them tumble down the stairs.

Prison guard is a pretty good job. Who's going to steal a prison?

I thought about going into politics, but I could never cheat on my wife.

I'm getting pissed off with my new psychiatrist. I'm sure he's only treating my paranoia for the money.

Hallowe'en is the by far the safest day to kill a person and leave them in a chair on your porch.

When you're driving, watch out for wild animals that are dead ahead.

We were born naked, wet and hungry. Then things got worse.

There are various ways to give up smoking – nicotine patches, nicotine gum, hypnotherapy. My auntie used to pour a gallon of petrol over herself every morning.

I'm at my most insecure when asked if I want to save changes made to a document when I am sure I did not make any changes at all.

Why is marijuana against the law? It grows naturally upon our planet. Doesn't the idea of making nature against the law seem to you a bit ... unnatural?

Any twelve people who can't get themselves out of jury duty are not my peers.

I keep forgetting – which Disney princess is it who solves all her own problems without trying to find a boyfriend?

I have some time to kill, but not enough to dispose of the bodies.

Air traffic control: 'What's your height and position?' Pilot: 'I'm 6ft tall and in the pilot's seat.'

I don't want to achieve immortality through my work. I want to achieve it through not dying.

Autocorrect has been around for centuries. I got mine when I married my wife.

My bank account was frozen. Well, let me rephrase that. My sock drawer is jammed.

You can fool some of the people all of the time. In politics, those are the ones you want to concentrate on.

Isn't it a bit unnerving that doctors call what they do 'practice'?

The neighbours just asked if I was stealing their Wi-Fi. It felt like such an invasion of my piracy.

I never win at Scrable.

What do you see when you drop a piano down a mineshaft? A flat minor.

Did you hear about the dyslexic paranoid? He thought he was following someone.

People say 'be yourself' like they don't even know me.

When I asked you for a flower, you gave me a garden... When I asked you for a stone, you gave me a statue... What are you – deaf?

Politicians and nappies have one thing in common: they should both be changed regularly, and for the same reason.

I have a phone interview tomorrow. What are some good questions to ask a phone?

I've enjoyed just about as much of this as I can stand.

I am actually quite pleasant until I'm awake.

I don't mind when someone writes 'wash me' in the dirt on my car. It's when they shave it on the dog that really steams me.

Finally, my coffee has arrived, despite not being what I ordered. Still ... better latte than never.

I've reached that point where I fear anything preying on my mind would starve to death.

Don't hate me because I'm beautiful. Hate me because your boyfriend thinks so.

Only a lack of imagination keeps me from immobilising myself with imaginary fears.

My garage band, Insufficient Memory, really needs a gig.

I'd have to say that my biggest downfall was about two flights of stairs.

The wife said she doesn't want much for Valentine's Day. She said, 'Just some chocolates and a few little surprises will do.' Kinder Eggs it is then.

The large flower on the end of your pen says, 'Think of me first if you must lay off professional staff.'

I can make a woman sarcasm. Repeatedly.

I've never been good at break-ups. Breakdowns, those I've got covered.

What happened when the dog went to the flea circus ? He stole the show.

My wife is constantly accusing me of being racist. I don't care what she says: I'm black, she's black – it should concern me that our baby is white.

Rap is 75 per cent crap.

My life is a never-ending string of, 'What was I going to do just now?'

You can lead the horse you rode in on to water but don't look him in the mouth.

'You make a very good cuppa,' she said. 'It's my special tea,' I replied.

As the poet said, 'Only God can make a tree.' Probably because it's so hard to figure out how to get the bark on.

I wish more people would give me the silent treatment.

I put the un in predictable.

Mistakes are proof that you're trying. And incompetent.

The secret to being funny is to say smart things stupidly. Or is it stupid things smartly? Whatever... It's not rocket surgery.

I'm sorry, Siri, but if I wanted my phone to talk to me I would answer my calls.

Some days just need to be schlepped through. I forget if it was the Buddha or Shakespeare who said that.

I am at my most photogenic when the pictures are of somebody else.

It was hard to come to terms with the death of my wife but eventually the assassin and I agreed on a fee.

What I look for in a relationship is how to ruin it.

A wise man once said nothing.

There aren't enough songs about the glory of middle age.

I don't wake up in the mornings... I come to.

Wisdom doesn't always come with age. Sometimes age just shows up by itself.

If a deaf person swears, does his mother wash his hands with soap?

Did you hear about the shrimp that went to the prawn's cocktail party? He pulled a mussel.

I have a hidden talent... I wish I could find it.

I'll bet wild hogs tell boaring stories.

Researchers have discovered that people will believe anything that you tell them researchers have discovered.

High-wire artists hate it when their cable goes out.

What does a fish say when it runs into a wall? DAM!

Work is the greatest thing in the world, so we should save some of it for tomorrow.

The good old days were when inflation was something you did to a balloon.

I can start a fire with two sticks. As long as one of them is a match.

I was talking to a fat lass with huge tits last night. 'My eyes are up here...' I said, as she looked down at the kebab in my hand.

Where do women pee? Because all I ever see on signs are men and Scottish men.

117

My wife says she's going to leave me for being too impatient. I can't wait.

The last time someone told me I looked hot it was 102° outside.

When James Bond is out of his home country of England, is he known as +44 07?

I rang up my local swimming baths. I said, 'Is that the local swimming baths?' He said, 'It depends where you're calling from.'

6:31 p.m. My wife is leaving me because of my obsession with *Big Brother*.

Did you hear about the five blondes who fell off a cliff? They were playing follow-the-leader.

If two people love each other nothing is impossible... Except deciding where to eat.

My dog has been sitting outside in front of the snowman for an hour, waiting for it to throw one of those twigs.

My great-granddad knew how to make ends meet. He invented the hula hoop.

My life is like a box of chocolates: hidden, so that my wife can't find me.

Dream big dreams: nap often.

A guy knows he's in love when he loses interest in his car for a couple of days.

'And so, God came forth and proclaimed widescreen is the best.' Sony 16:9

Twitter has saved me from a terrifying keeping-my-thoughts-to-myself addiction.

When I see who Twitter puts on my 'Similar to You' list sometimes, I realise how far my life has gone off course.

When I left home, my mum said, 'Don't forget to write.' I thought: 'That's unlikely – it's a basic skill, isn't it?'

Apparently, 'We were promised an open bar!' was not the type of objection to the wedding the priest was asking about.

Do you ever get the feeling that you're being watched? Because if it's bothering you, I'll stop.

I have a face for radio and a voice for Twitter.

I went to a general store. They wouldn't let me buy anything specifically.

What we should really fear is unidentified landing objects.

I posted on your wall. No, not Facebook. Look at the side of your house.

In school, I was never the class clown, but more the class trapeze artist... I was always being suspended.

I think it's pretty irresponsible that the newspaper companies don't post warnings when their Sunday comics contain Peanuts.

People used to say my dad's bark was worse than his bite. He was always crap at dog impressions.

No matter how loud car alarms are, cars never seem to wake up.

Be careful of your thoughts: they may become words at any moment.

Yo yo. A six-year-old's wish list or two gang members talking: you be the judge.

Some learn by observing, others by reading. Then there are the rest of us, who have to touch the fire to see if it's hot.

It seems to me that quintessential should mean five things that are super important.

Lord, if I can't be skinny, please let all my friends be fat.

I'm now day trading. I've got an extra Thursday if anyone has a Sunday or Wednesday they're not using.

The people who invented the Internet never would have got around to doing it if they'd had the Internet.

Sometimes you have to burn a few bridges just to keep the crazies from following you.

I'm in therapy at the moment. I don't need it, obviously, but I got all these psychiatrist gift vouchers for Christmas that my family clubbed together for. What I wanted was a crossbow.

My Facebook timeline is like a gift basket: full of assorted nuts and fresh fruits. Occasionally, a little jerky.

If a leper gives you the finger, do you have to give it back?

The world needs more people like us and fewer like them.

I'll accomplish something with my life as soon as my computer breaks and I lose my phone.

If you ever get caught sleeping on the job, slowly raise your head and say: 'In Jesus's name, amen.'

Just got a memory-foam pillow and I still can't remember my dreams. Lies!

My big Procrastination Project begins tomorrow.

I'm not on Foursquare. If I wanted something to constantly ask me to check in with my location, I would get a girlfriend.

A magician was driving down the road. Then he turned into a driveway.

Why is it called Alcoholics Anonymous when the first thing you do is stand up and say, 'My name is Peter and I am an alcoholic'?

The leading cause of death in mice is scientists.

Patient: 'I didn't care for the four-letter word the doctor used during my surgery.' Nurse: 'What was it?' 'OOPS!'

I cried uncontrollably when I found out that I had AIDS and HIV. I'm far too serious when it comes to Scrabble.

Receiving oral sex from an ugly person is like rock climbing: you should never look down.

Yes, Officer, I did see the speed-limit sign. I just didn't see you.

That awkward moment when a zombie is looking for brains and it walks right past you.

When I was younger, I always used to feel like a man trapped in a woman's body. However, that all changed when I was born.

You know who should be the most appreciative of mothers? Therapists, that's who.

The only really decent thing to do behind someone's back is pat it.

You try to fax a slice of cheese ONE TIME and just like that your privileges are revoked.

The secret of good journalism is to realise that some facts are just too good to be double-checked.

I bet you I could stop gambling.

A pessimist counting his blessings: 'Ten... Nine... Eight... Seven... Six... Five...'

Always bring a knife to a food fight. There will probably be cake.

I named my daughter Alexis because if I hadn't had her, I'd be driving one.

My wife said she needed some 'alone time'. So I made her a MySpace account.

'Oh! Oh! Oh!' – Dyslexic Santa

Nothing livens up a speed-dating event like a whoopie cushion.

Sign at the optometrist's office: 'If you don't see what you're looking for, you're in the right place.'

I went out with an Irish Catholic once. Very frustrating. You can take the girl out of Cork...

Inside every fat person there's a thin person looking to get out; they've just eaten them.

Age has its advantages. Too bad I can't remember what they are.

The police want to interview me. Strange, I didn't even apply for a job.

I wish I was on my wife's 'to do' list.

Apparently, sixty isn't the new thirty, and it gets you a six-month driving ban.

I don't trust my shrink any more. First he tells me to speak freely, then he charges me for listening.

The face of a child can say it all – especially the mouth part of the face.

It bothers me when I see tax money wasted on signs telling deer where to cross the road.

I saw six men kicking and punching my mother-in-law. My neighbour said, 'Are you going to help?' I said, 'No, six should be enough.'

I used to enjoy watching Larry, Moe and Curly but then I developed Stooge fright.

Yawning was originally meant for when you need to yell in a library.

I love flying. I've been to almost as many places as my luggage.

If a firefighter's business can go up in smoke, and a plumber's business can go down the drain, can a hooker get laid off?

I'm ageing like fine milk.

If Twitter had a swear jar we could cure cancer.

Everything in moderation. Especially fire.

I can't believe how much my wife spends on cosmetics. Why can't she just use Photoshop?

I can rise and shine. But not at the same time.

A true pessimist will look at a glass filled to the top and say the glass is too small.

If God had meant them to be lifted and separated, He would have put one on each shoulder.

I feel like we've met before. It must be a case of déjà who.

It's National Tell a Lie Day. So, just another day for every politician.

I'd be such a great womaniser if I could only get women to look at me.

If pro is opposite of con, then what is the opposite of progress?

I heard semen can reduce the ageing process, but I think that's rubbish. My socks look really old.

If you spin a Japanese man in a circle three times, does he become disoriented?

I've been scratching my head all day trying to figure out how I managed to get head lice.

I like to sugar-coat my words because I know I'm going to end up eating them.

I used to sell furniture for a living. The trouble was, it was my own.

Men who have piercings are better prepared for marriage. They've experienced pain and bought jewellery.

The first two slices of pizza cure depression and the last fourteen bring it right back.

Technically, all breakfasts are continental, unless you eat them in the ocean.

The average man spends seven years of his life in the bathroom. The average wife spends three years knocking and saying, 'Are you all right in there?'

You have the right to remain silent. And I wish you would.

My conscience never stops me from doing anything. It just stops me from enjoying it.

I went to the zoo the other day, but all I saw was a dog in a cage. It was a shih tzu.

I tried exercise, but I was allergic to it. My skin flushed and my heart raced. I got sweaty and short of breath. Very dangerous.

So if a dog breaks a mirror is that forty-nine years of bad luck?

Every Olympic event should include one average person competing, for reference.

You know you're an idiot when... Someone gives you a penny for your intelligence and you have to give them change.

Meet my colleague, The Boy Who Cried ASAP.

We'd find more missing kids if we posted their pictures on the T-shirts of large-breasted women instead of on milk cartons.

As I sat down next to a bloke he gave me a really strange look. Typical, I thought. The bus is empty, yet I still end up sitting next to a nutcase.

I spent my vacation in Las Vegas. I found out you can't beat the sunshine, the climate or the slot machines.

If I had a penny for every time I screwed up a cliché, I could lead a horse to water.

Promises are a bit like babies: fun to make but hard to deliver.

Technically, a slippery slope is the path of least resistance.

I'm as awkward with man hugs as I am at bowling. I never know when to let go.

Nurse: 'There's a man in the waiting room who claims he's invisible.'
Doctor: 'Tell him I can't see him.'

Windshield vipers don't clean your windshield very well, but they do protect your car from theft.

Tweeting in the car. Don't worry, I'm in the passenger seat. Which makes it harder to drive, but it fools the cops.

Progress is made by lazy men looking for an easier way to do things.

If you look like your passport photo, you're too ill to travel.

The problem with some people is when they aren't drunk, they're sober.

If women ruled the world there would be no wars. Just a lot of jealous countries not talking to each other.

Sacred cows make the best hamburger.

Eighty per cent of success is showing up.

We have so much in common. You want to travel... I want you to go.

If she says 'I love you just the way you are', just wait awhile.

Auctioneers are proof white guys could rap if they tried hard enough.

Whenever I'm on Amazon, I always get the shopping cart with one bad wheel.

You should never fear what you don't know, that's why I'm not afraid of anything.

I like to stand in phone booths and talk on my mobile.

Subtlety is the art of saying what you think and getting out of the way before it's understood.

It is far more impressive when others discover your good qualities without your help.

If I had a pound for every time my girlfriend moaned about equality, I'd give her 30p.

All a woman wants is a strong but sensitive, confident but not arrogant, trustworthy man. Who does whatever the hell she tells him to.

If you're a Repo Man, what you seize is what you get.

I've learned that the people you care most about in life are taken from you too soon and all the less important ones just never go away.

The Tories say we can't afford the same political games right now. They've invited Labour to play Battleships or Monopoly instead.

I have liver disease, caused by years of heavy drinking. My wife said I should go to BUPA, but I did the complete opposite. I went to APUB.

Why does water that has 'trickled through the mountains for centuries' have a 'use by' date?

My tee off time is 9.30 a.m. And maybe someday I'll even take up golf.

I put instant coffee in a microwave and almost went back in time.

My mate's wife asked him, if she died tomorrow, when would he start sleeping with other women? He said, 'About three years ago.'

I used that classic Liam Neeson line from *Taken* today: 'I will find you, and I will kill you.' My niece didn't want to play hide-and-seek anymore.

I hate seeing people walk on my lawn. Especially if they're coming up to the front door.

I'm fairly certain I could be arrested at any moment for being a serial time killer.

I like to have my pudding first, then my starter, then my main. Is that an eating disorder?

Karaoke bars combine two of the world's great evils: people who shouldn't drink and people who shouldn't sing.

I have a theory that the world will end in 5105, and we've been reading the Mayan calendar upside down.

The quickest way to get rid of a contractor is to hire him.

Please show your support of dyslexics and TR this.

Four fonts walk into a bar. The barman says, 'Oi – get out! We don't want your type in here.'

I appreciate the police escort but shouldn't they be in front of me?

You can have brains or beauty but you can't have all three.

You know your children are growing up when they stop asking you where they came from and refuse to tell you where they're going.

I admit it. You're stronger than I am. But breath isn't everything.

My boyfriend had a sex manual but he was dyslexic. I was lying there and he was looking for my vinegar.

After a holiday, the only thing that makes me glad to see the people I work with is having just seen the people I'm related to.

'This is pointless,' I said, as I handed the blunt dart back to him.

My mother told me, you don't have to put anything in your mouth you don't want to. Then she made me eat broccoli, which felt like double standards.

My mother was so overprotective we were only allowed to play rock, paper.

Are you always this stupid, or are you making a special effort today?

I gave my wife plastic surgery. I cut up her credit cards.

Inside every cynical person there is a disappointed idealist.

The police officer at your front door is never a stripper when you need them to be.

To be successful at fishing you should get there yesterday, when the fish were biting.

They said the baby looked like me until they turned it right side up.

Did you know? Line dancing was started by women waiting to use the bathroom.

My new exercise regimen is basically retrieving things I'm trying to teach the puppy to fetch.

By the time we get to the election, we're all just voting to make it stop.

I seek eloquence; I'd be satisfied with coherence.

If the world is really a stage then someone in casting needs to be fired.

You should never run away from your problems. Unless your problem is that you're being chased by a bear.

Would you *really* want to get on a non-stop flight?

When someone asks for feedback I make that microphone noise.

Why is lemon juice made with artificial flavour, and dishwashing liquid made with real lemons?

Getting sent off for a tackle in rugby is the equivalent of being fined for speeding in Formula 1.

There are limits to my friendship. I WILL: 1. Help you hide a body; 2. Provide an alibi. I WON'T: 1. Help you move.

I bought a life assurance policy today. Once a month someone calls me to assure me that I'm not dead.

The police got me a really big bouncy castle for my birthday. All I had to do was stand on a ledge outside my office.

I heard an advert offering twenty-four months with no interest. Just like my life.

I'm paranoid *and* needy. I think people are talking about me, just not as often as I'd like.

'I'm sorry. I just assumed if you wanted this project done quickly, you wouldn't have assigned it to me.'

I told my son about the birds and the bees. He then told me about the postman and my wife.

I often wonder what tomatoes did to make the other fruits disown them and force them to live as vegetables.

My mate said to me earlier, 'I challenge you to count 86,400 seconds.' I said, 'Get lost, that'll take me all day.'

I just asked my mate, 'What do you get if you remove an l and an i from oblivious?' 'I don't know,' he said. 'It's obvious.'

As I sat there licking my guitar, I thought to myself, 'I have a good taste in music.'

You know you need a boyfriend when everything you've hugged this week has had a flea bath.

My friend watched a *Batman* DVD with a girl on their ninth date. It went 'dinner dinner dinner dinner dinner dinner dinner dinner BATMAN'.

There are two types of people in this world, good and bad. The good sleep better, but the bad seem to enjoy the waking hours much more.

Drive-thru McDonalds was more expensive than I thought. Once you've hired the car…

A conclusion is the place where you got tired of thinking.

The last time I tried aromatherapy, I was caught in the lift with a bunch of uncles.

A transvestite is a man who likes to eat, drink and be Mary.

Yes, I know I looked different on my profile photo. I was trying to impress you with my Photoshop skills.

If my phone were really a smartphone it would have ended that call before I said 'I told you so' to my wife.

The more I try to unravel my life, the more I feel there's someone behind me, knitting like hell.

You have the capacity to learn from your mistakes. You're going to learn a lot today.

Cutting onions doesn't make me cry. I became indifferent to their suffering years ago.

All my friends keep telling me to never succumb to peer pressure. So I'm going to take their advice and not listen to them.

Three more cheeseburgers and I can join the Mile Wide Club.

Power corrupts, but batteries corrode. World domination is tricky.

The benefit of always going in to work late is that when you're on time, people think you're early.

If your feet smell and your nose runs, you're built upside down.

'How will I know when I've met the perfect woman?' 'She'll usually tell you.'

Sex is like football: it's always more satisfying when you come from behind.

On my first day of school my parents dropped me off at the wrong nursery. There I was ... surrounded by trees and bushes.

My wife just said, 'Your obsession with cats is totally out of control, so I've packed your bags.' I think she's kicking meeeowt.

Marriage is bliss. Ignorance is bliss. Ergo...

There are no winners in life... Only survivors.

The Internet: all of the piracy and none of the scurvy.

I don't want to get carried away here, but these security guards aren't really giving me a choice.

If it weren't for alcohol how would we even know when to call our exes?

Take a moment to unwind. It's far better for you than unravelling.

Years ago, timelines were something on your face.

Who was the first to see a cow and think: I wonder what will happen if I squeeze these dangly things and drink whatever comes out?

Apparently towels are the biggest cause of dry skin.

All this talk about death by chocolate, yet chocolate still roams free.

I never change the clock in my car. Six months of the year, I'm an hour late. The other six I'm two hours late.

I bought myself an oscillating fan, because I like to be comfortable 12 per cent of the time.

This next song is called 'Subtraction'. Take it away!

I don't know what my credit score is but I'm pretty sure I'm losing.

One cookie would just be afraid by itself in the dark, right?

My boss is one in a million. I'm just hoping this lightning storm thinks so too...

There's always one person in any organisation who knows what's really going on. This person must be fired.

When I had laryngitis, I was a hoarse whisperer.

What is ET short for? Because he's got little legs.

If a midget smokes weed, does he get medium?

Women will never truly be equal as long as they're smarter than men.

'Did you see the football today?' I asked my mate. 'No, I didn't', he said. I then informed him he was no longer our team's goalkeeper.

If I lunged out of bed to turn off the alarm clock, does that count as a workout?

Twice a week the wife and I go out for a nice relaxing meal. She goes on Mondays and I go on Fridays.

Cheat on your taxes and you'll end up in one of two places – jail or parliament.

As soon as I got a new lease on life, the rent was raised.

We could learn a lot from bees. Organisation, productivity, community sacrifice, stinging people who annoy us...

I hate it when my flatmate comes home drunk and pisses all over the toilet seat. Why can't she sit down to piss like other women?

I am super lazy. It's like normal lazy, but I wear a cape.

If you have such a problem with me hogging the covers at night then maybe you should get better locks on your doors.

It's not cellulite, it's my body's way of saying 'I'm sexy' in Braille.

'How many lawyers does it take to...' 'Ah, ah, ah. We'll sue.'

I've just got myself a sex doll but I don't want to fuck it yet. I'll leave it a couple of days – I don't want to seem desperate.

I got an email offer to buy used memory. How much should I ask for that time at band camp?

A German shepherd craps on my lawn each morning. Today, he even brought his dog.

The bright side of global warming is that 100 per cent of our great-grandchildren will own beachfront property.

Lawyer: 'Doctor! Doctor! Why do I feel sick every time I stand up to talk to the judge?' Doctor: 'Sounds like motion sickness to me.'

I wish I could understand what this computer guy is saying, but it's all geek to me.

Do not argue with an idiot. He will drag you down to his level and beat you with experience.

Found a hair in my spaghetti. But it was just angel hair.

The early bird might get the worm, but the second mouse gets the cheese.

We have enough youth, how about a fountain of smart?

It's still mystery to me why cops use drug-sniffing dogs rather than sober ones.

You can now buy a fridge with Wi-Fi... Like my cheese needs to be watching YouTube videos all day.

My biggest problem with the younger generation is that I'm not in it.

If bars can say no to drunk people, why won't McDonalds say no to fat people?

Let's play horse. I'll be the front end and you be yourself.

Supervision. Not as cool as it sounds.

Keep calm. Nobody else knows what they're doing either.

If genius is 1 per cent inspiration and 99 per cent perspiration, we should get cab drivers working on a cure for cancer.

UFOs are real. The Air Force doesn't exist.

Aim for the stars. But first, aim for their bodyguards.

Want to know what Slough was like in the 1970s? Go there now.

Every time your kid starts crying when they don't get what they want, just say, 'I don't negotiate with terrorists.'

Youthful indiscretions should be enjoyed by people of all ages.

I've been running round like a madman at work today... Naked with a chainsaw.

Ladies and gentlemen, if I could have your attention for a moment... I would be a better public speaker.

The pen is mightier than the sword and considerably easier to write with.

What's Irish and stays out all night? Patty O'Furniture.

Gardening is one person's effort to improve his lot.

You always remember your first crush. Mine was orange.

An optimist is a person who gets treed by a bear and enjoys the view.

Compromise is hard to swallow because it never tastes like chocolate.

All-knight diners were big during the Renaissance period.

Fish eyes are the windows to the sole.

If being sceptical is wrong, prove it.

I have an athlete's ability trapped in a dumpster's body.

I try to watch what I eat, but my eyes aren't fast enough.

I try not to think of it as a bad idea. I think of it as practice for a future good idea.

Men who don't understand women fall into two groups: bachelors and husbands.

My colleagues are exceptionally dedicated. You wouldn't believe how far some of them will go to annoy me.

Why didn't Noah swat those two mosquitoes?

I've learned to take life with a grain of salt, plus a slice of lemon and a shot of tequila.

Visitors to Las Vegas are divided into two groups – the 'haves' and the 'hads'.

It ain't what you don't know that gets you into trouble. It's what you know for sure that just ain't so.

Where's the daylight saving time setting on a five-year-old?

Love is a name, sex is a game. Forget the name and let's play that game!

Born free. Now I'm expensive.

I'd be more optimistic if I thought it would help.

I criticised my dad for using imperial measurements. He beat me to within 2.54cm of my life.

Sadomasochism – you're bound to enjoy it.

Following the explosion at the Elizabethan music shop, they've had problems with luting.

My girlfriend asked me to stop impersonating a flamingo. I had to put my foot down.

I don't get many compliments. So I was surprised when the phone company called to say I had an outstanding account.

Our eyes met, but the rest of us didn't.

Fight procrastination... Tomorrow.

I'd mind my own business if yours was a little less interesting.

I wasn't mad until you asked me if I was mad for the fiftieth time.

We never really grow up, we only learn how to act in public.

After the age of thirty-five, people start losing 7,000 brain cells a day. That number is tripled if they have a Facebook account.

I'm in favour of politicians doing two terms: one in office and one in jail.

Constipated people don't give a crap.

Our leaders can't see the forest or the trees.

My boss needs to stop holding secret meetings about my paranoia.

For sale: replica fisherman's knife (made to scale).

Chickens think rubber humans are hilarious.

When I was a child, I wanted to be a surgeon. But apparently I was too young.

999: 'What's your emergency?' I said, 'Two girls are fighting over me.' 'OK,' she paused. 'Well, what's the problem?' 'The fat one's winning.'

Few people realise that £1 pregnancy tests are 100 per cent accurate. (Results may take up to nine months.)

'What's done cannot be undone.' They obviously didn't have shoe-laces in Shakespeare's day.

At the stalker convention, everyone sleeps in the bushes outside the hotel.

Dear Women, We're not as dumb as you think we are. We're dumber. Love, Men.

I pride myself on being the most overrated of the underrated.

I think my gene pool may have been one of those above-ground ones.

My wife is a water sign. I'm an earth. Together, we make mud.

Stop me if I'm wrong... Why didn't you stop me?

Bad decisions often come back to haunt us. Especially since the creation of YouTube.

Police arrested two kids yesterday. One was drinking battery acid, the other was eating fireworks. They charged one and let the other one off.

For a lion to be a cannibal, he must first swallow his pride.

I love to go down to the schoolyard and watch all the little children jump up and down and run around yelling and screaming. They don't know I'm only using blanks.

If I save time, when do I get it back?

Never bite the hand that feeds you. Bite the hand that doesn't feed you.

I wish all these girls got as excited about me finishing in less than ten seconds as they do about Usain Bolt.

I used to do drugs. I still do drugs, but I used to, too.

With the advent of Twitter and Facebook, we have entered the Too-Much-Information Age.

All these programmes on TV about women being domestic goddesses are just not true, are they? I'd like to have a programme that truly represented how women approach housework. And if I did, it would be called, 'Fuck it, that'll do.'

I wonder if Google realise that 75 per cent of their traffic is made up of people using them as their emergency non-porn tab.

To err is human, to forgive is divine. In other words, the forgiving is somebody else's job.

There's a name for short female cops who drag me out of a bar with one hand: show-offs.

My wife's always walking into things and getting hurt. Yesterday it was our bedroom while I was fucking her sister.

The five second rule also applies to wearing sunglasses indoors.

Never be afraid to laugh at yourself. After all, you could be missing out on the joke of the century.

OK, here's the deal: you try not to look like that and I'll try not to laugh.

I love Mondays. It's when I take my weekly sarcasm class.

Calculating which type of bridge I cross more. It's a draw.

My wife asked me if we could have something more Christmassy on the television. So I put FIFA on and played in snowy conditions.

Liquor and beer, never fear. Beer and liquor, yadda yadda yadda, mugshot.

Five-year-old girl discovers 160 million-year-old fossil. Parents tell her it's not nice to talk about Grandpa that way.

I need a five-second delay between my brain and my mouth. Maybe ten. OK, minutes.

If I ever have an out-of-body experience, I'm going to try to come back to a different one.

The waiter said, 'Your table will be ready shortly.' This is the last time I'll be coming to IKEA's restaurant.

My body is a temple. No one worships here, though.

I remember when my better half had laryngitis. Fondly.

You may be recognised soon. Hide.

If the wolf is at the door, prevailing wisdom sends one of those pigs to answer it.

Marriage is a fine institution. But I don't think I'm ready to be put in an institution yet.

Don't worry. When I snap, you'll be the first to go.

For every action, there is a corresponding overreaction.

There are three ways a man can wear his hair: parted, unparted or departed.

I'm so vain, I joined the Navy so the world could see me.

Did pretty well on the scavenger hunt. Shot three scavengers.

The nice thing about being single is that I'm always there when I need me.

Women are the fairer sex, men are the laissez-fairer sex.

Autocorrect has to be my worst enema.

I finally hit my stride. It was in the driveway and I backed over it.

Getting older? Well, no sense crying over spilled nutritional supplement.

I don't have a problem with willpower. It's won't power I have a problem with.

My dinosaur name would have been Trainosaurus Wrex.

It doesn't matter how often a married man changes jobs, he still ends up with the same boss.

Copy editors are impotent.

Some see things as they are and ask, 'Why?' Others see things that never were and ask, 'Where's my medication?'

I've just been sentenced to twenty years for my part in a timeshare fraud. Luckily I only have to go to prison for two weeks every year.

Jealousy is the art of counting someone else's blessings instead of your own.

The only man who has never told his wife a lie is a bachelor.

I wish my uncle was still alive. He used to pull coins out of my ear and now I could really use the change.

'Angry Birds Suicide Hotline, which level are you stuck on?'

Cupid almost got me yesterday. I had an arrow escape.

What's the smoothest way to tell your dinner date that she has to get something of equal or lesser value?

I can trace my ancestry directly to the Tom who invented foolery.

I just read a book about Stockholm Syndrome. It started off badly, but by the end I really liked it.

I would be more willing to watch the nightly news if it were delivered by superheroes fresh from vanquishing their foes.

I used to hate it when old aunts came up to me after weddings and said, 'You're next.' They stopped doing that when I started saying the same to them after funerals.

Why is it so hard for women to find men that are sensitive, caring and good-looking? Because those men already have boyfriends.

I never understand women. Fake nails, fake tan, fake eyelashes, fake hair. All the effort I make, and they still won't go out with me.

Don't underestimate me... Unless you're trying to guess how old I am or how much I weigh.

Well, it seems cops don't like it when you ask them, 'Hey, you need some help?' Especially when you're wearing a Batman costume.

When people suck the life out of you, wouldn't it be nice if they took some fat, too?

I'm tired of watching my team from the sidelines. It's time we made a stand.

I went into the kitchen this morning and said to the wife, 'Is that coffee I smell?' She said, 'It is and you do.'

Did you hear about the paranoid guy with low self-esteem? He thought nobody important was out to get him.

Politics is the art of looking for trouble, finding it, misdiagnosing it and then applying the wrong remedies.

At what age does it change from 'pretending' to 'lying'?

I have a Supreme Court figure: no appeal.

My ex is a dyslexic amnesiac. She remembers everything.

Clearly, you are a person with an open mind. I can feel the breeze from here.

My wife suggested we just go crazy tonight but I think that's unfair. She'd have a huge head start.

Remember when Twitter was called 'graffiti'?

Wise people think all they say, fools say all they think.

I went to the doctor the other day and I said, 'Have you got anything for wind?' So he gave me a kite.

I had a crazy dream that I weighed less than a thousandth of a gram. I was like, 0mg!

My new band is called Free Beer, because when people see a sign that says 'Free Beer Tomorrow at 9 p.m.', they show up.

Scientists have just built the world's biggest supercollider, and they're doing experiments to see what makes up protons. I hope that if the experiment's successful, the whole of our reality will dissolve, and a big sign will up come that says: Level Two!

Some people just need a hug ... around the neck ... with a rope.

Adam came first, but then again men always do.

The closest most people ever get to perfection is when they're filling out a job application.

Why don't you slip into something more comfortable ... like a coma.

Alcohol is a perfect solvent: it dissolves marriages, families and careers.

The love between two mimes is an unspoken love.

The most reliable way to save face is to keep the bottom half of it tightly closed.

The wife and I just sat in a hot car and bickered for six hours. It was the same as going on holiday except we saved £1,000.

Youth is when we are always hunting greener pastures, and middle age is when we can barely mow the one we've got.

It isn't your jeans that make your bum look fat.

If time is money, I'm running out of time.

Build a man a fire and he'll be warm for a day. Set a man on fire and he'll be warm for the rest of his life.

Every time I take up exercising I meet new people. They're usually paramedics, but still, new people.

I was thinking I should see a psychic, so I figure a really good one should be calling any day now.

The difference between erotic and kinky: erotic is using a feather; kinky is using the whole chicken.

I spent my youth trying to attain wealth and now I'm spending my wealth trying to attain youth.

What was the best thing before sliced bread?

The reason grandchildren and grandparents get along so well is because they have a common enemy.

Squirrels: nature's speed bumps.

Just kicked my neighbour's car. Now I have to figure out how to get a smart car out of a tree.

A fraction of the population worries me, and that fraction is nine-tenths.

There's no fool like an old fool. But some of you young fools are showing real promise.

When I went shopping, I accidentally put my groceries in with my new Nintendo. Now my Wii smells of asparagus.

I prefer not to think before I speak. I like to be just as surprised as everyone else by what comes out of my mouth.

My imaginary friends are real. They just happen to be friends with other people except me.

My wife and daughter are out of town, which means I'm the man of the house now.

I finally got my head together, but now my body is falling apart.

Why does everyone say my name like it means 'shut up'?

Life has no remote. Get up and change it yourself.

Anyone who has never made a mistake has never tried anything new.

I used to own a motorcycle shop, but I had to sell it. I was always two tired.

My local bank wants a 'relationship', but I told them I have no interest.

She said she was approaching forty, and I couldn't help wondering from which direction.

It's Groundhog Day. But enough about the school lunch menu.

Arguing with women is like getting arrested: everything you say will be used against you.

I backed a horse last week at ten to one. It came in at quarter past four.

Sometimes I fear that my entire life is a mockumentary.

Sunny today, with a slight chance of me going outside to enjoy it.

Some of the most self-absorbed people I know are me.

A bullet may have your name on it, but a grenade is addressed 'to whom it may concern'.

Chicken and egg in bed, chicken has head on pillow, smoking. Egg rolls over, annoyed, saying, 'I guess we answered that question.'

You don't appreciate a lot of stuff in school until you get older. Little things like being spanked every day by a middle-aged woman. Stuff you pay good money for in later life.

I'm throwing caution to the wind. I hope it goes better than that spitting incident a while back.

Alcohol: because no good story started with someone eating a salad.

Mother-in-law's had her belly button pierced. Good place to hang the air freshener.

Recently my Visa card was stolen. Now it's everywhere I want to be.

She has a million-dollar figure but the top half is counterfeit.

I'm sick of being the guy everyone comes to when they want the money I owe them.

I was walking along the road the other day and on the pavement I saw a white baby ghost. However, come to think of it, it may have been a tissue.

Free puppies: part cocker spaniel, part sneaky neighbour's dog.

I put off doing more things by 9 a.m. than most people do all day.

Pushed too hard against my eardrum with a Q-tip and reset my brain.

Home is where you can say anything you want because nobody listens to you anyway.

For three days after death, hair and fingernails continue to grow, but phone calls taper off.

Pain is nature's way of saying, 'Don't do that.' Painkillers are mankind's way of saying, 'Just watch me.'

Sex is not the answer. Sex is the question. 'Yes' is the answer.

Hey NATO, my neighbour's testing short-range dry dog poop missiles again.

Anybody who thinks talk is cheap never argued with a traffic cop.

I'm so far behind I thought I was first.

Relationships with women are a challenge. They are tests, and I treat them as such: I cheat.

Some people hear voices. Some see invisible people. Others have no imagination whatsoever.

Sometimes I spice up my marriage by wearing a long black night-gown with buttons on it. It makes me look just like a remote control.

Into every life some rain must fall. Usually when your car windows are down.

Never trust someone that wears coloured contacts. They've already lied to you.

I'm buying my wife a matching belt and bag for Valentine's Day. We'll have that vacuum cleaner working in no time.

Lowercase letters: just like uppercase letters, but without the drama.

I'll never forget the first time we met. Although I will keep trying.

My friend died doing what he loved... Heroin.

I have a feeling I would be more successful had I worked harder, invested wisely and inherited more.

Why didn't Spiderman's enemies simply create a Spiderwoman to mate and eat him?

To err is human, to forgive, canine.

Children in the back seats of cars cause accidents, but accidents in the back seats of cars cause children.

The night before my wedding I had my hair cut into the shape of a deer. It was a stag 'do.

I love you with all of my butt. I would say heart, but my butt is bigger.

My body is a temple ... of doom.

I always cry at weddings. You know, 'cause I know what it's like to be married.

The ocean's salt would cover the earth 500ft deep, or flavour four cups of hot and sour soup.

A lorryload of tortoises crashed into a trainload of terrapins. What a turtle disaster.

'Do I come here often?' – Amnesiac hitting on a girl.

Some days you just have to fill the bath with Skittles and pretend to be Godzilla in a ball pit.

I saw this bloke chatting up a cheetah and I thought, 'He's trying to pull a fast one.'

Please, Lord, let me prove that winning the lottery won't spoil me.

Dragons sleep during the day so they can hunt knights.

Studies confirm that caffeine withdrawal (for me) can be fatal (for you).

I hate sex in the movies. I tried it once: the seat folded up, the drink spilled and that ice, well, it really chilled her mood.

Without Ray-Ban Wayfarer sunglasses, 98 per cent of all '80s saxophone solos wouldn't have happened.

It's much easier to be crazy and know it than to be sane and have some doubts.

I tried water polo, but my horse drowned.

The perfect housewarming gift is fire.

I've always wanted to barge into a dry-cleaner's and shout 'Stop the presses!'

You can lead a man to ponder, but you can't make him think.

I'm really a timid person – I was beaten up by Quakers.

Carrot cake plus Rohypnol equals passion cake.

This bloke said to me, 'I'm going to chop off the bottom of one of your trouser legs and put it in a library.' I thought, 'That's a turn-up for the books.'

I was expelled from school for cheating on my metaphysics exam. I looked within the soul of the boy sitting next to me.

I'm pretty sure if that dogs could talk their most common phrase would be, 'Are you going to eat that?'

When I see insane people on the street talking to themselves, I want to tell them about Twitter.

People who say they don't care what people think are usually desperate to have people think they don't care what people think.

I found a hole in my trainer that I can put my finger through. I've now been banned from the gym.

A lot of people are afraid of heights. Not me, I'm afraid of widths.

A secret is what you tell everyone not to tell anyone else.

It's the quiet ones that you've got to watch. Especially at mime shows.

This new sundial I bought is useless. It doesn't say whether it's a.m. or p.m.

I like birthdays, but I think too many can kill you.

A celebrity is someone who works hard all his life to become known and then wears dark glasses to avoid being recognised.

I was playing my air guitar and accidentally woke up a mime.

Screw up your courage. You've screwed everything else up.

My favourite yoga position is the downward-facing nap.

I wish I could autocorrect my life.

How do you know if it's time to wash the dishes and clean your house? Look inside your pants. If you find a penis in there, it's not time.

My wife will buy anything marked down. Last year she bought an escalator.

If you could watch my life backwards, you'd see a Weight Watchers success story.

Marriage is about give and take. You better give it to her or she'll take it anyway.

Jesus loves you, but everyone else thinks you're an arsehole.

No matter how much you give a homeless person for tea, you never get that cup of tea.

Watch repairmen always get to work on time.

Nostalgia isn't what it used to be.

Remember, if you smoke after sex you're doing it too fast.

I don't have an attitude problem. You have a perception problem.

Did you know that dolphins are so smart that within a few weeks of captivity, they can train people to stand on the very edge of the pool and throw them fish?

I'm a heavy smoker. I go through two lighters a day.

Still waiting for Google Earth to have a layer that shows lost frisbees.

So I phoned up the spiritual leader of Tibet, and he sent me a large goat with a long neck. Turns out I phoned dial-a-llama.

The first half of our lives is ruined by our parents, and the second half by our children.

I would have been here sooner, but I was avoiding you.

My girlfriend and I have an open relationship, and will continue to do so right up until she finds out.

What do you do when someone close to you dies? Move seats.

Seeing a spider is nothing. It becomes a problem when it disappears.

The main difference between an oral thermometer and a rectal thermometer is in the taste.

I think senility is going to be a fairly smooth transition for me.

I've been trying to hire a librarian, but they're all fully booked.

My kids have my wife's hair. The sink has mine.

Rain is just a bunch of humidity that's tired of living a lie.

A good friend will help you move, a great friend will help you move a body.

I never use body butter. I don't want to make myself irresistible to cannibals.

Why are haemorrhoids called 'haemorrhoids' instead of 'assteroids'?

If you think things improve with age, attend a class reunion.

I felt like a true gentlemen today, opening the door for my wife, but I was doing 70mph.

I've been knocking for ten minutes. Don't people answer their bathroom windows any more?

My body is like a temple. It takes staff to maintain, and sometimes the neighbours complain about the noise coming from it.

Never stand under a pumpkin tree.

The lights are on, but someone's been playing with the dimmer switch.

I dedicate this show to my dad who was a roofer. So Dad, if you're up there...

Unfortunately, putting a bow on your head does not make you gifted.

The only constant is change. Can you spare some?

I used to get strange looks for trying to use my phone on the bus. But then again, it was 1982.

It's not what you do. It's what you get away with.

The twenty-first century. When deleting history is more important than making it.

If a police dog is chasing you, try not to dive in a tunnel, then on to a seesaw, then jump through a hoop of fire. They're trained for that.

No matter how often I visit New York City, I'm always struck by the same thing: a yellow taxicab.

My boss has a heart of gold. Or whatever metal they're using these days to make robot hearts.

For sale: broken quiz machine. No questions asked.

Never agree to plastic surgery if the doctor's office is full of portraits by Picasso.

I went up to a girl and said, 'Hi, do you like the strong and silent type?' 'As a matter of fact I do,' she giggled. So I let out a fart and walked off.

One thing my dogs and I have in common is that we never want me to go to work.

I put tape on the mirrors in my house so I don't accidentally walk through into another dimension.

Doctor to patient: 'I have good news and bad news. The good news is that you are not a hypochondriac.'

I asked my date what she wanted to drink. She said, 'Oh, I guess I'll have Champagne.' I said, 'Guess again.'

Denial isn't just a river in Egypt.

If we really wanted to slow down Iran's nuclear scientists we'd introduce them to Angry Birds.

Drink coffee! Do stupid things faster with more energy!

Pre-marital classes should have a chapter on which way to hang the toilet paper.

If time is money, then how come someone like me, who has all the time in the world, is still broke?

I usually say all the right things. The problem seems to be that I say them to the wrong people.

Militant feminists: I take my hat off to them. They don't like that.

My wife was moaning because I always put her down because of her weight. Who does she think I am? The world's strongest man?

Nine out of ten doctors agree the leading cause of muffin tops is in fact muffins.

I drove my car until the day of wreckoning.

I need a backspace key for my mouth.

A bus station is where a bus stops. A train station is where a train stops. On my desk, I have a work station.

Ten years ago we had Steve Jobs, Bob Hope and Johnny Cash. Now we have no Jobs, no Hope and no Cash.

I was stood at the bar and I said to this girl, 'Do you come here often?' She said, 'Will you bugger off, this is the gymnastics final.'

If you want to know why the Brits are so good at cycling... Just take a look at the cost of public transport.

I ran into my old English teacher. He said, 'Goode to see ye!'

People are always asking me if I can do a negative tortoise impression. I'm going to stick my neck out and say no.

Is it true that cannibals don't eat clowns because they taste funny?

Five out of every three people have trouble understanding fractions.

I asked my girlfriend what she wanted for Christmas this year, and she said, 'Surprise me.' So I phoned her from Hawaii.

Children have so much energy because they siphon it out of their parents like tiny petrol thieves.

Study finds researchers study a lot of dumb things.

Why do banks leave their doors open and then chain the pens to the counter?

Seems like nothing in life has gone my way since that second face tattoo.

Right before I die, I'm going to say to whoever is next to me, 'I left a million dollars in the...'

I'm not ignoring you. I'm pretending you're dead.

My mates bet me a hundred quid I wouldn't take five Viagra tabs at once. I thought, 'How hard can it be?'

When it comes to affairs of the heart, I try to avoid EMTs, electric paddles and the word 'CLEAR!'

I don't know if you've ever fallen asleep while eating a plate of cauliflower and then woken up and thought you were in the clouds.

I told my wife the truth – I was seeing a psychiatrist. Then she told me the truth – she was seeing a psychiatrist, two plumbers and a bartender.

Researchers say trees are not adapting well to climate change, and they pine for a simpler time.

Many a man owes his success to his first wife and his second wife to his success.

Your mum's so fat they call her a pioneer. She's always breaking new ground.

Somewhere, a smart laser eye surgeon has an office full of brochures that are all slightly out of focus.

I hate it when people say, 'Oh, I'm a vegetarian except for fish.' Yeah? And I'm a non-smoker except for cigarettes.

I don't do drugs. If I want a rush I get out of the chair when I'm not expecting it.

Some of you need to give your inner child a time-out.

Right now I'm having amnesia and déjà vu at the same time. I think I've forgotten this before.

If you're talking about a creature that just wants to gulp down a huge meal and then sleep all day, then yes, I would call myself a cougar.

I went to a restaurant the other day called Taste of the Raj. The waiter hit me with a stick and got me to build a complicated railway system.

My wife said to me, 'I want you to whisper dirty things into my ear.' So I said, 'Kitchen, bathroom, living room...'

Cheating is such an ugly way to put it. I like to think of it as outsourcing my sex life.

I asked a Geordie hotdog seller for a frankfurter. He gave me a picture of Sinatra.

You remind me of somebody I don't want to know.

Some things have to be believed to be seen.

Some of us are wired differently. I think you should sue the contractor.

I walked up to reception in the hotel and said, 'Sorry, but I forgot what room I'm in.' 'No problem, sir. This is called the lobby.'

My kids' voices only work with caps lock on, apparently.

God must love stupid people. He made so many of them.

Next year, let's make the change to daylight saving time on a Monday at, say, 4 p.m.

The lottery: a tax on people who are bad at maths.

I've just bought a giant bonsai tree.

You call it multiple personalities, I call it social networking in my head.

I once had a goldfish that would hump the carpet ... but only for about thirty seconds.

At some point in my life I switched from acid to antacid.

I went to a restaurant that serves breakfast at any time. So I ordered French toast during the Renaissance.

I wish Twitter was real life, so women only had 140 characters to get to the bloody point.

'I'm going to a wedding in north-west London.' 'Maida Vale?' 'Nah, I'll wear a suit – wouldn't want to show the bride up.'

The toughest time for bakers is their hour of knead.

I'm not entirely sure why the kids call me 'Quasimodo', but I've got a hunch.

I was going to get married wearing flip-flops, but I got cold feet.

The optician just told me I'm colour-blind – that came as a bolt out of the green.

It's not the fall that kills you, it's the sudden stop at the end.

According to a new study, the moon is shrinking. Which proves a sad truth: balls everywhere in the universe shrink with age.

What goes 'ooooo'? A cow with no lips.

As I always say, fake it 'til you make it. Nurse, scalpel please.

My neighbours have inspired me to take up a new hobby... Building a moat.

What cheese would you use for hiding a horse? Mascarpone.

Don't be afraid to tell people what you think. Just be sure to ascribe it to someone else.

Somehow, when she dresses up like a witch one night a year, it's sexy. But when she's a witch every other day of the year ... nothing.

Thought I was having déjà vu but it turns out I do the exact same things every day.

I saw a man at the beach yelling, 'Help, shark! Help!' I just laughed. I knew that shark wasn't going to help him.

Why is gambling banned in Africa? Because there are too many cheetahs.

I've had a rabbit's foot for twenty years. My other foot is normal.

Words matter: you can hardly write a decent sentence without them.

Most people want a perfect relationship... I just want a hamburger that looks like the ones in adverts.

Hypnotists reckon they can cure alcoholism merely by implanting an idea in the drinker's head. It's a sobering thought.

579s84a831f9e94t67y89304. There's safety in numbers.

I can jump higher than mountains. You see, mountains can't jump.

I spit into the wind, but the wind spit back.

One thing you can say for kids, they don't go around showing everyone pictures of their grandparents.

Have you ever how noticed anybody going slower than you is an idiot, and anyone going faster is a maniac.

Grammar is important! Capitalisation is the difference between helping your uncle Jack off a horse and helping your uncle jack off a horse.

Why do people believe you when you say there are 4 billion stars, but check when you say the paint is wet?

Why do Americans choose from just two contenders for President, but fifty for Miss America?

The phrase 'Don't take this the wrong way' has a 0 per cent success rate.

Empty pockets teach you a million things in life, but full pockets can spoil you in a million ways.

If they make it illegal to wear the veil at work, bee keepers are going to be furious.

My wife is one of those people who keep talking when no one is interested any more... A school teacher.

I notice you have a razor-sharp wit. You know, someone should take that away from you before you cut yourself.

What's the only animal with an asshole halfway up its back? A police horse.

My eyes are bigger than my stomach. But my stomach is catching up.

When I grow up, I want to be my dog.

Just saw a sign for 'DUI classes'. That seems like an easy class.

I taught him everything I know and he's still stupid.

In case of fire, exit the building before tweeting about it.

Change is inevitable, except from a vending machine.

The four stages of man: Infancy, Childhood, Adolescence and Obsolescence.

A letter came from the bank. I could tell it was from the bank as it was written on a wreath nailed to the front door.

Cabbage patches are pointless. I can give up cabbage easily without them.

'My wife's gone to Jordan.' 'Amman?' 'No, she's just got big hands, but you're not the first to ask.'

My friend wanted me to help her start a dog collection. So I gave her a couple of pointers.

When people accuse me of being pretentious, I simply do what my spiritual forefather Friedrich Nietzsche would do and rise above it.

If it's true that our species is alone in the universe, then I'd have to say the universe aimed rather low and settled for very little.

If you want a successful relationship, find someone who likes the same thermostat setting you do.

If you lend someone £20 and never see that person again, it was probably worth it.

The secret to success is knowing who to blame for your failures.

Whatever you do in life, give 100 per cent ... unless you're donating blood.

My wife came home with a vibrator, started waving it about and screamed, 'I don't need you any more!' Guess who had to put the batteries in.

When I come to a fork in the road, I get hungry.
A shipment of Viagra was hijacked last week. Police are looking for two hardened criminals.

Once the shit hits the fan, the only rational choice is to sweep it up, package it and sell it as fertiliser.

A Canadian is just an unarmed American with health insurance.

What do you call a deer with no eyes? No idea.

I'm a cubic zirconia in the rough.

I always look my best when I wake up in the morning. Right up until I put my contact lenses in.

A friend said to me, 'I can never do the Welsh accent properly. Every time I try it, it sounds like Pakistani.' I said, 'You'll just have to try harder, Tariq.'

I'm against hunting. In fact, I'm a hunt saboteur: I go out the night before and shoot the fox.

What do you get the man who has everything? Might I suggest a gravestone inscribed with the words, 'So what?'

The lack of suspense is killing me.

Science flies you to the moon, religion flies you into buildings.

I hope my travel mug tells stories to all my stay-at-home dishes.

Never get into fights with ugly people: they have nothing to lose.

I wanted to be a milkman but I didn't have the bottle.

I lost my job as a cricket commentator for saying, 'I don't want to bore you with the details...'

As superpowers go, my being able to see 1.5 seconds into the future isn't particularly... DUCK!

The hardest thing to learn in life is which bridges to cross and which to burn.

Did you hear Superman's been arrested and he can't get bail? They say he's a flight risk.

I sought advice from a numerologist, but nothing she said added up.

I intend to live forever. So far, so good.

So what if Jesus turned water into wine? I turned a whole student loan into vodka once.

A boy can learn a lot from a dog: obedience, loyalty and the importance of turning around three times before lying down.

I'm bad with names – can I just ignore you?

Fun: find a box. Put it on your head. Walk around asking people to let you out.

Good friends don't let you do stupid things. Best friends don't let you do stupid things alone.

A jump lead walks into a bar. The barman says, 'I'll serve you, but don't start anything.'

My therapist says I have a preoccupation with vengeance. We'll see about that.

Sex is like a bank account. You deposit, withdraw and lose interest.

I love my six-pack. That's why I protect it with a thick layer of fat.

'Doctor! Doctor! How long do I have left to live?' 'Ten.' 'Ten what? Months? Years?' 'Nine... Eight... Seven...'

'Doctor! Doctor! I think I'm a smoke detector.' 'Calm down. There's no cause for alarm.'

I raked my neighbour's lawn while they were at church, and now Jesus will probably take all the credit.

Diamonds can't be a girl's best friend. I've never heard my wife talking about them behind their backs.

When my wife caught me using a penis enlargement cream, she laughed. I told her, 'There's no need to rub it in.'

I bought one of those anti-bullying wristbands when they first came out. I say 'bought' – actually I stole it off a short, fat, ginger kid.

My wife says I talk while I sleep, but I'm sceptical. Nobody at work has ever mentioned it.

At my lemonade stand I used to give the first glass away free and charge five pounds for the second glass. The refill contained the antidote.

You say sommelier, I say gainfully employed wino.

Why do seagulls live near the sea? Because if they lived near the bay, they'd be called bagels.

If there was an award for laziness... I'd probably send someone to pick it up for me.

I cleaned the attic with the wife the other day. Now I can't get the cobwebs out of her hair.

I said to the wife, 'I wish you wouldn't smoke in bed.' She said, 'But a lot of women do.' I said, 'Not bacon they don't.'

'Maintenant' is my favourite French word, for now.

I've got a joke about a group of small dolphins. It's multi-porpoise.

I broke up with my girlfriend when she told me she was 'really into Alan'. It's been a tough week, what with that and being diagnosed as dyslexic.

How many people with no sense of humour does it take to change a light bulb? One.

'Out, damned Spot! Out, I say!' – Lady Macbeth's dog takes a crap on the carpet.

What if birds are just alien cameras?

How many seconds are there in an hour? About eight if you take my wife to a buffet.

Be wary of strong drink. It can make you shoot at tax collectors ... and miss.

Cow-tipping safety tip: what looks like a sleeping cow might actually be a bulldozer.

Marriage: the only sport in which the trapped animal has to buy a licence.

My New Year's resolution for 2011 is to stop leaving everything so late.

Raising children is part joy and part guerrilla warfare.

I wish my best mate would hurry up and leave his cheating whore of a wife. Then I won't have to feel so guilty for sleeping with her all the time.

Does running away from your problems count as exercising?

Reckless abandon can be your friend. But never depend on it for bail.

My grandfather started walking five miles a day when he was sixty. Now he's eighty-five and we don't know where he is.

I'd like to keep the world at arm's length, but my arms don't seem to be long enough.

A generous spirit is its own reward, but I still prefer cash.

My action figure would come with action sold separately.

I just knew I was going to get thrown out of the optimism society.

I've got a party in my pants and the sprinklers just went off.

Can you guys keep it down? I can barely hear myself suffering in silence.

Insanity runs in my family. It practically gallops.

Human cannonballs should be rounder.

Time is that quality of nature that keeps events from happening all at once. Lately, it doesn't seem to be working.

A politician will find an excuse to get out of anything except office.

A tweet with a typo is like your ex: you notice it right after letting it go.

My wife isn't always right, but she's certainly never wrong.

I've never had a mentor. Unless tormentors count.

In the end it all boils down to one thing... Steam.

Haiku are easy. But sometimes they don't make sense. Refrigerator.

If life hands you lemons, break out the tequila.

'You won't catch me paying for sex,' I shouted, as I pulled up my trousers, grabbed my shoes and ran out of the brothel.

I joined a self-help group for people who talk too much. It's called On and On Anon.

'My wife is driving me to drink!' 'Consider yourself lucky, lad. Mine makes me walk.'

Men who stand in front of cars get tired. Men who stand behind cars get exhausted.

I'm ageing like a fine whiner.

Politicians divide their time between running for office and running for cover.

IKEA: prepare to self-construct.

I'll bet basketball players tell a lot of tall tales.

Most people are willing to strive for success if they can start from the top and then move up.

Never, under any circumstances, take a sleeping pill and a laxative on the same night.

Baseball and pancakes are alike because they both depend on the batter.

I'm not lost, I'm getting in touch with my disoriented side.

Men are like mascara: they run at the first sign of emotion.

I'm like a well-oiled machine that someone forgot to oil.

If steroids are illegal for athletes, shouldn't Photoshop be illegal for models?

I don't want to bore you but there's nobody else around for me to bore.

It's been a really bad day for me. First my girlfriend got run over by a bus. Then I lost my job at the bus company.

Light travels faster than sound. That's why some people appear bright until you hear them speak.

I've done a close-up sketch of a fish. It's a scale drawing.

Struggling to get your lizard up in the morning? You may have a reptile dysfunction.

My mate reckons he's got a thicker typeface than normal. It's a bold claim.

My girlfriend told me she was going commando tonight. Sounded great, until she smashed my window with a smoke grenade and released all my hostages.

I thought I wanted a career, but it turns out I just wanted pay cheques.

162

I'm 100 per cent against animal cruelty. Nothing makes me sadder than when my dog makes fun of me.

I didn't say it was your fault, I said I was blaming you.

To be or not to be... That's a trick question, right?

Nobody's perfect. Especially you.

With sufficient thrust, pigs fly just fine.

Statistics are like a bikini: what they reveal is suggestive, but what they hide is vital.

Turns out people are bad for the environment.

Life tip: it's always a good idea to get a second set of fingerprints on your weapon of choice.

I would be unstoppable if I could just get started.

Think of your flu jab as an ouch of prevention.

I'm still playing with a full deck. I just shuffle slower these days.

I see you're having a bad hair decade.

When someone texts 'ROFL', I always imagine Scooby Doo trying to say 'waffle'.

They say money can't buy you happiness... Guess they never heard about divorce.

I'll bet you £46,368.86 you can't guess how much I owe my bookie.

I just found bacteria growing on my chocolate bar. I guess there is life on Mars.

When staying at a public campground, a tuba placed on a picnic table will keep adjacent pitches empty.

Think of how stupid the average person is, and then realise half of them are stupider than that.

God gave us families to help us better appreciate total strangers.

If you worry too much about your job: stop it. You are not paid enough to worry.

I saw a woman wearing a sweatshirt with 'Guess' on it. I said, 'Thyroid problems?'

Three out of every five home improvement projects end in divorce.

Embroidery is a crewel lie.

I just put some LSD into a bag of dog food. Bitches were tripping.

Don't piss me off! I'm running out of places to hide the bodies.

The lady I'm married to has accused me of being impersonal.

If ignorance is bliss, there should be more happy people.

If you wear the right coloured apron, you can hand out free samples of whatever you want at the supermarket.

Coffee's not working – quick, throw a wolf in my lap.

Everyone is gifted. But not everyone opens their present.

I wish some conversations came with a fast-forward button.

Every day, man is making bigger and better foolproof things, and every day, nature is making bigger and better fools. So far, I think nature is winning.

Death is hereditary.

How can my mirror and my camera have such completely different ideas of what I look like?

I'm surprised that the hip-hop culture hasn't caught on with rabbits.

You can get a hot cup of Joe any time at the Cannibal Diner.

Sound: what you should remember to turn off when letting your mind go blank.

Jesus loves you, but everyone else thinks you're an idiot.

A shouting mother is the original surround sound.

One day in the scary film when the victim yells 'Hello?' I want to see the killer shout out 'Hey! I'm in the kitchen. Want a sandwich?'

Where there's a will, I want to be in it.

I always mean what I say. It's just that I don't always mean to say it out loud.

My son is allergic to peanuts. He breaks out in a rash every time I bring home my pay cheque.

Some days, I practise positive thinking. Other days, I'm not positive I am thinking.

I went on a girls' night out recently. The invitation said 'dress to kill'. I went as Rose West.

I found the key to success. Now I just need to find the lock.

Shopping centres have benches so that guys can sit down while they give up the will to live.

I've given up reading books. I find it takes my mind off myself.

Because of exams, I learn more in a week before I take the test than I learn during the entire term.

I like to watch horror films by pressing my face into my husband's arm and furiously whispering, 'WHAT'S HAPPENING?'

If I could be any person, living or dead, I'd definitely be a living person.

I'm zero for 145 at pulling random books on people's bookcases and having it lead to a secret passageway.

If my life was a spy thriller, I'd be the taxi driver broadsided in the first car-chase scene.

'Say hello to my little friend.' Great film quote. Terrible bedroom talk.

We have all heard that a million monkeys banging on a million type-writers will eventually reproduce the entire works of Shakespeare. Now, thanks to the Internet, we know this is not true.

Where do you see yourself in five beers?

The rules were already broken when I got here.

'What the hell?' my wife moaned yesterday. 'Football, tennis and Formula 1.' Turns out she didn't want PlayStation games for her birthday.

Why do bankruptcy lawyers expect to be paid?

There are two sides to every argument, but I don't have time to listen to yours.

Men think about sex every seven seconds. That's why I eat hotdogs in under six seconds – so it doesn't get weird.

A committee is twelve men doing the work of one.

Would you mind repeating the part where you weren't talking?

I always try not to judge people. Which is probably why I lost my job as a judge.

What I would give the woman who has everything? Well ... my phone number for a start.

I took my husband to the hospital yesterday to have seventeen stitches out. That'll teach him to buy me a sewing kit for my birthday.

I crossed the road today. Next I'm going to tick the pavement.

If your plan A doesn't work, don't sweat it. The alphabet has twenty-five more letters.

Chihuahua is an ancient Aztec word for 'never sit in peace again'.

If you ate pasta and antipasto, would you still be hungry?

Good news: girls think I have a magical power. Bad news: it's invisibility.

Cats make great pets. Out of their owners.

All of life's but a stage, and I think I missed my mark.

I like to go into the Body Shop and shout out really loud, 'I've already got one!'

If you ever hit rock bottom, bring some beer. I'm almost out.

No, I'm not single. I'm in a long-distance relationship because my girlfriend lives in the future.

I've just opened a shop specialising in shelves. They're flying off the... Selling really well.

I don't know how I got over the hill without getting to the top.

Twitter is worth $4 billion. And that's just in lost productivity.

Don't knock the weather. If it didn't change once in a while, nine out of ten people couldn't start a conversation.

I'm not that bright. The only way I'll ever get to say 'Checkmate!' is if I eat at a restaurant in Australia.

If you ever need anything, please don't hesitate to ask someone else first.

If the sky's the limit, then what is space? Over the limit?

I have kleptomania. But when it gets bad, I take something for it.

The results are in: 4 a.m. is officially the very best time to make decisions you'll regret later.

Is there another word for synonym?

I show a girl who the boss is by handing her a mirror.

So I went down my local ice-cream shop, and said, 'I want to buy an ice cream.' He said, 'Hundreds and thousands?' I said, 'We'll start with one.' He said, 'Knickerbocker glory?' I said, 'I do get a certain amount of freedom in these trousers, yes.'

My wife's leaving me because I have a terrible sense of humour. Ha ha.

Frisbeetarianism is the belief that when you die, your soul goes up on the roof and gets stuck.

Look, pal. You had best stay out of my way or you will quickly learn that I am absolutely no threat to you whatsoever.

My Rover broke down this morning. Something about 'always being the one doing the fetching'.

I've got ninety-nine problems, but the correct use of the verb 'to be' isn't one.

I just walked in on my manager vigorously masturbating. He told me to stop vigorously masturbating and to get out of his office.

If you think I'm pretentious, you should try talking to my sommelier.

I'm listening to a cassette of protest songs. It must be a demo tape.

Whoever said money doesn't grow on trees obviously never sold marijuana.

You know it's time to clean the fridge when something closes the door from the inside.

On my deathbed I want to leave this world surrounded by a beautiful loving family. So I've told my real one to stay away.

Walk into a gun store, buy three guns and a bunch of ammunition, then ask them if they have any ski masks.

Patient: 'Doctor, I think I'm addicted to Twitter.' Doctor: 'Sorry, I don't follow you.'

The pen may be mightier than the sword but the smart money is still on the sword.

A push-up bra is like a bag of crisps. You open it up and it's half empty.

Mirrors don't lie. Lucky for me, they can't laugh either.

If I brought one thing to a dessert island it would have to be a spoon.

Is reading in the bathroom considered multi-tasking?

If adult nappies are called Depends, then baby nappies should be called Definitely.

The next time there's an awkward silence, try whispering, 'Did you forget your line?'

Well, my brother says hello. So hurrah for speech therapy.

Know what the two pessimists did when they first met? They shook their heads.

My priest just told me I need more exorcise.

I went to see a psychic yesterday. He said, 'What's your name?' I said, 'I want my money back.'

Would I lie to you? Again, I mean.

Bubble wrap is like catnip for people.

I try to masturbate once a day for the health benefits. The other four times are just for me.

A caterpillar turns into a butterfly. Best Transformer ever.

I've just bought a guard dog and he's really good. I haven't been able to get inside my house for the past three days.

My wife asked this morning, 'How come you don't wake up with an erection?' I replied, 'Because you're the woman of my dreams.'

Non-alcoholic beer is like a vibrator without the batteries. It fills you up, but lacks the buzz.

There are more men than women in mental hospitals ... which just goes to show who's driving who crazy.

Some people deserve to have eggs thrown at them. Brick-shaped eggs ... made of brick.

My dog thinks if she can avoid eye contact she doesn't have to mind. I've found that also works well with my boss.

I told my friend, 'You're like a drug to me.' He said, 'You mean I'm addictive?' 'Please! I mean I can only take you in small doses.'

Normally you have news, weather and travel, but not on snow day. On snow day, news is weather is travel.

It's like each individual hair has its own hairstyle.

Sure, I'm willing to put in longer hours at work. As long as they're lunch hours.

Friendship is like peeing on yourself: everyone can see it, but only you get the warm feeling that it brings.

What do you have when you have two balls in your hands? A man's undivided attention.

I'm not needy. I'm wanty.

For adult education, nothing beats children.

I'm not getting old. I'm becoming a classic.

I know I'm drinking myself to a slow death. But then again, I'm in no hurry.

I have a strong will, but a weak won't.

The doctor told me I suffer with insomnia. I've lain awake all night worrying about it.

My lesbian neighbours gave me a Rolex. I think they misunderstood when I said, 'I wanna watch.'

I flirted with disaster last night. Now disaster won't stop texting me.

A bartender is just a pharmacist with a limited inventory.

I've started group meetings at my house for people with OCD. I don't have it, but I'm hoping one of them will be bothered enough to clean up.

If a pope goes to the bathroom, is it considered holy crap?

If I could be a superhero, I'd be Aluminium Man. My superpower would be foiling crime.

What's the difference between a lawyer and a bucket of shit? The bucket.

Honestly, who's got the time to teach a man to fish?

The only substitute for good manners is fast reflexes.

'You wouldn't steal a car.' I would if I could download it.

My brother came over to borrow the lawn mower. I told him she was still sleeping and he should come back in an hour.

A gymnast walks into a bar. He gets a two-point deduction and ruins his chances of a medal.

'That procedure doesn't work. Let's institute newer, more complex procedures to remedy this.' – Management 101

I don't suffer from insanity. I enjoy every minute of it.

I wish my wife would let me show her who's boss around here.

A miser is a hard person to live with, but he makes a fine ancestor.

You have two choices in life: you can stay single and be miserable, or get married and wish you were dead.

Just told my joke about Peter Pan again. Never gets old.

Dial M for Dyslexia.

Back in hospital for narcissism treatment again. I keep checking myself out.

How many immature people does it take to change a light bulb? Your mum.

Waiter brought me a plate of badger meat. Must have ordered from the sett menu.

Evidently my admirers are all secret.

Hell hath no fury. My wife has it all.

Old ladies in wheelchairs with blankets over their legs, I don't think so... Retired mermaids.

Increasingly, I'm feeling like a used car. My body's shot, my rear end's dragging and I can't keep my hood up.

I keep a well-stocked larder in case friends drop by. I could hide in there for days.

Bad memory: what is most responsible for the good old days.

I'm moving to Seoul. I was told it would be a good Korea move.

I stopped approving of political jokes the moment I realised how many of them were getting elected.

'LSD "helps alcoholics to give up drinking".' In the same way that a bullet helps you give up oxygen.

The imaginary enemy of my enemy is my imaginary friend.

The house is so quiet, I can hear myself think. Never mind, it's the toilet running.

My wife says I have a way with words: the wrong way.

At the age of six I lost both of my parents... What a card game that was.

There's too much emphasis placed on winning in life. I'm just trying for a participation ribbon.

Well, I see no one turned up for first day of ninja school... Or did they?

I'm nicknamed Spider. It sounds tough, but it's really because I'm more scared of you than you are of me.

I just sent both my kids to their rooms. So now I'm jealous of both of them.

'I drive like lightning.' 'You drive fast?' 'No, I hit trees.'

My girlfriend was furious when I said the reason I didn't go down on her was because it smelt fishy down there. Mermaids are so oversensitive.

I looked out the window and it was pissing down. I thought, 'Fuck it, I'm not going out in that. I'll pick the kids up from school tomorrow.'

To whoever invented the zero: thanks for nothing.

I just phoned the police because someone broke into my home and released thousands of house flies in it. They're sending out the swat team.

To catch a Swedish fish you have to use a gummy worm.

When you see a married guy talking to himself, you know he's just reliving an argument he already lost.

The really scary part of middle age is that you know you're going to grow out of it.

I enjoy using the comedy technique of self-deprecation – but I'm not very good at it.

There is no right way to do the wrong thing. But there is usually an easier way.

There's no fool like an old fool. But some of you young fools are showing real promise.

Wanted: person to inflate balloons. The ideal candidate knows how to blow things out of proportion.

Women may not hit harder, but they hit lower.

I saw a cougar. In leopard-print tights. Driving a Jaguar. No lion.

Snowboarding: all the fun of surfing and almost no shark attacks.

I have two imaginary lovers. It's a mirage à trois.

I can't even teach new dogs new tricks.

If you wake up feeling funny, you should call in shtick.

Why is it called tourist season if we can't shoot them?

Special Show! Ivan the Narcoleptic Trapeze Artist! One Night Only!

I thought coq au vin was love in a lorry.

I tell people exactly what I think. Silently.

I'm not lazy, I'm energy efficient.

Women are too hard to read. Take my wife for instance. You can pick her up whenever you'd like.

This guy was so computer illiterate, when I asked him to turn on the computer he said, 'Where am I supposed to rub it?'

If you must choose between two evils, pick the one you've never tried before.

Please do not disturb me. I'm disturbed enough already.

I've just heard that yesterday one of the seven dwarves kissed a giraffe. According to various sources, the other six put him up to it.

Don't judge me until you've stumbled a mile in my shoes.

Last night a horse asked me if I was planning on driving home. There might've been a police officer on top of it.

The road to ADHD is paved with bad attentions.

I can't afford studio family portraits so I loaded the wife and kids into the back of the truck and ran a red light.

You're not actually the stupidest person on the planet. But if he were to die...

You can pick your friends, and you can pick your nose, but you can't flick your friends out the car window.

If it's true that we're here to help others, then what exactly are the others here for?

A bus is a vehicle that runs twice as fast when you are after it as when you are in it.

On a scale of nine to ten, how would you rate me?

You don't need a parachute to skydive. You only need a parachute to skydive twice.

'My sister used to love dressing up as *Star Wars* characters.' 'Leia?' 'What kind of sicko do you think I am?'

Every time I see the term 'POW camp', I can't help but think it's where Batman learned to punch.

'He that is without sin among you, let him first cast a stone.' – The world's worst trigonometry teacher.

Nitrous Oxo – a laughing stock.

Work through lunch? I don't even work through work.

An advert begs me to try 'the toothbrush most dental professionals use' and I think, 'That's gross; I'll buy my own.'

The number-one cause of divorce is wanting somewhere to send the kids every other weekend.

You can learn a lot about a person just by watching them through binoculars twenty-four hours a day.

There are times when I miss you so bad I wish I could remember where I hid your body.

I'd love to have a sex change. Preferably from 'none' to 'absolutely shitloads'.

It's been one day since my last confession and they still won't let me go.

'Doctor! Doctor! I feel like an old sock.' 'Well, I'll be darned.'

I have enough money to last me the rest of my life, unless I buy something.

There's no I in team, but there are two in schizophrenia.

The most adventures I get is visiting Amazon on my Safari.

There aren't too many banks left with the word 'trust' in their name, are there?

Sunrises are just as beautiful as sunsets, just less crowded.

But I don't want to do-it-myself. The last time I tried that I ended up superglued to the cat.

You seem like a woman with a lot of unresolved issues. Would you like to get married?

Looking fifty is great – if you're sixty.

I'm sorry. Did the middle of my sentence interrupt the beginning of yours?

A smile is a curve that sets everything straight.

Apparently dyslexia is not a good excuse for driving 53 in a 35 zone.

Prison is peculiar. All the pros are cons.

Say what you want about drunk people, but at least they've had all their shots.

I have to exercise early in the morning before my brain figures out what I'm doing.

What's orange and sounds like a parrot? A carrot.

Violence doesn't solve anything. It is, however, a fine temporary fix in some situations.

'Goldfish have a memory that only lasts for five seconds.' If Internet Explorer had that, I'd still be in a relationship.

Never judge a man 'til you've driven a mile with his wife.

I'm a humble person, really. I'm actually much greater than I think I am.

Boobs are the proof that men can focus on two things at once.

We have a beautiful little girl who we named after my mum. In fact, Passive Aggressive Psycho turns five tomorrow.

Will you be my 'it's complicated' on Facebook?

Your pepper spray is making it difficult for me to see you home.

If you can't continually answer a question with a question, then marriage may not be for you.

She told me it was her thirtieth birthday. So I put thirty candles on her cake arranged in the shape of a question mark.

They call it golf because all the other four-letter words were taken.

The difference between a champ and a chump is U.

I have a few skeletons in my closet. Every single one of them deserved it.

So I got lost shopping in IKEA, and now I work here.

The favourite music of Irish teenagers is sham-rock.

I'm a very persuasive person. I can convince myself of anything.

Know who doesn't want to be online right now? Fish.

I think cow tipping is probably the most aggressive form of lactose intolerance.

Wallpaper strippers are often only doing it to pay their way through collage.

I just got a new job in Scotland. Stirling work.

I once dated a French girl called 'Rien'. She meant nothing to me.

'What do we want?' 'Less pedants!' 'Actually, it should be "fewer pedants".'

I hooked the world's biggest fish last night. I'm still reeling.

As a contortionist, when things don't go right I usually get bent out of shape.

The grass may be greener on the other side but I tell myself it's just from envy.

Jokes about dyslexia are as easy as A, C, B.

Knowledge is power, and power corrupts. So study hard and be evil.

My kids start day camp today. Or, as they call it, 'locked out of the house for the rest of the summer'.

Anything seems possible when you don't know what you're talking about.

I'm trying to find myself. But to make it interesting, I'm wearing camouflage.

Who would be your dream dinner-party guests, living or dead? I'd choose living.

Heat causes things to expand. Thus, in summer, the days are longer.

My best relationship advice: make sure you're the crazy one.

There are free things in life I'll never understand: spelling and counting.

Dogs have masters. Cats have staff.

If anyone lost a big stack of banknotes with a rubber band around it... I found the rubber band.

I must have been really pissed when I drove home last night. We don't own a tractor.

Karate seems like a good skill to have if you're ever attacked by a stack of boards.

I got tired of taking it on the chin. So I started swallowing.

I'm always either self-conscious or unconscious.

I wish my cat would stop thinking outside the box.

Living with a toddler is like using a blender with no lid.

Women are reasonable. You don't have to agree with us as long as you admit we're right.

Stun: the only necessary setting a laser printer doesn't have.

A bikini is an outfit where 90 per cent of a woman's body is exposed. The amazing fact is that men are so decent, they only look at the 10 per cent that isn't.

Not being able to see the forest for the bears is a lot worse.

What if all conspiracy theories are started by the government in order to cover up what they're really doing?

The first five days after the weekend are always the hardest.

What do you do when you see an endangered animal eating an endangered plant?

Women shouldn't have children after forty. Because, really, forty children should be enough.

Some mistakes are too much fun to only make once.

Only I can make fun of my wife, because I live with her. If you ever make fun of my wife... I'll make you live with her.

I can't stress enough the importance of stretching the truth before running for political office.

Can you imagine a world without men? No crime and lots of happy, fat women.

Life is a journey ... but one where it's good news when you lose your baggage.

I always tell my wife, 'I love you just the way you are.' But she never listens. She just goes and puts on more weight.

I hate when people say, 'Here's a picture of me when I was younger.' Every picture is a picture of you when you were younger.

A woman walks into a bar and asks for a double entendre – so the barman gives her one.

I am in complete control of my life. But please don't tell my wife, my boss or my kids.

Friends may come and go, but enemies tend to accumulate.

Lord, give me the superpowers to change the things I cannot accept with serenity. Amen.

I'm currently writing a book about my love of dogs and gardening. It's called *Bitches and Hoes*.

Only dead fish go with the flow.

I used to have super powers but my psychiatrist took them away.

You can do more with a kind word and a gun than with just a kind word.

A fool and his money are never around when you need them.

Cocaine is God's way of saying you're making too much money.

I live life in the fast lane ... with a stream of cars behind me, horns blaring.

Middle age is when your age starts to show around your middle.

I couldn't believe it when I found out I could fly. All I took was a passport and a plane ticket.

Photons have mass? I didn't even know they were Catholic.

I tried to hang myself with a bungee cord. I kept almost dying.

Butterflies are not what they used to be.

A baby is an angel whose wings decrease as his legs increase.

I went to a Blunt Weaponry Fan Club party last night. I got really hammered.

My doctor told me: 'I can't do anything for your illness. It's hereditary.' So I told him to send the bill to my father.

The amount of sleep required by the average person is five minutes more.

My girlfriend's legs look great in hold-ups. It's the way they shake as she's handing over the money.

There's a section in tomorrow's paper about the Catholic approach to birth control. It's a pull-out.

Bloke in the pub kept calling me 'Sat Nav'. I told him where to go.

Anger management courses – they're all the rage.

My wife left me because she said I'm addicted to oxymorons. She was pretty ugly anyway.

Deposed kings get throne away.

Police station toilet stolen. Police have nothing to go on.

I'm not sure what I'll do if opportunity ever does decide to knock, but I'll burn that bridge when I come to it.

A paper cut is a tree's last revenge.

My wife has a contract to give lectures. It's called a marriage licence.

My doctor emailed me asking if I knew my 'blod group'. I replied, 'Typo.'

Reporter: 'To what do you attribute your old age?' Old man: 'To the fact that I was born in 1900.'

Pride, commitment, teamwork: words employers use to get you to work more for less money.

We'll be attending the National Schizophrenics Convention. Anybody who's everybody will be there.

Autocorrect: I hate it. The person who created that is a blooming can't.

My cosmetic surgery might have gone wrong, but I'm smiling on the inside.

Remember, boys and girls: do not handle any fireworks. Leave them to the adults who've been drinking all day.

It's useless to hold people to what they say when they're in love, drunk or running for office.

Don't you think it's time we stopped blaming our problems on people in our past and started blaming them on people in the future?

I saw a disclaimer that said 'don't try this at home', so I tried it at my neighbour's house.

Some bloke was acting all hard in the pub. I thought, 'I'm going to take that bastard out!' So I did and we had a lovely time.

I can make the phone ring just by shoving the last oversized bite of burger into my mouth.

As I look around the town I live in, I'm forced to ponder... Who's fattening us up and when will they eat us?

It's so simple to be wise. Just think of something stupid to say and then don't say it.

'What's my birthday present?' 'You see that yellow Ferrari over there?' 'OMG YES?!' 'Well, I got you a notebook in the same colour.'

If you're looking for sympathy, you'll find it in the dictionary between shit and syphilis.

Whenever I read a really stupid tweet I think, 'What an idiot. Why did I write that?'

If someone with multiple personalities threatens to kill himself, is it considered a hostage situation?

I just read an article about the wages of alcoholism. I didn't know you could get paid for that.

He spiked my drink with speed. I didn't mind so much – I got loads of hoovering done.

A clean desk is a sign of a new employee.

The rich and the poor are alike: they both complain about taxes.

Recent research has shown that six out of seven dwarves aren't happy.

If you want me to walk a mile in your shoes, you're going to have to buy the insoles, ointments and powders.

A woman is like a fine wine: you have to let her breathe.

Unlike the others, I have twenty-seven cats for normal reasons.

Have you ever heard your neighbours having sex and thought to yourself, 'If they knew I was under their bed...'?

It's you and me against the world, and I'm switching sides.

My missus just left me after saying I think about football more than her. I was gutted: I've been with her for five seasons.

I was just hugged and then mauled by a bipolar bear.

Women are smarter than men, but men have the advantage of not knowing this.

Never trust a dog to watch your food.

I've gained twenty pounds of belly fat since I landed a desk job. I think of it as my industrial waist.

I before E, except after C: disproved by science.

A friend like you is worth a million dollars. So, if you don't mind ... can I sell you?

Why should I try touching my toes when my knees are so much closer?

When I was younger I had everything handed to me on a plate... Soup was a nightmare.

I once had a dream that came true. I dreamt I was awake and when I woke up I was.

I have all the money I'll ever need – if I die by 4 p.m. today.

Yawning is your body's way of saying '20 per cent battery remaining'.

'What do we want?' 'A cure for Tourette's!' 'When do we want it?' 'Squirrel!'

In my house, multi-tasking means screwing up several things at once.

Smother your wife with love and affection... And if that doesn't work, use a pillow.

I try to stay in touch with reality but lately it won't return my calls.

My satnav keeps saying, 'Go back twenty years and enter law school.'

I've reached the age where birthdays aren't what they used to be. You know ... fun.

There are two types of people I hate: racists and Norwegians.

You don't need training to be a rubbish collector. You just pick it up as you go along.

Remember, there are two words in life that will open a lot of doors for you: 'push' and 'pull'.

I have a large homosexual following. I have to walk slowly though, so that he can keep up.

Spot the Obvious Mistake – possibly the cruellest book in the Spot the Dog series.

The inventor of the ballet skirt was struggling for a name, until he finally put tu and tu together.

The first rule of Freudian Slip Club? You don't wank about Freudian Slip Club. TALK! I meant talk!

Do you have a MySpace account? Then I have a typewriter and a pager you may be interested in purchasing.

The difference between this place and that yogurt is yogurt has a live culture.

I fell in love at first sight. I should have looked twice.

Ever notice when people reach a certain age they repeat everything they say? They repeat everything they say.

I've had to cancel my appointment at the impotence clinic. Something's come up.

Did you sleep well? No, I made a couple of mistakes.

God, I hate waiting in lines. I wish this woman would hurry up and pick a suspect.

Shouldn't window boxes be made out of windows?

I'm an optimistic pessimist. I look forward to thinking the worst.

Some things are just really hard to hear. Especially if the people at the next table are whispering.

E will be the end of me.

I started so many fights at my school – I had that attention deficit disorder. So I didn't finish a lot of them.

If at first you don't succeed, blame someone else.

How many people here have telekinetic powers? Raise my hand.

My imaginary friend keeps staring at me. Bloody weirdo.

Shouldn't it have been 'Robbin' Hood?'

I bought a cross-trainer to keep fit. I suppose that it's not enough to just buy it.

Never do a runner from a Kenyan restaurant.

Insulting me gets you nowhere. Plus, it makes you look fat.

What a gorgeous day to walk around outside staring at my phone.

Husband: 'I love you.' Wife: 'Is that you or the beer talking?' Husband: 'It's me talking ... to the beer.'

I'm not against half-naked girls – at least not as often as I'd like to be.

Archaeologists have dug up a book called *Irish Dancing Part Two: What to Do with Your Arms*.

When push comes to shove try not to be standing on the edge of anything.

You're never too old to learn something stupid.

My ex-wife is spreading false rumours about me being schizophrenic. Well, three can play at that game.

How do you find Will Smith in the snow? You look for fresh prints.

I want a zombie that likes me for more than just my brains.

Lots of people try to avoid lazy stereotypes on St Patrick's Day, but it hardly matters. Most Irish people will be too drunk to notice.

Getting some strange looks at work today. I was always told 'dress for the job you want, not the one you have'. I want to be an astronaut.

My wife has the body of a woman half her age. I suppose I should call the police.

How many pedants does it take to change a light bulb? Is it a bayonet or a screwcap?

If lemons hand you life, you're probably dyslexic.

What's the difference between in-laws and outlaws? Outlaws are wanted.

Old man: 'My memory's shot. Would you mind telling me your name again?' Older man: '... how soon do you need to know?'

A little boy asked his father, 'Daddy, how much does it cost to get married?' His father replied, 'I don't know son, I'm still paying.'

The trouble with doing something right the first time is that nobody appreciates how difficult it was.

Intelligence tests are biased toward the literate.

I was cleaning my flat today when suddenly I thought... Why don't I just buy a new tyre?

The letter Q needs to get a real job.

Crowded lifts smell different to midgets.

I remember that Beatles song like it was 'Yesterday'.

My accountant recently came up with so many tax deductions, I had enough left over for bail.

My opinions may have changed, but not the fact that I am right.

It appears my window of opportunity has been painted shut.

I wonder how many of those cocaine-sniffing dogs have to go to rehab.

Word on the street is that the ice-cream van guy has been around the block a few times.

Wow, what a rush – I was just recognised in public! I didn't think that wanted poster was still in circulation.

After I found out my tailor had been sleeping with my wife I screamed, 'I don't ever want to see you again.' He replied, 'Fine, suit yourself.'

Love means never having to say anything because you're both look ing at your smartphones.

At the bank, I told the cashier, 'I'd like to open a joint account please.' 'OK, with whom?' 'Whoever has lots of money.'

Nurses are workin' for the weakened.

'Doctor! Doctor! My arm is broken in three places.' 'Well, stay out of those places.'

I hate when people don't watch where I'm going when I'm walking and texting.

How come no supervillain has ever tried to kill Spiderman with insect repellent?

I want to hang a map of the world in my house. Then I'm going to put pins into all the locations that I've travelled to. But first, I'm going to have to travel to the top two corners of the map so it won't fall down.

The difficulty with a research grant is that if you solve the problem, you're out of a job.

Whoever coined the phrase 'quiet as a mouse' has never stepped on one.

Atheism is a non-prophet organisation.

If drugs are ever legalised, I can't wait to see what the adverts will look like.

What a beautiful day for sticking a cucumber through someone's letterbox and shouting, 'Help, help, the Martians have landed!'

I spent an hour explaining how Wi-Fi works to my dad and my dog. The dog gets it.

If you're dating in the office pool, you're going to drown.

I always keep my chin up. If I don't, people might find out that I have more than one.

Weddings would be worth all the trouble if they didn't end in marriage.

Marriage is like a late-night phone call. You get a ring and then you wake up.

In marriage, as in war, it is permitted to take every advantage of the enemy.

Love may be blind but marriage is a real eye-opener.

My girlfriend said I wasn't supportive enough. So I cupped her boobs.

Assisted suicide? Oh, you mean marriage.

I WENT TO THE DENTIST AND NOW I'M USING ALL CAPS.

I was chatting to this girl on the net yesterday. I said, 'Do you fancy going out for a drink later?' She said, 'Get lost, I'm trying to play tennis.'

Pity the man with multiple children at university, for he is getting poorer by degrees.

A clear conscience is usually the sign of a bad memory.

For a totally balanced day, do tai chi in the morning and drink chai tea before bed.

Enter a café. Ask to see the menu. Say, 'Have you got anything a mouse would like?' When they say no, whisper into your sleeve and leave.

In the case of the negligent babysitter, charges were dropped.

I found out that my uncle was gay during a family outing.

There's nothing wrong with meeting your partner on a dating site. Unless of course you're already married to them.

If God is watching us, the least we can do is be entertaining.

I went to the corner shop – came back with four corners.

Nothing makes a fish bigger than almost being caught.

I measure my fitness level by whether or not my bath towel still fits around me.

I'm off for a quiet beer. Followed by fourteen noisy ones.

Better the devil you know than the devil who makes you guess his name.

My wife was kidnapped and held to ransom in a case of mistaken identity. The kidnappers mistook me for somebody who might care.

Just because nobody complains doesn't mean all parachutes are perfect.

Not much concerns me. In fact, about the only time I have something on my mind is when I'm wearing a hat.

Notice in a library: 'While reading the Kama Sutra, please hold the book with BOTH hands.'

I had a ploughman's lunch the other day. He wasn't very happy.

It would be more fun to watch out of shape people compete in the Olympics.

Tell a man there are 400 billion stars and he'll believe you. Tell him a bench has wet paint and he needs to touch it.

I entered the word 'moron' in my satnav to see what happens, and guess what? I'm outside your place.

The best way to make a fire with two sticks is to make sure one of them is a match.

A fine is a tax for doing wrong. A tax is a fine for doing well.

It's OK if your wall safe is easy to crack if all you keep in it is a spring-loaded boxing glove.

My wife stopped pretending to have orgasms years ago. That's all right with me though – it meant I could stop pretending that I cared.

Believe in reincarnation? When you die, don't put RIP on your gravestone, put BRB.

Where do I see myself in five years? I would hope in a hologram but it will probably still be in the mirror. Stupid scientists.

My blonde girlfriend said, 'I think the man that invented the clock is a genius!' I said, 'Why?' She said, 'Well, how did he know what time it was?'

You can tell a lot by the way a woman walks. Like, if she walks away, she's probably not into you.

It's that time of the month where my wife is miserable and you can't go anywhere near her. She'll be OK next week though: that's when I get paid.

One-night stands in hotel rooms just don't do it for me any more. That's why I always ask for a bed with two nightstands.

I may be a schizophrenic. But at least I have each other.

No one ever gives me a hand, but I often get a finger.

The only difference between the people I've dated and Charles Manson is that Manson has the decency to look like a nutcase when you first meet him.

What's the difference between being hungry and being horny? Where I put the cucumber.

I just bit my lip. I hadn't even realised I was hungry.

Whenever one office door closes, fifty browser windows open.

My new house has a circular driveway. I can't get out.

I didn't know how to tell my wife that I'd cheated on her, so I just told her I was the fastest animal on the planet.

If you ever buy a large TV, remember to put the box in your neighbour's dustbin so they get robbed and not you.

I have no idea why I walked in to the short-term memory clinic.

Judge: 'You understand that you have sworn to tell the truth?' 'I do.' 'You understand what happens if you commit perjury?' 'My side wins.'

If things get better with age, I'm approaching magnificent.

Help keep Britain beautiful. Stay in your house today.

Nothing ever works out for me. The way my luck is running, if I was a politician I would be honest.

A sailboat in need of repairs is nothing but a big woe boat.

If you're going to keep fishing for compliments, I think you'll need some better bait.

To lose one parent may be regarded as a misfortune. To lose both looks to me like you've murdered your parents to claim your inheritance.

My friends have entered me in an innuendo contest.

I've got a great joke about shoehorns. I just wish I knew how to work it into conversation.

Blind auctions leave lots to the imagination.

My bloody neighbour banged on my front door at two-thirty this morning. Thank God I was still up playing the drums.

Why do politicians envy ventriloquists? ...Because ventriloquists can lie without moving their lips.

My girlfriend came in complaining that I never lift a finger around the house... So I did: the middle one.

Always give 100 per cent at work: 12 per cent on Monday, 23 per cent on Tuesday, 40 per cent on Wednesday, 20 per cent on Thursday and 5 per cent on Friday.

I really need to start meeting my goals. Can someone introduce me to them?

I have an inquiring mind. Mostly it asks 'Huh?'

'Doctor! Doctor! Help me, I'm shrinking.' 'Just wait a minute and be a little patient.'

You should know you'll get loud when you start drinking. It says right there on the label: 'alcohol by volume'.

When my wife tells me how to drive, I don't even hear her. It's like I have an auto immune disease.

The last time I was involved in sex, I was a sperm.

If I have to work for an idiot, I might as well work for myself.

Society needs both optimists and pessimists. For example, an optimist invented the aeroplane while a pessimist invented the parachute.

She was a lifeguard at the beach; she kept the buoys in line.

For those who recognise Morse code – I bet Irish dancing drives you mad.

If a pig loses its voice, is it disgruntled?

I took the wife's family out for tea and biscuits. They weren't too happy about having to give blood though.

Laugh and the world laughs with you. Snore and you sleep alone.

Tupperware lids are like snowflakes: no two are alike.

I've decided to go on a glutton-free diet.

Budget: a record of where your money should have been spent.

Plant puns: weed 'em and reap.

At a four-way stop, it's obvious that the vehicle bearing the most duct tape goes first.

We had to say goodbye to our German shepherd yesterday. Auf wieder-ersehen, pet.

Don't flatter yourself, I do have a banana in my pocket.

The last time someone wanted me for my body I was filling out an organ donor card.

One thing I know about the speed of light: it always gets here way too early in the morning.

I can please only one person per day. Today is not your day. Tomorrow isn't looking good either.

Every room I'm in is a panic room.

First rule of gun safety: don't piss me off.

I would never pose nude for a magazine. I'd just use money to buy it, like a normal person.

3.14 per cent of sailors are pi rates.

I read recipes the same way I read science fiction. I get to the end and I think, 'Well, that's not going to happen.'

Talking to me in the morning is like trying to dribble a ball with not enough air in it.

Some people talk in their sleep. Lecturers talk while other people sleep.

The Czech engine light is always on in my Yugo.

So I met a gangster who pulls up the back of people's pants. It was Weggie Kray.

When I see a Goodfellas pizza in the freezer, I assume it's there because it betrayed the other pizzas.

My friend and I are moving into a tree house together. I just hope we never fall out.

I'm terrible at phone sex. Apparently I sound like I'm having a stroke.

Spending an entire day on the sofa is effete in itself.

So I rang up British Telecom and said: 'I want to report a nuisance caller.' He said: 'Not you again.'

My mother-in-law's in hospital. They say she's not looking too good. No word on her condition yet, though.

Recipes are like online dating websites. They never end up looking like the picture.

Archaeologist: someone whose career lies in ruins.

Just because they're the fairer sex doesn't mean that women play fair.

Some people are like clouds. Once they move on, it's a great day.

The UK army has lost over £6 million worth of equipment. That's the problem when you cover everything with camouflage.

I'm a very overprotective mother. I never let my kids outside of my body.

I got this powdered water – now I don't know what to add.

I have faith in fools. My friends call it self-confidence.

How does a play in Glasgow end? The hero gets the heroin.

I'll always remember my wife's dying words: 'I can't swim you idiot!'

A friend asked what I would regret most if I were to die in my sleep. Probably going to bed.

Women love a man brimming with confidence. Because without that, what's to destroy?

So I rang up a local building firm and said, 'I want a skip outside my house.' He said, 'I'm not stopping you.'

I try not to limit my madness to March.

Even Popeye didn't eat his spinach until he absolutely had to.

Do unto others before they undo you.

I don't feel old. In fact, I don't feel anything until noon. Then it's time for my nap.

Whatever doesn't kill you only counts as attempted murder.

To save time, let's just assume I know everything.

My friends used to say they'd copulate with anything that moved. I never saw a reason to limit myself.

Driving to work is more fun if you just pretend it's Grand Theft Auto.

They shouldn't call it 'office politics', if you can't really vote out the bosses.

I've successfully been starting my diet tomorrow for 1,095 days.

My wife said, 'You always blame everyone else when things go wrong.' I said, 'And whose fault is that?'

Psychology: the art of pulling a habit out of a rat.

I'm getting slower in my old age. My wife asked me to help her move some furniture around and it took me twenty minutes to think of an excuse.

I'm sick and tired of my computer being the only one of us getting naps and cookies.

While the optimist and pessimist argue over the glass of water, the opportunist sneaks in and drinks it.

Be kind to nurses. They choose your needle and catheter sizes.

At the stroke of midnight, Neil wept softly, cradling the sour cream as it expired.

My whisky kept going missing so I confronted the wife. She told me that the guilty party was the family dog. I found it staggering.

I would definitely do one of those staycations as long as everyone else left.

Jack looked at Jill after they got the water and knew it was all down-hill from there.

If my death is extraordinary as my life, at least I'll go quietly in my sleep.

Marriage is the process of finding out what kind of man your wife would have preferred.

If video games make you violent, does Monopoly make you a millionaire?

I feel like I'm coming down with a case of narcissism. Seriously, I just don't know what's come over me me me.

Why do they lock petrol station bathrooms? Are they afraid someone will clean them?

Origami takes patience, focus and no social life whatsoever.

Life is unsure... Always eat your dessert first.

As soon as women see me, they want to get in shape to impress me. So they start running.

In my ideal relationship, neither of us would be wearing the trousers.

My last girlfriend left after she caught me wearing her favourite dress. I said, 'Please don't go, I can change.'

Revenge is a dish best served cold, I said, forcing my boss's lifeless body into the freezer.

I'm so clever that sometimes, even I can't figure out what I'm doing.

Remember when phones were stupid and people were smart? Good times.

Breaking news: 'The Kodak Film company have filed for bankruptcy.' More details to come as the story develops.

If the government was really serious about stopping terrorism they would hire six-year-olds to be interrogators.

I don't recommend chasing your dreams. You're in no shape to be running.

I'm calling it a night ... because it's dark outside.

The toughest part of a diet isn't watching what you eat; it's watching what other people eat.

My mum said she wanted to talk to me about my obsession with Football Manager. But I didn't want to attend, so I sent my assistant.

I only had four pints last night and this morning I've got a terrible hangover. That's the last time I'm drinking whisky.

I was at an ATM and this old lady asked me to help check her balance. So I pushed her over.

There's nothing wrong with teenagers that reasoning with them won't aggravate.

The best librarians are certified in reshushitation.

They say you should test your fire alarms once a month. It's cost me a fortune in houses.

Half of the world's misery comes from ignorance. The other half comes from intelligence.

My boss has told so many unfunny jokes today, I've forgotten what my real laugh sounds like.

Stop kicking yourself. Let me do that.

If someone says 'I love you' and you don't feel the same way, say 'I love YouTube' really fast.

I before E except after 'Old MacDonald had a Farm'.

I put my chips on the table knowing that she was about to fold. She said, 'Move your dinner while I sort these clothes out.'

Girls are like phones. They love to be held and they love to be talked to, but if you press the wrong button you'll be disconnected.

Good chance of showers today. – Bathroom forecast.

In archaeology you uncover the unknown. In diplomacy you cover the known.

I liked you when we first met, but now you've talked me out of it.

Hey guys... Need a last-minute gift for mum or the wife? Put the toilet seat down.

Everyone remembers where they were when they heard that JFK had been assassinated. I was in a history class.

I've just been to an exhibition at the National Poor Trait Gallery. It was lazy and uninspired.

Girls' names are like passwords. Get it wrong; access denied.

Never underestimate the power of stupid people in large groups.

My signature move is 'recline'.

My New Year's resolutions are: 1. Stop making lists. B. Be more consistent. 7. Learn to count.

To err is human. To blame someone else is politics.

If you want to know what life would be like if you were rich, look at your cats.

I won't take a bullet for anyone. If I have time to jump in front of a bullet, you have time to move.

Employee of the month is a good example of how somebody can be both a winner and a loser at the same time.

I'm not very influential. Last time I pulled some strings my jumper unravelled.

I just shagged a bird with schizophrenia. I'm claiming it as a threesome.

Trouble defies the law of gravity: it's easier to pick up than to drop.

When a newly married couple smile, everyone knows why. When a fifteen-year-married couple smile every wonders why.

Don't steal. That's the government's job.

Of course I can keep a secret. It's the people I tell it to who can't.

I could do great things if I weren't so busy doing little things.

Having a few drinks on the plane pretty much guarantees that I'll fit comfortably under the seat in front of me.

Make crime pay. Become a lawyer.

I've just been winding my watch up. I joked about it having three hands.

Beware websites who charge to see someone have sex with a stringed instrument. I think it's a fiddle.

At my yoga class today I achieved a new level of consciousness: un.

My girlfriend left me because of my obsession with Linkin Park. But in the end, it doesn't even matter.

I always wanted to be a footballer when I was at school, but I was crap at drama.

I was raised as an only child, which really annoyed my sister.

If I'm ever on life support, I hope they remember to try switching me off and then back on again.

The wife's gone and left me due to my obsession with glass. I'm shattered.

I'm worried about my financial future. Even daylight has a better savings plan than me.

Sometimes I take the low road because the path has been cleared so well before me.

People who live in stone houses shouldn't throw glasses.

You can tell a lot about a man by the colour of lipstick he wears.

Fact: mountaineers rope themselves together to prevent the sensible ones from going home.

Life is like a game of chess. It's long, boring and I don't really know what I'm doing.

Poker's like a séance. You sit around a table holding hands, and one guy profits from everybody else's loss.

I've got ninety-nine problems, and my obsessive need to keep count of them is one.

Anyone else ever wondered how long it would take a giraffe to throw up?

I have so much allergy medicine in my body right now that I could probably sell myself to a meth lab.

There are two kinds of people who don't say much: those who are quiet and those who talk a lot.

Why is a newspaper ten times more interesting when the person across the aisle is reading it?

I'm having awful car trouble. The car won't start and the payments won't stop.

I've just seen my first snake of the summer. He was canvassing the neighbourhood and passing out election brochures.

Do you know what I find interesting? Neither does this guy who keeps talking to me.

I said no to drugs, but they just wouldn't listen.

Instead of 'single' as a marital status, it should be 'independently owned and operated'.

The worst part of the server crashing is that she was carrying my starter.

Every time I hear of someone being attacked by a shark, I think, 'Didn't they hear the music?'

Experience is what you get when you didn't get what you wanted.

Don't you know it's rude to talk while I'm interrupting?

Just about the time when you think you can make ends meet, somebody moves the ends.

I think it's adorable how children start looking like their owners.

The later I get, the drunker it is.

Actually, I'm not getting smaller. I'm running away from you.

The only people who really love change are wet babies.

Never bring a ladle to a knife fight. You'll be able to dish it out but you'll never be able to take it.

Being married to me gives my wife something to live for: a divorce.

Knowledge is power: the power to make other people feel stupid.

You know that tingly feeling you get when you like someone? That's common sense leaving your body.

Don't insult my intelligense.

Muscle relaxants go straight to my tongue.

Every cigarette you smoke takes five minutes off your life. According to my calculations I should have died in 1879.

What's green and sings? Elvis Parsley.

My psychic friend just thanked me for his surprise birthday party. Looks like I'll have to plan one now.

No one ever answers my questions, but they always question my answers.

The only normal people are the ones you don't know very well.

Ever since my beak transplant, I've had a fowl mouth.

My checking account is like the Sistine Chapel: overdrawn.

I just saw a guy using a payphone. I can only assume he's being told where to deliver the ransom money.

Robots are never anxious. They have nerves of steel.

If you pass the same 'turning point' in your life twice, get yourself a new satnav receiver.

Asking a pessimist his opinion is like asking a fire hydrant how it feels about dogs.

You can't expect me to stick to my resolution to give up drinking. I was drunk when I made it.

The honorary doctorate is to the PhD as the Burger King crown is to the monarchy.

I took my parents for granted until I had kids of my own. I don't know what I'd do if they weren't here to raise them.

The quickest way to double your money is to fold it in half and put it back in your pocket.

Changes are ahead: I'll keep you abreast once I figure out what is afoot.

Some people have a way with words, others not have way.

I'm a work in regress.

Don't judge. God hates competition.

Warnings are so stupid. Like on this deodorant: 'Avoid contact with eyes.' Too late, I've already seen it.

A New Year's resolution is something that goes in one year and out the other.

If you're worried that your kids aren't loud enough, you can always put them in a swimming pool.

Men have a basic understanding of complex ideas. Women have a complex understanding of basic ideas.

If Jesus was a Jew, how come he has a Mexican first name?

Sometimes there's no nicer feeling than peeing into a bottle. But other times I hate my job at the beer factory.

Hey cowboys: thanks for all your herd work.

My wife keeps complaining about her nine-to-five job. I must admit, 4.51 p.m. is a strange time to start work.

Time is a great healer, but a terrible beautician.

Ask not for whom the bell tolls. Let the voicemail get it.

Feed a cold, starve a fever, drown a problem.

Wedding rings are bad for your circulation.

If it's free, it's advice. If you pay for it, it's counselling. If you can use either one, it's a miracle.

Silence doesn't mean your sexual performance left her speechless.

The closest I ever got to a 90 per cent in university was my blood alcohol content.

Have you hugged an idiot today? Me neither, come here!

Cleavage is like the sun: you can look, but it's dangerous to stare.

When I'm in the mood to hear how fat I sound, sometimes I'll sit in a wicker chair.

The last guy who broke my heart was hard to get over. At least until I shifted the truck into four-wheel drive.

Hard work has a future pay-off. Laziness pays off now.

All I want is a little more than I'll ever get.

I was born to be a pessimist. My blood type is B negative.

Being paranoid means never having to think that you're alone.

When I'm lying on my deathbed, my one big regret will be that I'm lying on my deathbed.

I've been chained to my desk all day. My fault for working in an S&M club.

You can't fire me, I'm not even loaded.

Marriage means commitment. So does insanity. Coincidence?

What's yellow and looks funny on your mother-in-law? A JCB.

Do mimes observe a brief moment of talking when a fellow mime passes away?

If you're one in a million, there are six thousand people exactly like you.

Where there's smoke, I'm fired.

I've always been a very vocal advocate of nonviolence towards me.

Patient: 'The problem is that obesity runs in our family.' Doctor: 'No, the problem is no one runs in your family.'

'Whose knickers are these?' screamed my wife as she held them up in front of her face. 'Get off!' I said. 'You're giving me a wedgie.'

I tried to drown my sorrows, but they were strong swimmers.

Wooden spoons are great. You can either use them to prepare food. Or, if you can't be bothered with that, just write a number on one and walk into a pub.

The world is a dangerous place. Only yesterday I went into Boots and punched someone in the face.

She goes shopping to see things she can't afford and imagine what it would be like to have them. Same reason he goes to a topless bar.

I make my own luck. It's mostly bad, but still.

Deep down, I knew scuba diving wasn't for me.

I just dropped a jar of mayonnaise on my foot. The last thing the wound needs is dressing.

Isn't it odd the way everyone automatically assumes that the goo in soap dispensers is always soap? I like to fill mine with mustard, just to teach people a lesson in trust.

Funny... I don't recall being absent-minded.

Look, I'm trying to rant here. Stop interrupting me with 'facts' and 'reason'.

I get in trouble because there are only two kinds of secrets: those that aren't worth keeping and those that are too good to keep.

Things are gradually falling into place ... on top of me.

I think I'm allergic to chocolate. My bum and thighs are showing definite signs of swelling.

After seeing how poor the Chinese were at the running events at the last Olympics, I'm going to try my luck and not pay for my takeaway tonight.

Bad job for a procrastinator: ice sculptor.

I'm not a vegetarian because I love animals; I'm a vegetarian because I hate plants.

Recently I've learned that 'cholesterol' is just a clever word for 'flavour'.

Now that the face transplant is being perfected, have you given it any thought?

What's the difference between a duck and an elephant? You can't get down off an elephant.

I'm trying to get back to my original weight. 7lb, 9oz.

With age comes new skills. You can laugh, cough, sneeze and pee all at the same time.

I wanted to be a farmer at one time, but it turned out to be the wrong field for me.

When a man talks dirty to a woman, it's sexual harassment. When a woman talks dirty to a man, it's £3 per minute.

I went to a karaoke bar last night that didn't play any '70s music. At first I was afraid, oh, I was petrified.

I hope I never meet the girl of my dreams. She's seen me in a lot of awkward situations.

I'm looking at my laughter lines and thinking ... what was ever that funny?

Senile is not just a tourist location in Egypt.

I don't have a 'can do' attitude, I have an 'aaah, that'll do' attitude.

Definition of anxiety: half of the time you're worried about the other half of the time.

My mate Dave drowned. So at the funeral we got him a wreath in the shape of a lifebelt. Well, it's what he would have wanted.

Procrastination has its good side. You always have something to do tomorrow.

These new spider silk pyjamas are great, except the flies keep getting stuck.

I cried myself to sleep every night for ten years until I found out that someone had stuffed my pillow with onions.

Any waiter is a singing waiter if you hit him in the right place with the pepper mill.

I respect giraffes, but I always get the impression they're looking down on me.

The Waste Land is a littery masterpiece.

I see smoke on the horizon. God, I hope it's Monday burning to the ground.

I was so ugly that they sent my picture to Ripley's Believe It or Not Museum and he sent it back saying, 'I don't believe it.'

When my wife gets a little upset, sometimes a simple 'calm down' in a soothing voice is all it takes to get her a lot upset.

How's this for a political platform? Don't lie through your teeth.

The best things in life are other people's.

The owner of the local cinema passed away. His funeral will be at 2:00, 4:30, 7:00 and 10:00.

New app on sale: the phone box locator.

My body is a temple. Do you want to come over for midnight mass?

A man stole a case of soap from the corner store. The police said he made a clean getaway.

Bacon and eggs: a day's work for a chicken, a lifetime commitment for a pig.

If I want something done right, the last thing I would do is do it myself.

My girlfriend broke up with me and sent me pictures of herself in bed with her new boyfriend. Solution? I sent them to her dad.

A parking warden is simply a prefect who reached their full potential.

A really hot girl asked me for my number today and all I had to do was hit her car with my car.

My dad's motto is 'neither a borrower nor a lender be', which is why he lost his job at the British Library.

Breaking up is hard to undo.

I hate being left out almost as much as I hate being included.

I'm ageing like a fine wine that someone left uncorked.

Seven days of HTML makes one geek.

To err is human... To rub it in is divine.

My dad strikes me as an angry drunk.

I called the paranoia society. The guy on the phone said, 'How the hell did you get this number?'

It's easy to spot people who can't count to ten. They're in front of you in the supermarket express lane.

I would love to change the world, but they won't give me the source code.

You're everything I've ever wanted in a vague acquaintance.

People tend to make rules for others and exceptions for themselves.

I pointed to two hags sitting across the bar and told my friend, 'That's us in ten years.' She said, 'That's a mirror.'

It's like these advertisers know what I want even before I do!

Thanks to plastic surgery, anyone can now look like an elderly teenager.

I'm looking forward to the day when my to-do list becomes my ta-da! list.

The best year for any wine is the year you drink it.

My auntie has a traditional remedy for Tourette's. She swears by it.

I'm just like everyone else. I put the words in my mouth one foot at a time.

How do you make a goldfish age? Take away the G.

The theory 'if you want something done right, do it yourself' didn't pan out too well with my last surgery.

I told the Inland Revenue I didn't owe them a penny because I lived near the seaside.

Time waits for no man, especially not a snowman.

Learn from your parents' mistakes: use contraception.

I'm a creature of habit. All bad.

I like to think my lack of common sense enhances my other senses.

People who say smoking takes away your sense of taste are right. My uncle smoked for years, and now he wears sandals and votes Conservative.

I've swallowed a lot of wisdom, but all of it seems to have gone down the wrong way.

When a woman wears leather, a man goes crazy and gets weak in the knees... She smells like a new truck.

I was raised half Jewish and half Catholic. When I went to confession I'd say, 'Bless me, Father, for I have sinned, and you know my lawyer, Mr Cohen.'

We're having creative differences. I'm creative and you're different.

I bet other birds are always accidentally asking penguins to get them drinks at parties.

I've got some reliable inside information about Apple's next product: I won't be able to afford it.

How do you call a prison inmate? Use a cell phone.

If at first you don't succeed, try drinking beer while you do it. You'll be amazed at how much less you care.

Sleeping with prostitutes is like making your dog dance with you on its hind legs. You know it's wrong, but you try to convince yourself that they're enjoying it as well.

My relationship with my ex wife was very psychological... She's a psycho and I'm logical.

I lied about making £4,000 a month from home, and so can you!

My wife was shocked when she found out that I switched her vibrator with a taser.

I've discovered the secret of life: breathing.

If it's the Psychic Network, why do they need a phone number?

I'm sure wherever my dad is; he's looking down on us. He's not dead, he's just very condescending.

The first time I see a jogger smiling, I'll consider it.

Immortality jokes never get old.

I must say you really have an open mind. And a mouth to match.

For guys, it doesn't matter whether we win or lose. We're going to lie about it anyway.

If you've lost every bet you've ever made, congratulations! You're now qualified to work on Wall Street.

My mental pool has a deep end, but most of the water is gone.

Tact is the ability to describe others as they see themselves.

I'm winning the argument I'm having in my head with my fiancée right now, by a mile.

Put L-plates on your car and suddenly nobody suspects you of drunk driving.

My body is a temple. But I'm not religious, so it's run-down and dilapidated.

I got myself a new Labrador retriever today. The kid next door said he'd go out and find my dog if it ever got lost.

I've never really minded the morning rush at all. Unfortunately my Ecstasy addiction did cost me my job in the end.

No story that begins with 'He had never drunk tequila before' ever has a happy ending.

My friend drowned in a bowl of muesli. A strong currant pulled him in.

I'm not a vegetarian, but I eat animals who are.

I can see my breath today. So either it's cold out here or I need a better mouthwash.

If I was rich, I'd do nothing all day from a much nicer armchair.

After the success of my first restaurant, Karma, I've decided to expand my food business and open Karma 2. We serve just desserts.

You know you're an adult when you suddenly start taking Bert's side over Ernie's.

Roosters are just edible alarm clocks.

My Indian princess name is Running Late.

I do all my own stunts, but never intentionally.

We are the anti-abortionists... You will never de-foetus.

I've decided to follow the health advice given in the news recently and avoid alcohol three days a week. Now I just have to decide which week.

It usually only takes four or five attempts for me to get something right on the first try.

What part of 01001110 01101111 don't you understand?

How does a man define a fifty-fifty relationship? She cooks. He eats. She cleans. He gets dirty. She irons. He gets it wrinkled.

Ninja mode is not a plausible excuse for not being seen at work.

Does Hallmark make a Get Well card for a boss that suggests there's no real hurry about it?

I play all my country-and-western music backwards: your lover returns, your dog comes back and you cease to be an alcoholic.

A recent survey shows that nine out of ten men prefer big boobs. The tenth man prefers the other nine men.

My body is less beefcake and more cheesecake.

The great thing about gingerbread men is that each one is a new chance to bite somebody's head off.

I don't really balance my bank account so much as capsize it.

Life's like a bird: it's pretty cute until it craps on your head.

The best way to save a frog's life is to clamp his mouth shut so he can't croak.

The only man who doesn't reap what he sows is the amateur gardener.

Calories make the world go round.

What do you call a kid with no arms and an eyepatch? Names.

Just noticed a sign on a pub door saying 'Guide Dogs Only'. Possibly the most exclusive pub ever.

A babysitter is a teenager acting like an adult while the adults are out acting like teenagers.

Women love watching babies. Men love watching football. Which is why we need baby football.

Did you hear about the constipated mathematician? He worked it out with a pencil.

I'd tell more jokes about sex, but I don't know much about it. I'm a married man.

Life is like a hot bath: it feels good while you're in it, but the longer you stay, the more wrinkled you get.

Just say NO to negativity.

I went to the doctor's the other day and he said, 'Go to Bournemouth, it's great for flu.' So I went – and I got it.

I'm currently dating a couple of anorexics. Two birds, one stone.

Four out of five bubble baths result in Santa Claus beards.

Sometimes the grass is greener on the side with the most bullshit.

It's all fun and games until someone loses a tooth. Then it's hockey.

I wish there were an easier way to tell which of these emo kids are the tickle-me ones.

Your gene pool could use a little chlorine.

The computer screen says I need to upgrade my brain to be compatible with my new software.

My Internet bride got delivered today, she's the Wi-Fi always dreamt of.

I took part in the sun-tanning Olympics – I got bronze.

I've perfected my beauty regimen: drink six martinis before looking in the mirror.

The only time I've ever had a chip on my shoulder was when I tried to pour the entire bowl into my mouth at once.

My wife accused me of showing favouritism towards one of our children, but that's rubbish. I love Dave and not-Dave exactly the same.

Boomerangs and attention deficit disorder don't mix.

I remember every minute of my recent trip to Las Vegas. I was there for five days and two nights.

Life is full of complications. Even when you're born there's a string attached.

The sole purpose of a child's middle name is so he can tell when he's really in trouble.

Satire is being silly about the serious. Sport is the exact opposite.

Sardine fishermen buy special fishing nets from the Inland Revenue. They allow big fish to swim and catch all the little ones.

Age is just a number... Yeah, and jail is just a room.

Cows are such moorons.

I had a dream last night that I was cutting carrots with the Grim Reaper. Dicing with death.

Alcoholism is the only disease that tries to convince you that you don't have it.

Our dog can find anything. It's a Labragoogle.

I always try to learn from my mistakes. So now I'm having my son teach me guitar.

I need a job sleeping, with lots of overtime.

Hundreds of kids are shipped off to mime boarding school every year, never to be heard from again.

I'm not saying my wife is fat, but our memory foam mattress has started pretending to have Alzheimer's when she gets into bed.

I think my smart car and my smartphone are conspiring against me.

I've recently stopped using products that are tested on animals. My dog hasn't had a meal in two days.

I want to tell you all about my new drill, but don't worry – I won't bore you with it.

I have all my ducks in a column. I really wish I knew how to use Excel.

Just off to my appointment with the optometrist. I know there's a joke in there somewhere, but I can't see it.

'Knock knock.' 'Who's there?' 'Grandpa.' 'Wait! Stop the funeral!'

I like calling the Psychic Hotline and asking them what I'm wearing.

You should see my dog: he can do tricks. Watch him destroy this £2,000 sofa.

I only make mental bets. And, coincidentally, I've lost my mind.

I'm the guy that people see with a beautiful woman and think: 'Rich or funny, that's the only way.'

I just got a torrent of abuse. Which was really bad because that's not what I thought I was downloading.

An optimist is someone who just doesn't have much experience.

An optimist has a condom in his wallet. A realist has a photo of his wife. I'm a pessimist: I have a photo of a condom.

The best way to lie is to tell the truth: carefully edited truth.

Vegetarian: Native American definition for lousy hunter.

It's all fun and games until somebody loses an eye. Then it's a life of piracy on the high seas.

'Goodnight honey', I said as I got up to go to bed. I'm trying to make the marmalade jealous.

The other day I sent my girlfriend a huge pile of snow. Then I rang her up and said, 'Did you get my drift?'

'Doctor! Doctor! I can't stop singing "The Green Green Grass of Home"!' 'That's what we doctors call Tom Jones Syndrome.' 'Oh, really? Is it common?' 'It's not unusual.'

Big shout-out to slugs! Those little guys are out there every day, doing all the same stuff as snails but without helmets.

My second childhood would be a lot better if I didn't have to do it in my first body.

Once in a while I take the blame when the dog farts, just to repay him.

I almost had a psychic girlfriend but she left me before we met.

I used up all my sick days, so I'm calling in dead.

My wife and I are getting along great at the moment. She's not home.

Who ever invented knock knock jokes should get a No-bell prize.

A police recruit was asked during exam, 'What would you do if you had to arrest your own wife?' He said, 'Call for backup.'

I've never paid for sex. Which has pissed off quite a few prostitutes.

I admire the Pope. I have a lot of respect for anyone who can tour without an album.

The most uncomfortable coffee shop in the world is probably Starebucks.

I really need to stop talking to my cat. Right meow.

I've heard you're a ladykiller. They take one look at you and die of shock.

7/24 is much more my ratio.

I think it's OK for dorks to stare at beautiful women. I mean, it's not like they can see us anyway.

Life is full of disappointments and I'm full of life.

I went to the paper shop, but it had blown away.

I can't believe I've mixed their Valentine's Day cards up. My girlfriend now thinks I love her and my wife thinks I want to fuck her.

Apparently men think about sex every seven seconds. Luckily I wrote this in sex.

Today, my wife walked in on me screwing her sister in front of the mirror. I said, 'I know what it looks like...'

When I die, I'd like the word 'humble' to be written on my statue.

I had an out-of-body-wash experience in the shower today.

'How fast do you think you were going?' '60mph, Officer?' 'Try 135.' So I shut the door and drove as fast as I could.

What do church mice believe in? Cheeses.

If you learn from your mistakes, you must be a freaking genius.

Marriage is Stockholm Syndrome in reverse.

What's the difference between fiction and reality? Fiction has to make sense.

I went golfing this morning and made a hole in one. Too bad it was in a windshield.

Entrail mix: for cannibals who love the outdoor lifestyle.

Life is like a doughnut. You're either in the dough or in the hole.

Lance Armstrong has denied ever using drugs, but he has admitted pedalling.

What's the best thing about babies? Making them.

I would take a bullet for my wife, unless it was fired out of a gun.

My dad's dying wish was to have his family around him. I can't help thinking he would have been better off with more oxygen.

Fact: heat makes objects expand. So there you have it: I'm not overweight, I'm just overheated.

As I get older, women dress me with their eyes.

Save the earth. This is the only planet with beer on it.

I applied for a new lease on life but I didn't pass the credit check.

I like the way you move. Away from me.

I just laughed so hard milk came out of the nose of the guy sitting next to me.

My friend was a pro at Russian roulette: he only ever lost once.

Even crime wouldn't pay if the government ran it.

My wife came home today and said, 'Here I am, just back from the beauty parlour.' I replied, 'What's wrong? Was it closed?'

If a man said he'll fix it, he will. There's no need to remind him about it every six months.

Kilometres are shorter than miles. So I'm taking my next trip in kilometres to save on petrol.

I'm getting fed up with my girlfriend's OCD. She's insisting that I arrange my DVDs alphabetically. I can't put *Up* with *It* any longer.

When I was seventeen I thought my parents were the stupidest people in the world. At twenty-one I was amazed at how much they had learned in four years.

My mate's been hanging out at the gym. I told him he should wear bigger shorts.

No, no, no. It's 'absinthe' makes the heart grow fonder.

People claim to be into recycling, but watch their faces as you rinse out a condom.

The recruitment consultant asked me, 'What do you think of voluntary work?' I said, 'I wouldn't do it if you paid me.'

Déjà vu: when you think you're doing something you've done before, it's because God thought it was so funny he had to rewind it for his friends.

At the gym, I'm always trying to impress the girls. One time I managed to lift 750kg... Until my forklift broke down.

I passed a drugs test recently. Which was strange, because I don't remember eating one.

Danger is my middle name. First name: Avoids; last name: Completely.

My workplace is like Oz: my boss doesn't have a heart, my colleagues don't have brains, and I don't have the courage to quit.

Why do I self-sabotage? Because some jobs are too important to be left to amateurs.

The most precious thing we have is life. And yet it has absolutely no trade-in value.

Sleep is at the top of my list of places I'd like to go back to.

There was a big fire at work today. It was OK though: I opened the fire escape and it left.

Why do they have fences around graveyards? Because everyone is dying to get in.

I'm getting a little sick of these email alerts from my bank implying that I'm unbalanced.

I saw the world's biggest fan last week. It blew me away.

If I was doing yoga right now, the position would be called 'downward spiral'.

Before you wed that lawyer, remember: you're about to marry someone who's been professionally trained to argue.

Played frisbee with my dog in the park. Waste of time – I think I need a flatter dog.

I've just bought a Border collie. The one I already had wasn't bored enough.

The road to failure is the path of least persistence.

The right to bear arms is slightly less ludicrous than the right to arm bears.

Most children threaten at times to run away from home. This is the only thing that keeps some parents going.

You autocomplete me.

I've been sacked from my job. Or as I prefer to think of it, I'm on eternity leave.

My first stand-up attempt was a disaster. Mind you I was only ten months old at the time.

Every once in a while, it's important to show my kids who's boss. I do this by pointing to my wife.

If you're looking for someone to disappoint you, I won't disappoint you.

I want my children to have the things I never had. Then I want to move in with them.

Monogamy leaves a lot to be desired.

Once I dared my little brother to drink a cup of acid. He hasn't spoken to me since.

My wife isn't crazy about my new household slogan: 'Slam Beers Not Doors.'

'Doctor! Doctor! I swallowed a bone.' 'Are you choking?' 'No! I'm serious.'

I don't drink champagne any more after a really bad experience. We had it at my wedding.

My plastic surgeon nose very me well.

A man walked into the doctor's, and the doctor said, 'I haven't seen you in a long time.' The man replied, 'I know, I've been ill.'

Remember: what doesn't kill you makes a great story.

Sometimes all it takes to inspire me is seventeen cups of coffee and a defibrillator.

I really hope that dead cockroach I found in the basement died of loneliness

I used to live the life of Riley. Until Riley discovered his credit cards were missing.

Discretion is being able to raise your eyebrow instead of your voice.

Hard work never killed anyone, but why take the chance?

Who are you? How did you get in here? (When did I put that mirror there?)

To be sure of hitting the target, shoot first and call whatever you hit 'the target'.

Middle age is having a choice between two temptations and choosing the one that will get you home earlier.

I cna ytpe three hundred wrods pre mniuet.

'Sir, could you please step out of the vehicle?' 'I'm too drunk, you get in.'

The optimist sees melting snow. I see grass that will have to be mowed.

A good way to stand out from the competition at a job interview is to bring your CV on a floppy disc.

The horn of plenty is usually driving right behind me in traffic.

Nobody ever shows up at the Agoraphobics Anonymous meetings.

I needed a password eight characters long so I picked Snow White and the Seven Dwarves.

Damn, I think I took a wrong turn somewhere. Looks like I'm going to have to backtrack twenty-five years.

The glass is always cleaner on the other side.

I overheard my girlfriend on the phone to her pal saying she wants to get engaged on Valentine's Day. I hope she finds someone nice.

A criminal's best asset is his lie ability.

Meeting disappointment head-on. Or as I like to call it, waking up.

'Jesus loves you.' A nice gesture in church. A horrific thing to hear in a Mexican prison.

I walked into a pub in Glasgow. It was so rough even the arms on the chairs had tattoos on them.

My wife left me because of my neediness for approval. She's a total bitch, right guys? Guys?

The early bird gets the worm. But so does the bird that stayed up all night.

The easiest job in the world has to be coroner. Surgery on dead people. What's the worst thing that could happen? If everything went wrong, maybe you'd get a pulse.

All this talk of genetically modified food being contrary to nature is rubbish. Today I had a delicious leg of cod.

I've had my share of combat experience... After all, I'm married to a loose cannon.

I'm getting pretty nervous about my maths exam. I think I've got a 40–40 per cent chance of passing.

If I had a pound for every time I was told that I wasted time collecting useless statistics, I'd have £847.

The trouble with my budget is there are far more ways to get into debt than there are to get out of it.

Some people are motivated by carrots, others by sticks. But nobody is motivated by carrot sticks.

A nice way to fire someone is to throw them a surprise going-away party.

Twitter provides the technology for my thoughts to be ignored by far more people than ever before.

Just checked my piles out using a mirror. Maybe I should have waited 'til the lift was empty.

The only way I'm going to make a mark on the world is if I take a felt-tip pen to a globe.

If you leave alphabet soup on the stove unattended, it could spell disaster.

They say that half the secret to success is just showing up. But they won't tell me where.

The worst part of the recession is, I lost half my stuff and still have my wife.

On the aeroplane descent I felt my ear pop and out came that last coin the magician forgot to remove when I was eight.

Kleptomaniac Superman is the Man of Steal.

For all the things done in its name, Love should complain more about identity theft.

It's so quiet in here I can hear myself think. No good can come of this.

What do you call a sheep with no legs? A cloud.

Music has the charm to soothe a savage beast. But I'd try a cricket bat first.

Why isn't there any aspirin in the jungle? Because the parrots-ate-'em-all.

You can learn many things from children. How much patience you have, for example.

The hair of the dog can be a cheap and effective solution to both a hangover and a comb-over.

When rabbits get divorced, it's called splitting hares.

I always seem to hurt the ones I love the most. Probably because I've got a huge dick.

My maths teacher accused me of cheating. It's true, I did, but I can't help that the English teacher is sexier.

Parting is such sweet sorrow. Especially if you're bald.

I've just got Sky TV – ask me anything about sharks or Nazis.

If actions speak louder than words, why can't I hear mimes?

I used to be indecisive, but now I'm not so sure.

The captain and I are not seeing aye to aye.

Beer is a gateway drug to aspirin.

If you're in a car with someone who talks a mile a minute, will going 60mph in reverse shut them up?

My life is like a Lamborghini: it's going too fast, and it costs too much.

My wife and I had words but I never got to use mine.

'I'm having trouble finding myself.' – Where's Wally in therapy.

'Doctor! Doctor! What did the x-ray of my head show?' 'Nothing.'

I wanted more communication and she wanted less. So we compromised and now we communicate more or less.

My wife is driving me to drink. I hope she remembers to pick me up when I'm done.

I'm not an alcoholic. I can stop drinking any time I've got no money.

'I ain't got no fancy book learning' is a double negative. We still believe you though.

By the time you learn the rules of life, you're too old to play the game.

I tried to write a drinking song, but I couldn't make it past the first few bars.

Exit signs? They're on the way out.

Live a life of service to others. You can start by refilling this cup of coffee.

If you love something, let it go out with the guys once in a while.

Albinos – you can't say fairer than that.

Roses are dead, violets are dead, I'm crap at gardening.

I don't think all these guys with aviator glasses actually know how to pilot a plane.

It's a tough job, but someone's gotta do it. Not me, of course. Someone though, definitely.

Toddlers are the storm troopers of the Lord of Entropy.

I do what the little voices inside my wife's head tell me to do.

You are such a good friend that if we were on a sinking ship together and there was only one life jacket... I'd miss you heaps and think of you often.

I just gave some rohypnol to my girlfriend. I didn't sleep with her, I just wanted some peace and quiet.

If you want my opinion you'll have to ask my wife for it.

People say, 'I'm taking it one day at a time.' You know what? So is everybody. That's how time works.

Technically, Humpty Dumpty died a crackhead.

Just saw a politician trying to save both faces.

Some of us learn from the mistakes of others. The rest of us have to be the others.

If you're looking for drama, find the girl who's yelling 'I hate drama!' the loudest.

I was watching the London Marathon and I saw one runner dressed as a chicken and another dressed as an egg. I thought, 'This could be interesting.'

Like my car, I'm flat tired.

Responsible. Who wants to be responsible? Whenever anything bad happens, it's always 'Who's responsible for this?'

I just weighed myself. I think I'm retaining beer.

Typical cops. They caught me running with a bag of money. But where were they ten minutes beforehand when someone was nicking my getaway car?

Should crematoriums give discounts for burn victims?

I just caught my dogs going through my rubbish. I think they're working for one of the tabloids.

My husband: 'It'd be nice to have a wife who cooked breakfast.' Me: 'Can we get one?'

If God is watching us, the least we can do is be entertaining.

There are a lot of special women in my life, but Betty Crocker takes the cake.

My wife has given up sex for Lent. Now I know the true meaning of Palm Sunday.

To be intoxicated is to feel sophisticated but not be able to say it.

Never own a pet shop. Shops make terrible pets.

Let's role-play. You be a person with low standards and I'll be myself.

When you really want to slap someone, do it and yell, 'Mosquito!'

Living on Earth is expensive, but it does include a free trip around the sun.

I heard most accidents happen at home. Maybe I should move.

They say age is all in your mind. The trick is to keep it from inching its way into your body.

My neighbours listen to some excellent music. Whether they want to or not.

I love sleep. My life has the tendency to fall apart when I'm awake.

Losing weight doesn't seem to be working, so I'm concentrating on getting taller.

All the world's just going through a stage.

My wife has finally left me because of my history obsession, even though I told her that it's all in the past.

You are as pretty as a flower. Unfortunately, it's a cauliflower.

I was mugged by a man on crutches wearing camouflage. I thought, you can hide but you can't run.

One spelling mistake can destroy your life. Husband sent a message to his wife: 'I'm having a wonderful time, wish you were her.'

It's always darkest before dawn. So if you're going to steal the neighbour's newspaper, that's the time to do it.

So it turns out that if you bang two halves of a horse together, it doesn't make the sound of a coconut.

I cut my drinking in half by eliminating the orange juice in these screwdrivers.

There are only two types of criminals: those who get caught and the rest of us.

Someone told me it was May Day. I immediately launched my fleet of lifeboats and helicopters.

A dyslexic man walks into a bra.

If those NASA scientists were so smart, how come they all counted backwards?

More than anything, doughnuts have contributed to my personal growth.

Do plumbers have pipe dreams?

Two antennae met on a roof, fell in love and got married. The ceremony wasn't much, but the reception was excellent.

'Knock, knock.' 'Who's there?' 'Dyslexia.' 'Dyslexia how?'

When food falls on the floor, the Little Germs scream, 'Let's get it!' and Mama Germ says, 'No, we must wait five seconds.'

A hamburger walks into a bar. The bartender says, 'Sorry, we don't serve food here.'

If you are what you eat, I'm dead meat.

My upstairs neighbour made a groundbreaking discovery last night. He can't fly.

A unicorn and a cyclops. That's an accident waiting to happen.

I had so much coffee I made it to work in under four minutes, but I forgot to bring my car.

Taxes and death are certain, but at least death doesn't get worse every year.

Life is way more exciting in your forties. At any point you could sneeze wrong and end up getting emergency back surgery.

I'm not saying she was stupid, but I asked her how to spell Mississippi and she said, 'The river or the state?'

If I wanted your opinion I would have married you.

If every day is a gift, I'd like to know where I can return Mondays.

I treat all email marked 'treat very urgently' with the utmost urgency, deleting it as fast as I can.

I hate it when you're making your way home drunk, just minding your own business, and someone steps on your fingers.

I knew the wife would be annoyed when I told her I didn't bring the dog's ball along to the park. I took some stick.

If you're not supposed to misuse cough syrup, then why does it come with a little plastic shot glass?

My mate rang me and asked, 'What are you doing at the moment?' I said, 'Probably failing my driving test.'

My girlfriend said she's tired of my obsession with martial arts. So I kicked her out.

A man came up to me and said, 'Sorry, sorry, sorry, sorry.' I said, 'That's very annoying.' He said, 'Well I can only apologise.'

Old MacDonald had a really bad Scrabble hand... E–I–E–I–O...

My favourite part of attending a marathon is watching the reaction of runners who grab my plastic cup of vodka.

I made my computer password 'Yes', because my wife apparently doesn't know that word.

Musicians are always getting themselves in treble.

I was such an ugly kid, when I played in the sandpit the cat kept covering me up.

It's a shame that 99.9 per cent of politicians give the rest a bad name.

The closest I get to multi-tasking is ignoring more than one thing at a time.

The wife said to me, 'If you throw enough shit, some will stick.' I said, 'Can't we just paint the kitchen?'

I got lost on the road to nowhere.

From now on I'm going to put all my eggs in one basket. Then I won't look so stupid walking round Asda.

Why does a dog smell worse than a human? Because a dog has four armpits.

Behind every successful man is a woman who didn't marry me.

You can put lipstick on a pig, but make sure you wipe it off before the RSPCA arrive.

Sometimes I Google myself just to see what I've been up to.

I could take you with both hands tied behind your back.

Don't count your chickens. And don't blame my cat. He has an airtight alibi.

If nobody knows the troubles you've seen, then you don't live in a small town.

The first thing a man notices in a woman are her eyes. And when her eyes aren't looking, he notices her tits.

People said I'd never get over my obsession with Phil Collins. But take a look at me now.

Anyone who says an onion is the only vegetable that will make you cry has never been hit in the face with a turnip.

I slept like a rock last night. I woke up in the flower bed with the house key under my belly.

My body isn't a temple, it's a maximum security prison for fat.

Good grammar skills is something in which I excel in.

The family that sticks together should bathe more often.

The biggest difference between my wife and a bear is that sometimes, if I play dead, the bear will leave me alone.

I think I'm having a no-life crisis.

Beware when taking a magician's exam: the test is loaded with trick questions.

People often say to me, 'What are you doing in my garden?'

I have a date with destiny. I hope she likes hot dogs and mini golf.

I'll tell you what I love doing more than anything: trying to pack myself in a small suitcase. I can hardly contain myself.

I'd do anything for her: swim the deepest river, climb the highest mountain. She's now left because I'm never at home.

Jesus is on Twitter. Mind you he's only got the twelve followers.

I never lie. OK, I do, but not to you. Well, maybe to you, but not about this. Trust me.

Your call to action went straight to voicemail.

This orange juice says concentrate, but it doesn't say for how long.

I've just finished making the first episode of a murder mystery series set on an aeroplane. It was the pilot.

I like a 'knows-nonsense' type of gal.

My wife kept complaining that she needed more space. So I locked her outside.

I thought I finally found my groove. Turns out, it's a rut.

New social media sites keep popping up, but Facebook is still the best way to keep in touch with people you don't want to keep in touch with.

If you don't pay your cab driver after the ride, that's no fare to him.

Got a new job working at the police station, sketching pictures of suspects. I'm a con artist.

I'm on a forgotten-name basis with quite a lot of people.

A man may be a fool and not know it. Unless, of course, he is married.

Build a man a fire and you keep him warm. Set a man on fire and you get one phone call.

Apple pie isn't American unless you eat the whole thing in one sitting.

I don't remember the words 'anything you say can and will be used against you' being in my marriage vows.

The moment for calm and rational discussion has passed. Now is the time for senseless bickering.

When taking a cruise the best places for whale watching are the buffet lines.

I ordered a wake-up call the other day. The phone rang and a woman's voice said, 'What the hell are you doing with your life?'

The most distracting fish in the sea is the red herring.

My earliest memory is nine months before I was born. I went to a party with my dad and left with my mum.

Support bacteria. They're the only culture some people have.

There are three stages to a person's sex life: tri-weekly, try weekly and try weakly.

I got a tattoo of a digital watch on my wrist. I regretted it literally one minute later.

Materialism: buying things we don't need with money we don't have to impress people that don't matter.

Can we really afford another economic crisis? Can't we just use one of the old ones?

A man goes to the doctor with a strawberry growing out of his head. The doctor says, 'I'll give you some cream to put on that.'

I remember in 1995 when I went to an Oasis gig with my sister and my brother. I shouted, 'Go Oasis!' Then my sister left.

Thank you for your automated email from 'Do Not Reply'. Permit me to introduce you to my automated filter, 'Did Not Read'.

Today I bought cupcakes without sprinkles. Diets are hard.

An overweight man went to the doctor, who advised him to try a keep-fit DVD. But the guy wasn't keen on that idea. 'Well,' suggested the doctor, 'try something that leaves you a little short of breath.' So he took up smoking.

I want to be treated like a queen. Just not Marie Antoinette.

Respect your elders. They made it through school without Google or Wikipedia.

I love the look on people's faces, standing soaked in the rain at the bus stop as I drive past... It's partly why I became a bus driver.

Being popular on Twitter is like sitting at the cool table in the cafeteria at a mental hospital.

Good health is merely the slowest possible rate at which one can die.

You may have a heart of gold, but so does a hard-boiled egg.

I've thought long and hard, and have finally decided on my New Year's resolution: 1024x768.

If olive oil comes from olives, where does baby oil come from?

If you want to avoid the flu, stay away from the fireplace.

Watching the global financial crisis unfold is rather like watching my dad being molested by a clown. I know it's going to affect me, I'm just not entirely sure how.

I'm not saying my wife's fat, but I got on top of her in bed last night, and my ears popped.

If at first you don't succeed, sigh, sigh and sigh again.

I've given up begging my girlfriend to swallow. From now on, she can deal with her anorexia on her own.

This is the Camouflage Association. Didn't you see the sign?

Looks like my get-rich-painfully-slow scheme isn't working either.

I should have never wished for better hindsight.

The only way that raising children could be any harder is if they decided to unionise.

The vet looked at me and said, 'I'm afraid your cat won't last long: it's the big C.' 'What? Cancer?' I replied. 'No,' he said, 'curiosity.'

My son has eighteen maths questions for his homework. He says he did five at school. That leaves ... uh ... a few more to do tonight.

My best childhood memory was falling asleep on the sofa and waking up in bed thinking, 'Wow, I can teleport.'

I can't help think how unfortunate it would be if your name was 'Beermat'. The drinks would always be on you.

But you must believe in free will. You have no choice.

I just saved lot of money on my car insurance by switching ... my car into reverse and driving away from the accident.

Where does the road paved with bad intentions go?

I could tell you the first rule of Spite Club, but I won't.

My life coach told me I'd have to get one before he could coach me on it.

I bet mimes are really good at drawing a blank.

Note to self: next time I leave my wife a message that I'm in a three-some all afternoon, specify that it's golf.

Some people say I'm a dreamer, others say, 'If you fall asleep at work again we're going to have to let you go.'

Why don't we ever see this headline: Psychic Wins Lottery?

First rule of telepathy club:

I've found the secret of happiness – total disregard of everybody.

According to my neighbour's diary I have 'boundary issues'.

Say what you like about the deaf...

There are two kinds of people I don't trust: schizophrenics.

All I really want is to be understood. That's why I'm yelling.

The lifts are broken and I work on the twenty-seventh floor. I'm pretty sure I'm the first person ever to use the phone in reception to call in sick.

Keep the dream alive; hit the snooze button.

I took drugs last night with my shoelaces undone. Big mistake – I was tripping all night.

A Buddhist goes up to a hot-dog stall and says, 'Make me one with everything.'

Two silkworms had a race – it ended in a tie.

Lots of girls can be had for a song. Unfortunately, it often turns out to be the 'Wedding March'.

If it weren't for law enforcement and physics, I'd be unstoppable.

The closest I get to dating now is guessing someone's age.

Compromise: an agreement whereby both parties get what neither of them wanted.

Ask me about my narcissism!

If you suck at playing the trumpet, that's probably why.

If you watch an Apple store get robbed, are you an iWitness?

An attractive woman with no personality is like a clear sky on a 10° day: looks good in pictures, but no one wants to live with it.

The secret of our marriage is chemistry. She's on Valium and I'm on Prozac.

The biggest threat to my job security is a boss who walks quietly.

Just be yourself. All the good personalities are taken.

These days, my happy hour is a nap.

I'm on the 'starts tomorrow' diet.

The worst thing your wife can catch you doing is nothing.

'What do we want?' 'We'd like to buy a vowel!' 'When do we want it?' 'Nw!'

The bar was closed when I got there, with a sign that said, 'The door is alarmed.' I said to myself, 'How do you think I feel?'

I'm thinking of starting a non-profit organisation to wipe out natural causes.

Why do they call it multiple choice when you only get to pick one?

Having a multivitamin with a beer for breakfast is the same thing as eating a bowl of Weetabix, right?

I was thinking of getting contact lenses. But I always think my face looks a bit blurry without my glasses

All women have an hourglass figure – it's just that they all carry around different amounts of sand.

I have manners. They're just all bad.

I surveyed 100 women and asked them what shampoo they used when showering. Ninety-eight of them said, 'How did you get in here?'

So I got home and the phone was ringing. I picked it up and said: 'Who's speaking please?' And a voice said: 'You are.'

I wish all my electronics came with as much memory as a girlfriend or wife.

I've got a great gadget that allows keyless entry into any car. It's called a hammer.

A clock with a mirror? Time for reflection.

How many booze-addled layabouts does it take to... Never mind, I got it done.

I'm not saying you're a turkey, but how do you manage to survive every Christmas?

I tell women what they want to hear. Usually something like, 'Well, I'm going to go now.'

I've been meaning to tell you about your breath. It's got to stop.

I like to keep my girlfriend on her toes. So I've been teaching her ballet.

Hope: the feeling you have that the feeling you have is temporary.

Efficiency is a highly developed form of laziness.

I wish people cared about Earth as much as they cared about who they believe created it.

I was mugged by an acupuncturist. Stabbed four hundred times. Slept well and woke up feeling great.

Kinstipation: the painful inability to get visiting relatives out.

I've been up all night interrogating an egg... I think he's about to crack.

The world was my oyster. Then I found out I was allergic to shellfish.

Why do dogs always think the knock at the door is for them?

When in doubt, take the high road. There's less traffic.

They say playing video games is a waste of time, but I credit Tetris for the speed and agility I display when packing my suitcase.

I'll be impressed when I see a hypnotist get a chicken to act like a human.

I'll take the high road. You take the psycho path.

I don't call it lying down; I call it landscape mode.

Warning: asking people about their weekend may result in them telling you about it.

I'm very English really. I even ordered a book on the Internet called *How to Have Absolutely Nothing to Do with Your Neighbours*. Unfortunately I was out when it was delivered.

It's not the bullet that kills you, it's the hole.

My girlfriend answered my booty call last night. Fuck knows what she was doing with her sister's phone.

Cats have nine lives. Which makes them ideal for experimentation.

If they gave out gold medals for laziness, my teenage daughter would have me go up on the podium and receive it for her.

It takes forty-three muscles to frown, and yet it's still not an Olympic event. Ridiculous.

I asked my blonde girlfriend last night who she thought is the biggest selling band of all time. 'That's easy,' she said. 'The elastic one.'

I'm a workaholic but I've been in recovery for years.

The advantages of amateur origami are two-fold.

Pigeons keep showing up uninvited in our garden and eating food that isn't meant for them. Just like relatives.

All those interested in seeking an appointment with God ... kindly text while driving.

I like using Latin phrases when speaking in English and vice versa.

I have a lot of respect for women who can juggle work, and kids, and a husband, and a chainsaw.

If you would ever like to know what each and every one of your faults are, try criticising the wife sometime.

If the doctor says you only have six months to live, get married immediately. This will make the six months seem like forever.

We are shaped by what we love – especially dessert.

I distrust camels, and anyone else who can go a week without a drink.

They say memory is the first thing to go. The second thing to go is memory.

If we're not supposed to have pillow fights, why do they call them throw pillows?

During sex, my girlfriend always wants to talk to me. Just the other night she called me from a hotel.

As I sat down in front of the PC and had a wank, he calmly added an indecency charge.

Seasickness usually comes in waves.

I no longer need to punish, deceive or compromise myself. Unless, of course, I want to stay employed.

I hate the moments right before take-off when I'm on a plane. My head gets filled with thoughts of impending zoom.

When I grow up I want to be a kid.

I saw a documentary on how ships are kept together. Riveting!

I'm less of a catch, and more a 'catch and release'.

Teach a man to watch television and he'll find the fishing channel.

I just saw the little boy next door licking whipped cream off his cat. Pretty sure he heard something he shouldn't have.

I went to the dentist. He said, 'Say ahhhh.' I said, 'Why?' He said, 'My dog's just died.'

News: 'The war on drugs has failed.' Obama will be surrendering to some potheads later today.

With the price of gold this high I'm starting to seriously consider wishing I had some.

Turn the tennis up on your TV – make your neighbours think you're getting laid.

My psychiatrist told me I was crazy and I said I wanted a second opinion. He said, 'OK, you're ugly too.'

Mountain climbers are curious types. They always want to take another peak.

Grammar: the difference between knowing your shit and knowing you're shit.

I walked past a shop that was selling microscopes. So I went in for a closer look.

A couple of lads tried to get into my car last night so I attacked them with a cricket bat. I'm not cut out to be a taxi driver.

My wife complained that I never take her anywhere expensive. So I took her to the petrol station.

I used to work as a trapeze artist, until I was let go.

I spend a lot of time at the hospital nursery. I like meeting new people.

Everyone seems to have a problem with me texting and driving; especially the people on this pavement.

Actions speak louder than words, but talk is cheap and you have to consider that in this economy.

I try to avoid trouble but I think it likes me.

My mother-in-law fell down a wishing well. I was amazed: I never knew they worked.

Are you really leaving or are you just trying to brighten up my day?

If sex is a pain in the ass, you're doing it wrong.

This weekend I'm attending an animal rights barbecue.

What do you call someone who hangs around with musicians? A drummer.

Relationships between snowmen and snowwomen are frosty at best.

Money means nothing to me. If you don't believe me, ask me for money. You'll get nothing.

Drive carefully! Remember, it's not only a car that can be recalled by its maker.

My wife left me after she caught me measuring my penis. It just reaches the back of her sister's throat.

People who say I'm hard to shop for don't know where to buy beer.

In America any child can grow up to be President, and I suppose it's just one of the risks they have to take.

The first rule of mud wrestling is: fight dirty.

I don't think my parents liked me. They put a live teddy bear in my crib.

I decided to write a joke about restraining orders. This is the closest I could get.

Take my advice. I'm not using it.

As a kid I was made to walk the plank. We couldn't afford a dog.

I'm not lying, I'm Photoshopping the truth.

Democracy is three wolves and one sheep voting on what to have for dinner.

All pistachios come from broken homes.

Delusions are simply the ability to remember things exactly as they never happened.

Hospitality: making your guests feel like they're at home, even if you wish they were.

I quit my job at the helium balloon factory. I refuse to be spoken to in that tone.

What are the first three letters of the Greek alphabet? I. O. U.

Togun has thirty-eight chocolate bars. He eats twenty-eight of them. What does Togun have now? Diabetes. Togun has diabetes.

Carrots may be good for a human's eyesight, but they're even better for a snowman's sense of smell.

I put £2,000 on a horse today. When I got back it was gone.

Hindsight shows you how a mistake looks from the rear.

If you notice a person is deceiving you, they must not be deceiving you very well.

I saw a flying saucer today. It appeared right after the flying cup that my girlfriend threw at me.

A plastic surgeon gets paid way more than a tyre mechanic, even though they both get paid to fix flats.

Her: 'Tell me that you love me and will never lie to me.' Him: 'OK, you're going to have to make up your mind.'

If people were influenced by video games, then the majority of Facebook users would be farmers by now.

The BMW 314i has a 3.14 litre engine. Finally, a car that runs on pi.

Ever since I misplaced my dictionary, I've been at a loss for words.

Even doctors make mistakes. Mine asked me to undress.

Knowledge is knowing that a tomato is a fruit. Wisdom is not putting it in a fruit salad.

Why do couples hold hands during their wedding day? It's just a formality, like two boxers shaking hands before the fight begins.

If Einstein hadn't come up with the Theory of Relativity, somebody else would have. It was only a matter of time.

My chiropractor said I needed a posture alignment but I think she was just pulling my leg.

My wife's been giving me the silent treatment today. I just wish I knew what I did to upset her, so I can do it again when she starts to talk.

Me: 'This strobe light you sold me doesn't work properly.' Shop assistant: 'Have you tried switching it off and on?'

I'm sick of everyone calling me lazy, so I've decided I'm going to commit suicide. I've hired a hitman for the job.

I'm happy to report that I have achieved my New Year's resolution of making commitments I don't keep.

Why did the Marxist only drink herbal tea? Because proper tea is theft.

Due to circumstances beyond my control, I will no longer be controlling any circumstances.

Today I went to my first Stalkers Help Group meeting. I was surprised to find that I knew a lot of the people there. They didn't know me, though.

I used to jog five miles a day... But then I found a shortcut.

A coffin? That's the last thing I need!

Nanotechnology is going to be huge.

If dentists make their money from looking after our unhealthy teeth, why would I trust a toothpaste four out of five of them recommend?

The shinbone is a device for finding furniture in a dark room.

You are only your worst critic until you become my friend.

The leading cause of erectile dysfunction is the phrase, 'We need to talk.'

Married men should forget their mistakes. There's no sense in two people remembering the same things, right?

A lot of children think their parents are all no-ing.

I couldn't pull out of my parking space. I had to use my back-up plan.

Two Eskimos sitting in a kayak were chilly. But when they lit a fire in the craft it sank, proving once and for all that you can't have your kayak and heat it.

Is it too much to hope that my good cholesterol will be a positive influence on my bad cholesterol?

Throwing money at your problems won't work. Especially if your problem is a charging rhinoceros.

Walking in on your parents having sex is very distressing. Although your parents were more concerned that I had keys to their house.

A computer lets you make more mistakes faster than any invention in human history, with the possible exceptions of handguns and tequila.

The neighbourhood watch is having a meeting about the creepy guy and I'm the only one not invited.

I'm in shape. Just the wrong one.

'Leave them wanting more' pretty much sums up my customer service skills.

I'm as nervous as a postman at a dog show.

Spelling is a lossed art.

My wife says she'd like us to renew our vows. I told her I try not to make the same mistake twice.

Losing a husband can be hard. In my case it was almost impossible.

Life is what happened while your favourite song was going from heavy metal to classic rock to the oldies channel.

If I ever get taken in for questioning, I hope there's no algebra.

It's bad luck to be superstitious.

I hate people who use metaphors that are physically impossible. They make my blood boil.

My new girlfriend just told me she wants to have my children. She's going to be so surprised when I bring her my three-year-old.

You know who else likes that full-bodied flavour? Cannibals.

My Internet went down. By which I mean, my neighbours changed their password.

With a calendar, your days are numbered.

Velcro? What a rip-off!

The doctor says I'm healthy enough for sexual activity, but not attractive enough.

Having sex is like playing bridge. If you don't have a good partner, you'd better have a good hand.

I've never been wined and dined. I have been beered and snacked though.

Guilt: the power of punitive thinking.

Friends are like condoms: they protect you when things get hard.

Love is like a fire. Sometimes it warms your heart. Sometimes it burns down your house.

I think I've been watching too much porn on my computer. I logged on last night and got a message saying, 'Not tonight, I've got a headache.'

A lot of people say I'm indifferent, but I don't care.

It isn't the pace of life that concerns me. It's the sudden stop at the end.

If you can't make a simple question sound like an accusation, you're not qualified to be married.

My penis was actually in *The Guinness Book of World Records* once. But the librarian found out, and she kicked me out.

It takes a long time for a giraffe to swallow his pride.

My idea of yoga is taking my bra off without removing my shirt.

Yesterday I read an article about the dangers of drinking too much: it scared the shit out of me. So I've decided I'm never reading again.

Warning: if you do it right the first time, they'll ask you to do it again.

I went on a staff training course last week. Mine failed, so he's still only a stick.

I went down the local supermarket. I said, 'I want to make a complaint – this vinegar's got lumps in it.' He said, 'Those are pickled onions.'

You're really not as bad as people say. You're much, much worse.

There is no rest for the wary.

'I live life on the edge.' – Humpty Dumpty

You know you've gone to a bad psychic when the first thing she says is, 'Why are you here?'

Insanity means never having to say 'I'm guilty'.

You are like a dream to me: I forget pretty much everything about you a few minutes after seeing you.

As I do more laundry, nudists seem less crazy.

To err is human, to arr is pirate.

My wife tried to leave me because she thinks I'm too immature. But she didn't know the secret password so I couldn't let her out the front door.

Anyone can get old: all you have to do is live long enough.

Don't think of it as a flu jab. Think of it as installing virus protection software.

I believe in looking out for number one. Especially if the dog hasn't been house-trained yet.

I might not be my mother's favourite child, but I am her only one, so that makes me kind of special.

I feel like I've had this spell cast on me before. It's like déjà voodoo all over again.

Airline hostesses show you how to use a seat belt in case you haven't been in a car since 1958.

The only time my wife runs her fingers through my hair is when she cleans the shower drain.

Don't break anyone's heart; they only have one. Break their bones, they have over 200 of those.

If you order my new cash flow system now, I can start making money right away.

I discovered my wife in bed with another man, and I was crushed. So I said, 'Get off me, you two!'

If it wasn't for my granddad, we'd be speaking German now. He was a really awful German teacher.

My wife is 10 centimetres dilated! No, no, she's not having a baby. It's her mouth. it never shuts.

I hate when people tell me how to drive. Thanks Officer, have a nice day.

I can always tell when I meet a particularly smart person. They always have the same opinions as me.

I think that we can all agree that the best way to load the dishwasher is the way you do it.

Your beauty is so rare, no one can find it.

I'm on the sex diet: the more sex I have, the more weight I lose. So far I've gained 7kg.

A man went into a chemist's shop and said, 'Have you got anything for laryngitis?' And the chemist said, 'Good morning, sir. What can I do for you?'

Some brains are like the Bermuda Triangle. Information goes in, never to be seen again.

The Karma café has no menus. You get served what you deserve.

My wife and I both made a list of five people we could sleep with. She read hers out and there were no surprises: 1. George Clooney, 2. Brad Pitt, etc. I thought, 'I've got the better deal here'... Your sister.

'Man on the street' interviews are dangerous. They should really hold them on pavements.

It's a humbling moment when you realise your dog or cat has actually trained you to do something.

Today's pay cheque has more deductions than a Sherlock Holmes story.

After Monday and Tuesday, even the calendar is like W T F.

I ran three miles today. Finally, I said, 'Lady, take your purse.'

The best way to get a youthful figure is to ask a woman her age.

My muscle tone needs autotune.

The last person to question my masculinity got a face full of piping hot lavender tea.

I hate people who speak for other people, and so do you.

The best thing about being single is sleeping around. You can sleep all over that lonely bed of yours. Left, right, middle, whatever.

I'm thinking of having the lawn carpeted, so the puppy will know where to pee.

Never go to bed angry. Stay awake and plot your revenge.

Pollution costs us millions every year. Grime doesn't pay.

I'll worry about being replaced by a computer when they make one that grovels.

I want that job pushing shy skydivers out of planes.

I'm fairly certain I'm suffering from male pattern blandness.

Married men live longer than single men, but they're a lot more willing to die.

If a turtle doesn't have a shell, is he homeless or naked?

There must be a special discount clothing shop for builders. Their jeans are always 50 per cent off.

The key to surviving a stock-market crash is liquidity. So I'm off to the bar.

I helped organise my lawyer's funeral this week, but apparently he has to be dead before we can go ahead with it.

It seems like every girl I date owns a not-in-the-mood ring.

I wish there was some kind of rollover plan for childhood naps I refused to take.

A bear hug isn't truly a bear hug unless it's administered by a real bear.

Machiavelli said, 'It is better to be feared than to be loved if you cannot be both.' Something to bear in mind when you embark on Internet dating.

The human tongue weighs practically nothing, but very few people can hold it.

Hypnotists reckon they can cure alcoholism merely by implanting an idea in the drinker's head. It's a sobering thought.

Men: 'A woman, without her man, is nothing.' Women: 'A woman: without her, man is nothing.' Punctuation is powerful.

I'm having a bit of car trouble ... mainly because I can't afford to put petrol in it.

Am I the only one who thinks a flash mob should contain nudity?

I am correct 97 per cent of the time. Who cares about the other 4 per cent?

Chewbacca just did something wrong; total Wookie mistake.

All generalisations are false, including this one.

Very few things upset my wife. So it makes me feel rather special to be one of them.

'Doctor! Doctor! I snore so loudly, I wake myself up at night.' 'Have you tried sleeping in another room?'

I just made my hamster a strong coffee. I don't want him falling asleep at the wheel.

Gambling is an excellent way of getting nothing for something.

Some things are best kept between you and the neighbours. Like a fence, for example.

A surprise party is a great way to show your wife how convincingly you can lie to her.

Romance often begins by a splashing waterfall and ends over a leaky sink.

My girlfriend came over earlier. 'Look, I need to talk to you about your fixation with faeces,' she said. 'Pull up a stool,' I replied.

My brother was a victim of his own success. His trophy cabinet collapsed on him.

I used to be afraid of the dark. Now I'm terrified of the electricity bill.

What is small, red and whispers? A hoarse radish.

My new dustbin is too small. I can't get the old one in it.

I've got my first Gamblers Anonymous meeting tomorrow. I rang them today to check the time. It's ten to one.

I want my tombstone to say: 'Don't just stand there, water my flowers.'

No man goes before his time... Unless the boss leaves early.

My husband wants me to have a sex change. He wants me to change no to yes.

Research shows that 80 per cent of men don't know how to use condoms. These men are called DADS.

What's got a trunk, four legs and lots of keys? A piano up a tree.

I said to the gym instructor, 'Can you teach me to do the splits?' He said, 'How flexible are you?' I said, 'I can't make Tuesdays.'

My new credit card has this great theft protection scheme where it just says 'declined' whenever you try to use it.

It was the least I could do. I always do the least I can do.

Never tell a parrot your secrets.

I drew a line in the sand but what I should really do is sweep this place.

Pronouns: like normal nouns, just highly trained.

Life is like a box of chocolates: sometimes it makes you sick.

My girlfriend just asked me, 'When we go to Egypt, can we go on a camel?' I said, 'No, it would take ages to get there on a camel.'

Did you hear about the guy whose whole left side was cut off? He's all right now.

Drinking and drugs will not solve all your problems. That's what chocolate is for.

I forgot to pay my exorcist. Ended up being repossessed.

Why aren't atheists any good at exponential equations? Because they don't believe in higher powers.

I left my wife for a bin man. But he wouldn't take her.

I haven't had sex for about two years, six months, fourteen days, thirteen hours and fifty-six minutes. It doesn't bother me though.

I'm writing a book. I've got the page numbers done.

You only get one chance to make a first impression, unless you're precise with your rolling pin.

There are only two levels in lion taming: 'expert' and 'cat food'.

To me, a beautiful woman is like a fast car: I've never had one.

If you have a split personality I can't be friends with you. Or you.

Fool me once, shame on you. Fool me twice, shame on you again. And stop picking on me, I'm clearly an idiot.

I thought I saw Shaggy walking past earlier. It wasn't him.

If all the dinosaurs had had such a wide vocabulary, maybe they would have survived like the thesaurus did.

When a cowboy breaks his leg, I think his horse should be allowed to shoot him.

At night I hear the voice of pie and sometimes that of ice cream calling to me from the kitchen. Broccoli is strangely silent.

When I was driving the other day, I couldn't find my favourite CD, so I decided to listen to something I don't usually listen to for a change. My wife.

I got a part in the film *Cocaine*, but I only had one line.

The hardest thing about learning to ride a horse is the ground.

I wanted to complain about the service in a restaurant last night. But I couldn't find a waiter.

I assume full responsibility for my actions. Except the ones that are someone else's fault.

I am yet to bite a moose that tastes like chocolate.

Protect your bagels. Put lox on them.

At my company, we put the the 'k' in kwality.

'Doctor, I don't know what's wrong with me.' 'Take these pills, I don't know what they're for.'

I was riding a horse and its leg broke, so I had to shoot it. I'm not allowed on the carousel any more.

I've been totting up my alcohol units for the month. I've checked into three so far.

People usually get what's coming to them... Unless it was sent through the post.

Being married is like having a best friend who doesn't remember anything you say.

Someone called me gay for wearing heels the other day, but I was hardly going to wear trainers with that dress.

I just met Darth Vader's corrupt brother, Taxi Vader.

Money can't buy you friends, but you get a better class of enemy.

There's a kid outside playing tennis using a big bass drum. What a terrible racket.

I just checked the height/weight chart at the gym. Apparently I'm four inches too short.

The five stages of Monday: denial, anger, bargaining, depression, wine.

I don't have a beer gut, I have a protective covering for my rock-hard abs.

I'm taking Viagra and drinking prune juice – I don't know whether I'm coming or going.

I can't say that my wife is outspoken... At least, not by anyone I know of.

I married Miss Right. I just didn't know her first name was Always.

I have an advanced degree in sensationalistic journalism. My boss calls it a doctor-it degree.

I'd kill for a Nobel Peace Prize.

Coal diggers would probably make more money if they could mine their own business.

If I had a hammer, I'd hammer in the morning. If I had a hammer, I'd hammer in the evening. My neighbours would hate me.

I don't know why the boss calls it a week's wages when it only lasts for a day.

The key to knowing when to panic is to start moments after someone says, 'OK, don't panic.'

Irony: working for an aluminium company and getting canned.

Can you sue a Chinese restaurant for damages incurred as a result of bad fortune cookie advice?

I found thousands of letters in my post box today. That's the last time I order a dictionary from IKEA.

I was told the training process for cats is quite difficult. It wasn't. My cat had me trained in two days.

Screw up your courage! You've screwed up everything else.

All forms of gambling are frowned on by most religions. Except, of course, marriage.

Cocaine dealers are always sticking their business in other people's noses.

The difference between the Pope and your boss is, the Pope only expects you to kiss his ring.

Reaching under the couch for something is the closest I'll ever get to yoga.

I don't mind when older folks decide to relax and slow down. I just wish they wouldn't do it in their cars.

Black Beauty? Now there's a dark horse!

I'm all for saving the world – just not necessarily the people.

Have you ever gone on one of those murder mystery weekends? Did you get caught?

An empty box of tissues is nothing to sneeze at.

The trouble with real life is that there's no danger music.

Why limit happy to just an hour?

When you choke a Smurf, what colour does it turn?

Why was the Energizer Bunny arrested? He was charged with battery.

I used to work at a recycling plant. My job was to crush cans. It was soda pressing.

Sometimes the best helping hand you can give is a good, firm push.

The best person for a job is generally the one who understands it well enough to not want it.

You know you're getting old when your wife gives up fooling around for Lent and you don't notice until Easter.

The only way to keep your health is to eat what you don't want, drink what you don't like, and do what you'd rather not.

I'd rather be an unsolved mystery than a foregone conclusion.

I just sprayed a mosquito with mosquito repellent. Now he'll never have any friends.

Who invented the brush they put next to the toilet? That thing hurts!

Have you noticed how the top and bottom biscuit in the packet are always broken? I don't know why they bother putting them in.

I'm saving myself from marriage.

Now that winter's almost over, I bet the trees will be releafed.

I had an out-of-body experience today. My inner child ran away.

I went to the shop the other day to buy six cans of Sprite. Only when I got home did I realise I'd picked 7Up.

I play a lot of catch with my daughter. This time it was a sinus infection.

Remember: it takes forty-three muscles to frown and only four to pull the trigger of a decent sniper rifle.

I went to buy a goldfish, and the man in the pet shop said, 'Do you want an aquarium?' I said, 'I don't care what star sign it is.'

I caught the Easter Bunny laying eggs. All I can say is, they're way too small and they don't taste anything like chocolate.

I'm not afraid of hard work. You can tell by the way I fight it.

If you're going to a party tonight, try not to get carried away. In fact, try to leave without any help at all.

For sale: parachute. Only used once, never opened, small stain.

It's less of a bald spot and more of a helipad for mosquitoes.

Short story using religion, sexuality and mystery: 'Good God, I'm pregnant. I wonder who did it?'

My mate dared me to take a dump on a Honda today. I think I'll do it on my own Accord.

A TV can insult your intelligence, but nothing rubs it in like a computer.

I hate my supervisor. Behind her desk it says, 'You don't have to be mad to work here, but it helps.' Mind you, she's written it in her own shit.

Last Monday's meeting of the Apathy Group has just been cancelled.

Don't put words in my mouth. I keep my feet in there.

The surest sign that a man is in love is when he divorces his wife.

I just want people to accept me for who I pretend to be.

I realised I was dyslexic when I went to a toga party dressed as a goat.

How many hard-of-hearing people does it take to screw in a light bulb? Watt?

Ghosts and demons hang out together on Hallowe'en because demons are a ghoul's best friend.

My wife is a sex object. Every time I ask for sex, she objects.

My negative outlook has held me back for far too long. It's time to let my low self-esteem take a turn.

I was diagnosed with anti-social behaviour disorder, so I joined a support group. We never meet.

You can always spot a guy who masturbates a lot by his hands. If you look closely, you'll see he's wearing a wedding ring.

I don't believe in astrology. I'm a Sagittarian, and we're sceptical.

After years of research, Irish scientists have announced why the dinosaurs went extinct. It's because they all died.

I always go the extra mile. The restraining order says I have to.

I've decided I'm not going to focus on my past any more. So if I owe you money, tough shit.

The primary reason bar soap has declined in popularity is because most people don't want to smell like bars.

Procrastination is like masturbation: in the end, you're just screwing yourself.

Sometimes I get the feeling that pets are just using us for our thumbs.

What is invisible and smells like carrots? Rabbit farts.

I tried to donate blood today. I didn't realise you had to give your own.

A computer once beat me at chess, but it was no match for me at kick boxing.

Before I lose my temper I always count to zen.

It's been a lifetime struggle for me to stop spending my lifetime struggling.

The severity of the itch is inversely proportional to the ability to reach it.

My drinking team has a bowling problem.

I'd think more of you if I heard less of you.

I went to buy some camouflage trousers the other day but I couldn't find any.

Statistically, 132% of all people exaggerate.

This just in: bees caught in sting operation.

I've quit my new job as a postman. They handed me my first letter to deliver, I looked at it and thought: 'This isn't for me.'

I believe in sharing the road with other drivers. They can have the part behind me.

If a double-dip recession is so bad, why did they make it sound so delicious?

I love this comfy bed so much that every night I sleep with it under my pillow.

Have they invented a cure for morning people yet?

My wife told me she'd like me to last longer in bed. So I quit my job.

'Carpe diem' is Latin for 'seize the day'. Anybody know the Latin for 'throw it back'?

Just renewed my gin membership.

This tweet is brought to you by Oil of Olay, the favourite oil of Spanish bull fighters.

I was feeling bold but then I lost my b.

This day is pregnant with possibilities, but I just found out they're not mine.

I knew that was a mistake. I recognised it from all the other times I made it.

The only way I will go the extra mile is if I took a wrong turn somewhere.

I like to write 'wake up' on my to do list so I can start the day off by accomplishing something.

My body is a temple. That is, it looks and feels like something that was destroyed by the Romans some 2,500 years ago.

Spending two hours getting ready every morning really brings out your natural beauty.

Women always worry about the things men forget. Men always worry about the things women remember.

I never listen to voicemail that starts with: 'We need to talk.' I just called my girlfriend. She said we broke up three years ago.

Saying, 'Sorry, can we just be friends?' is like saying, 'The dog died but can we keep it?'

Before you get married maybe you should try to assemble some IKEA furniture together first.

The wife and I just got divorced. We split the house: I got the outside.

How did it ever cross the scarecrow's mind that he didn't have a brain?

Monday, Tuesday, Wednesday, Thursday, Friday, Saturday, Sunday... Those were the days.

Beauty is in the eye of the beer holder.

Looking up 'obsolescence' in the Encyclopedia Britannica.

The ninja diet involves eating whatever you want and never getting caught.

I bought some of that emo grass seed the other day. It's brilliant. The grass cuts itself.

I asked my wife if she could let me know the next time she's about to come. She said, 'I don't like ringing you when you're at work.'

When I die, I'm leaving my body to science fiction.

The real moral of 'Rudolf the Red-Nosed Reindeer': if the boss loves you, everybody loves you.

I was not a particularly small child. I was the one who always got picked to play Bethlehem in the school nativity.

I tried to share a kebab with a homeless guy I saw sitting on a bench last night. He told me to get lost and buy my own.

I'm not allowed on cruise ships ever since that whole 'poop deck' misunderstanding.

A guy just yelled at me for texting and driving. I told him to get off my bonnet and mind his own business.

Hearing aid for sale. Give me a shout if you're interested.

My wife and I have decided we don't want any children. If anybody else does we can drop them off tomorrow.

I decided to call my penis 'period', because the wife always moans when she's on it.

If Barbie is so popular, why do you have to buy her friends?

My neighbour knocked on my door and accused me of stealing her underwear off her clothes line. I was so shocked I nearly shit her pants.

It's best not to marry a man who refers to the rehearsal dinner as 'The Last Supper'.

The wife just asked, 'What's that pile of clothes doing on the bathroom floor?' I said, 'It's a dead Jedi.'

My mate likes having sex with goats. Only kidding.

A pessimist is merely someone who recognises that every silver lining is attached to a cloud.

How much money do I need before I can ignore the laws of physics?

Lying about my age is easier now that I have trouble remembering what it is.

A fool and his money are never around when you need them.

One, two, three, four... Does anyone even remember what started the thumb war?

Ever get the feeling we're all in the same handbasket?

The only job in which I could see myself taking my work home with me would be sommelier.

Guys think every girl's dream is to meet the perfect guy. Every girl's dream is to eat without getting fat.

Behind every successful man is a woman. Behind the fall of a successful man is usually another woman.

I can always count on you to be totally unreliable.

Ignore that anchor. It'll go a weigh.

I stood in some dog shit earlier. My mate said, 'Urgh, dude, that's not cool!' So I lit up a cigarette and stood in it again.

When the clock factory burned down there was some second-hand smoke.

Hell hath no fury like a woman who says, 'Nothing's wrong.'

The Wizard of Oz is really just a cautionary tale about the lengths a woman will go to for the right shoes.

My girlfriend says I keep pushing her buttons... She's right: I'm looking for the mute button.

I don't have psychotic episodes. They're more like feature-length presentations.

What do you call a dog with no legs? It doesn't matter what you call him, he isn't going to come.

What's black and white and eats like a horse? A zebra.

Once you start making Freudian slips, it's just one after a mother.

I nearly invested money in the Egyptian tourism industry. But then I realised it was just a pyramid scheme.

With me, things are seldom cut and dried. Most are slashed and burned.

The pen is mightier than the sword and I'm generous. So if we ever duel, I'll let you have the pen.

I'm a bit condescending. That means I talk down to you.

I got slapped by the new girl at work today. I only asked if she spits or swallows. It seemed like a reasonable question considering we work as wine tasters.

Five more minutes' sleep, that's all I ask. But please don't start the countdown for another two hours.

They call me Mr Rhetorical. Can you guess why?

It's OK to have an imaginary friend. But more than one and they can have a quorum and make decisions without you.

They say cheese gives you nightmares. Ridiculous! I'm not scared of cheese.

From my handwriting identification skills, I have carefully deduced that Santa is my secret Valentine every year.

Why is it so hard to find an exercise bike with a nice little basket where I can put my nachos?

If the shoe fits, your mouth is too big.

My doctor said I need to work out with dumbbells. Would any of you like to go jogging with me?

In order to be successful in life, I think we all need to ask ourselves one question... Who can I sue?

Nobody likes surveys. I don't know how I know that.

I never worry about money. What's the use of worrying about something you don't have?

When we were together, you always said you'd die for me. Now that we've broken up, I think it's time you kept your promise.

I once threw a rock 5,280 feet. It was a milestone.

I can't believe it's been five years since the day I stopped smoking. It was the worst twenty-four hours of my life.

An apple a day may keep the doctor away, but I can't afford to buy new iPods every week.

The knack of flying is learning how to throw yourself at the ground and miss.

I love the turtleneck I got for Christmas. Whenever someone starts to ask me something I just retract my head.

I hope my New Year's resolution to only say nice things about people isn't misinterpreted as a vow of silence.

I'm not crazy, I'm a lover. That's why I'm in a jacket that lets me hug myself.

I used to hate eating my greens as a kid. For some reason they tasted much worse than the other crayons.

'I want to be a millionaire, just like my dad.' 'Wow, your dad's a millionaire?' 'No, but he always wanted to be.'

My wife just called me insane. I don't care, she doesn't exist anyway.

A bartender walks into a church, a temple and a mosque. He has no idea how jokes work.

You're only young once. If you act like a fool after that, you're going to need a new excuse.

A man walks into a bar with a roll of tarmac under his arm and says, 'Pint please, and one for the road.'

I go for a stress test on Monday and I should do pretty well. I've been cramming for it my whole life.

How do you get holy water? Boil the hell out of it.

If money doesn't grow on trees then why do banks have branches?

Calling me 'socially awkward' makes it seem like there's a place where I'm not awkward.

I don't think my hairline is going to survive this recession.

I probably wouldn't kill so many houseplants if they could scream for food and water the way my children do.

I just joined a two-step programme because I'm addicted to square dancing.

A dry sense of humour is better than slobbering all over the place.

You know what they say... 'Those who don't learn the lessons of history are doomed to fail their exams.'

My job security clearance is so high that when my wife asks me how my day was, I tell her, then I shoot her.

I try to play it cool with women by pretending not to notice when they're not noticing me.

It's hard to believe that the newest version of Monopoly doesn't come with a government bail-out option.

I have a black eye in karate.

What's easier to pick up the heavier it gets? Women.

The traffic light is always greener in the other lane.

Falling in love is like riding a bike. There's always a chance you might get run over.

Let's get married and blame all our problems on each other.

Is the Origami Society still around? I heard they folded.

Monday is an awful way to spend one-seventh of your life.

I didn't fight my way to the top of the food chain to be a vegetarian.

What is the most important thing to learn in chemistry? Never lick the spoon.

It's difficult to have a committed relationship with a schizophrenic. They're always seeing other people.

Live every day like it's your last. But pay your bills and dress appropriately, just in case it isn't.

I dated an opera singer once, but it was always mi mi mi mi mi.

During a performance at a concert hall in Bermuda last night, the man playing the triangle disappeared.

My wife spends hours in the bathroom teasing her hair. She's a blonde, so I doubt her hair gets her jokes.

I almost forgot to update my status to say I'd been to the gym. What a waste of a workout that would have been.

Men have two emotions: hungry and horny. If you see him without an erection, make him a sandwich.

I'm a keeper. So don't give me anything you want back.

A fool and his money are the best partners in a ménage à trois.

To make a mistake is human; to blame it on somebody else shows management potential.

My ex called to ask some travel advice. I was very adult about it and suggested he take a train to Hawaii.

If bees could talk, I bet they would just drone on and on.

Police officer: 'How do you explain all the cannabis in your loft?' Suspect: 'Someone must have planted it there.'

A positive attitude may not solve all your problems, but it will annoy enough people to make it worth the effort.

The voices in my head may not be real, but they have some good ideas.

I have a feeling these birds wouldn't be so angry if we'd stop firing them through the air.

Rationalisation is Procrastination's spin doctor.

How is it that one careless match can start a forest fire, but it takes a whole box to start a campfire?

The only way I'd be ripped is if I tore a tendon.

I don't like country music, but I don't mean to denigrate those who do. And for those who like country music, denigrate means 'put down'.

I don't think all those screwdrivers really belong to Philip.

I took an IQ test and the results were negative.

I quit Facebook the day I posted a picture of a burger I was about to eat and my doctor poked me and advised against it.

Your face is fine. But you'll have to put a bag over that personality.

The fact that no one understands you does not make you an artist.

I try to see the best in everyone. They, however, are trying harder to hide it from me.

I once went to one of those parties where everyone throws their car keys into the middle of the room. I don't know who got my moped but I've been driving that Peugeot for years.

Yesterday, my new girlfriend and I went on a date to the skating rink, but we were kicked out. We had started to break the ice.

What happens if you get scared half to death twice?

I bought a Christmas tree today. The guy asked me if I was going to put it up myself. I said, 'No, I'll probably put it in the living room.'

Nudists need to be exposed for what they are.

If you can stay calm while all around you is chaos, then you probably haven't completely understood the situation.

I'll live in the moment later.

Women will never be equal to men until they can walk down the street with a bald head and a beer gut and still think they're sexy.

Any machine is a smoke machine if you use it wrongly enough.

If I had a pound for every time I lost count of something, I'd have...

I hate it when my fingers go through the toilet paper. Apart from that I like my job at the nursing home.

Let's be frank here. I'll be Sinatra and you be Zappa.

It's never too late to make a bad impression worse.

If you want to make people angry, lie to them. If you want to make them absolutely livid, tell them the truth.

Things have been so uneventful lately that when I die, I'm hoping someone else's life gets flashed before my eyes.

Let's grow old together. You go first.

'Have I made myself clear?' said the chameleon, as he stood in front of a sheet of glass.

Is the Prime Minister ever going to let that policeman in? He's been at his door for days.

A man walks into a Bar. He's now a qualified law professional.

Say no to drugs when the drugs start asking you questions.

My dad has a weird hobby: he collects empty bottles. Which sounds so much better than saying he's an alcoholic.

I've started keeping two lists: 'to do' and 'too late'.

If money can't make you happy, you won't like poverty either.

I'm not being condescending, I'm just too busy thinking about far more important things you wouldn't understand.

What do we want? A cure for short-term memory loss! When do we want it? When do we want what?

I just can't seem to get a girlfriend even though I can speak two languages fluently. English and Klingon.

I know there are plenty of fish in the sea, but how did I end up on the catch and release list?

I just met John and Jane Doe and their lovely children, Play, Tornay, Potay and Alfred.

Someone asked me recently, what would I rather give up – food or sex? Neither! I'm not falling for that one again, wife.

When I was six my family moved to a new city, but fortunately I was able to track them down.

Wife: 'See that devoted couple? He kisses her every time they meet. Why don't you do that?' Husband: 'I don't know her well enough.'

Time: don't spend it all in one place.

Sorry, Officer. I thought you wanted to race...

Did you hear about the new farmers' dating site? It's full of hoes.

A man has been jailed for forging banknotes. He also got a big fine which he immediately paid in crisp £9 notes.

My wife is leaving because of my weird sexual obsession with legal contracts. I'm still coming to terms with it.

I phoned the local ramblers club today, and this bloke just went on and on.

If the recipe calls for crushed ice, just tell the cubes they'll never amount to anything.

I don't like it when you berate yourself. It's sad, self-pitying and undercuts my efforts.

I roasted a duck last night, but I don't think he got the jokes.

Saying 'I forgive you' is the kindest way to tell someone, 'I still think it's your fault.'

There are two theories to arguing with women. Neither one works.

I'm pretty sure my computer's 'error reports submissions' end up the same place as letters to Santa.

Despite the old saying, 'Don't take your troubles to bed', many women still sleep with their husbands.

Doctor: 'The best thing you can do is give up drinking and smoking and start eating healthy foods.' Patient: 'What's the second best thing?'

A wife is somebody who won't tell you what to do but will get mad when you don't do what she wanted you to do.

How can you give your word and also keep it?

Studying for finals is like playing Tetris: just when you seem to get the facts to fit together, all that you thought you'd learned disappears.

I don't mind being suspect, but I do try to avoid being a defendant.

I would never eat my own words. I'm too full of myself.

My mum's so pessimistic that if there was an Olympics for pessimism, she wouldn't fancy her chances.

You have to remember all the trivia that your girlfriend tells you, because eventually you get tested. She'll go: 'What's my favourite flower?' And you murmur to yourself, 'Shit, I wasn't listening... Self-raising?'

A man who likes to lie in bed can usually find a girl willing to listen to him.

Me: 'Why is that drawer always locked?' Wife: 'Oh I keep Buzz and Woody in there. I lock it so they don't escape.' How naive is she?

The doctor asked me if I ever got lonely. I said, 'No, don't be silly.' After that I got bored playing hospital, and put my dolls away.

I am extremely wise with credit cards and only use them to buy the things I could never afford otherwise.

I choose butter over margarine because I trust cows more than I trust chemists.

If the world doesn't end on 21 December 2012, I have a feeling there will be a lot of babies born on 20 September 2013.

He who lives by the sword shall die by the sword if he is not very good with the sword.

I used to go out with a Welsh girl that had 36DDs. It was a ridiculously long name.

I tried making a couple of quick bucks. It cost me my job when the other scientists caught me injecting the laboratory rabbits with steroids.

Proofreading: checking the alcohol content.

We're equal partners in our marriage. I'm the silent one.

The evening news is where they begin with, 'Good evening', and then proceed to tell you why it isn't.

When the hospital botched my brain surgery I had half a mind to sue.

I killed a mime the other day. I shot him using blanks.

'Press any key to quit' is a lot easier than writing those resignation letters.

One of my family has just been diagnosed with Alzheimer's. If only I could remember who.

Hard, durable, tough... Sorry about the strong language.

I quit smoking using nicotine patches. I put six of them over my mouth.

The fight we had last night was my fault. My wife asked me what was on the TV and I said, 'Dust.'

Your denial is beneath you, and, thanks to the use of hallucinogenic drugs, I see through you.

Consciousness: that annoying time between naps.

I can't put into words how much I love my wife. I'm illiterate.

Sure, I have my little hang-ups just like everybody else. Usually with telemarketers.

Hey, drunk! I'm everybody!

I'm so sick of people lying to me. I've asked three people for the time today and they've all told me something different.

I'm never travelling Virgin Atlantic. I don't want to get on a plane that won't go all the way.

We are all time travellers moving at the speed of exactly sixty minutes per hour.

The world is round, so it has no point.

A Smurf walks into a bar. The bartender says, 'Why so blue?'

It matters not whether you win or lose: what matters is whether I win or lose.

Don't drink and drive. You might hit a bump and spill your drink.

The best way to communicate with a fish is to drop it a line.

A careful driver is one who just saw the car ahead of him get a traffic ticket.

Nature abhors a vacuum, which is why my floors are such a mess.

If you think your dog can't count, try putting three dog treats in your pocket and then give him two of them.

They keep saying the right person will come along. I think mine got hit by a truck.

Wrong-number calls are annoying but not nearly as annoying as right-number calls.

The deification of domestic pets in our culture is out of hand. It's reigning cats and dogs.

I tried sniffing coke once, but the ice cubes got stuck in my nose.

A dog asks a cat, 'How come I've never seen cats making love in public?' The cat says, 'Do you want humans to steal our style like they did yours?'

Crime in multi-storey car parks: that's wrong on so many different levels.

First day of my levitation course today, and I went straight to the top of the class.

If Microsoft Word has taught me anything, it's that if I want to get a point across, I need to use bullets.

I got this new calorie-counting app. Each day I go for a new high score.

A guy tried robbing me at knife-point, but luckily I managed to disarm him. I'd just bought a chainsaw.

Organ doner – worst kebab I've ever had.

A man walks into a bar wearing a tie fastener. The barman says, 'Sorry, we don't like your tie-pin here.'

I don't understand how crows can fly so straight when there are so many crowbars around.

I met my missus at a singles bar. Odd – I thought she was at home looking after the kids.

I don't think playing catch with the kid was the problem so much as the fact that I kept dropping him.

I got kicked out of the dentist for using all the nitrous oxide. Needless to say, I had the last laugh.

Whenever I fill out an application, in the part that says, 'In case of emergency, notify:' I put 'doctor'. What's my mother going to do?

It was so cold this morning I actually saw a politician with his hands in his own pockets.

I love oral sex... It's the phone bill I hate.

I'm in shape. Round is a shape, isn't it?

How do crazy people go through the woods? They take the psychopath.

Déjà moo: the feeling that you've heard this bullshit before.

I won't say ours was a tough school, but we had our own coroner.

I discovered I scream the same way whether I'm about to be devoured by a great white shark or a piece of seaweed has just touched my foot.

Optimism: the eternal belief that you're always one-third of the way to a threesome.

Sex is like comedy: most of the time I don't get it, but I act like I do.

First it's one little white lie. Then they get easier and easier to tell. The next thing you know, you're a lawyer.

I've been way too busy today. Now I can't remember if I lost my dog or if I found a dog leash.

Just bought a head of lettuce. Now I'm wondering what they do with their bodies.

I don't have a licence to kill, but I do have a learner's permit.

I got a cookbook for roadkill. Lovely dinner. Didn't tell me what to do with his bike, though.

I went to the butcher's the other day and I bet him fifty quid that he couldn't reach the meat off the top shelf. He said, 'No, the steaks are too high.'

I have a nut allergy. When I was at school the other kids used to make me play Russian roulette by force-feeding me a packet of Revels.

On a scale of zero to one, how much do you love binary?

Without me, it's just aweso.

I can tell there were birds on my roof from the eavesdroppings.

You know what my sexual fantasy is? To have sex.

What do you call a fish with no eye? A fsh.

She stopped speaking to me when I wouldn't open the car door for her. It's not my fault – I just panicked and swam to the surface.

I'm going to invent a satnav for kids that says, 'We're not there yet... We're not there yet... We're not there yet...'

When people ask me if I'm working hard or hardly working, I like to stab them with a pen and ask if they're hurting hard or hardly hurting.

First the doctor told me the good news – I was going to have a disease named after me.

I joined the Tourette's Society today. It only took a minute to swear me in.

I once dated a butcher. She gave me the cold shoulder.

I saw the most useless guide dog I've ever seen today. It knew nothing about the history of the town; it just sat there, licking its bollocks.

What if there were no hypothetical questions?

I'm in training for a movie marathon.

The easiest way for me to tell if my wife is really listening to me is if she rolls her eyes.

'I'm going to make love to you all the way into next week!' I said to my wife, at 11.59 on Sunday night.

If you think life is unfair, you're not going to be too thrilled about death.

I just sold a lawn mower on eBay. That'll be the last time my neighbour wakes me up on a Saturday.

The main ingredient in hand sanitiser is paranoia.

My doctor told me I should get outside more, so I took up smoking.

How many Marxists does it take to change a light bulb? None. The light bulb contains the seeds of its own revolution.

Want an anagram of 'rodeo incidents'? Consider it done.

Girls love a guy who can make them laugh. How lucky I am to be blessed with such a small penis.

A relationship is the period of time between 'I love you' and 'Everything you do pisses me off'.

In a new poll, 80 per cent of Japanese women admitted to having faked origami.

I really like left-handed gloves. Although, on the other hand, I don't.

My apathy is at an all-time whatever.

I'm always a little disappointed when I walk away from my car and it doesn't explode after I press the lock button.

What do you get if you cross a road with a chicken? Questioned, apparently.

The 'check engine' light came on, so I did. Yep. Still there.

What did the bra say to the hat? You go on a head, I'll give these two a lift.

Two lions are walking down the aisle of a supermarket. One turns to the other and says, 'Quiet in here today, isn't it?'

I enjoy watching wrestling a lot more if I think of it as competitive hugging.

I tried runway modelling once. It was a huge disaster. Now I'm not allowed back at the airport.

Emoticons are the mimes of the Internet.

My Twitter feed mirrors my diet. A little too much junk.

'Must you really lick the knife?' 'Sorry, force of habit,' I said. 'Loads of people do it though, don't they?' 'Yes, but not during surgery, Doctor.'

I found a present for my mother-in-law in the loft – I'll take it up to her later.

Baby snakes probably throw a lot of hissy fits.

Women don't want to hear stories about your ex unless it's the one where she gets chased by a bear after eating three doughnuts.

In Paris, they just stared when I spoke to them in French. I never did manage to make those idiots understand their own language.

I'm ageing like fine wine: I spend a lot of time lying down on my side.

Pornography is often frowned upon, but that's only because I'm concentrating.

If I had to describe myself in one word, it would be 'bad at following directions'.

I was once dating a girl who worked for an organ donor clinic, but I had to dump her. She only wanted me for my body.

I'm at the age where I need to start watching what I eat, so I spend a lot of time looking at food.

Optimist: 'The glass is half full.' Pessimist: 'The glass is half empty.' Conspiracy theorist: 'The government is hoarding the water!'

I thought my girlfriend might be The One, but after finding police, nurse and maid uniforms in her wardrobe, I realised she can't hold a job down.

My wife treats me like a god: she barely notices I exist until she wants something.

Many a wife thinks her husband is the world's greatest lover. But she can never catch him at it.

Sex is like air: it's not that important unless you aren't getting any.

I used to own a balloon company, but I couldn't keep up with the high cost of inflation.

I met the fella who invented the crossword the other day – can't remember his name, it was P something T something R.

Actually, Officer, if you factor in the earth's rotation, we were all speeding.

DNA: Association of National Dyslexics.

I keep trying to ostracise people but I can't get their attention.

Tomorrow: a mystical land where 99 per cent of all human productivity, motivation and achievement is stored.

Corduroy pillows: they're making headlines!

Optimism: where there's a will, there's a way. Pessimism: where there's a will, someone died.

My lawyer said he wanted a retainer, but I'm not sure why I should have to pay for his dental work.

Some guy waved to me and then walked up and said, 'Sorry, I thought you were someone else.' I said, 'I am.'

You'd think the self-checkout lanes would have more mirrors.

Bulldozer: someone who can sleep through a politician's speech.

I just finished masturbating under the sheet. I hope the barber didn't notice.

I can stop a speeding bullet. Once.

As an alternative to dieting, simply refer to yourself as 'value-sized'.

I was playing chess with my friend and he said, 'Let's make this interesting.' So we stopped playing chess.

'Doctor! Doctor! I'm scared of Father Christmas.' 'Not to worry. You're just a little Claus-trophobic.'

I poured Spot remover on my dog. Now he's gone.

What has four legs and an arm? A happy pit bull.

An avalanche is what happens when all hill breaks loose.

Did you hear about the blonde accountant? She absconded with all of the accounts payable.

I don't think I've ever been told I'm a bad listener.

My wife's going through 'The Change'. We're going to be late for dinner, I just know it.

I called my girlfriend a whore during sex once. She made me pay for that afterwards.

I don't like the way this guy in the mirror is looking at me.

My word is my bond, and that word is 'glue'.

Any food can be a superfood if you put a little cape on it.

My contacts have really been bothering me lately. So I deleted them from my phone.

Some people are so incapable of self-loathing you can't help but do it for them.

I should've known it wasn't going to work out between my ex-wife and me. After all, I'm a Libra and she's a bitch.

Italics are a bit forward aren't they?

If the police arrest a mime, do they tell him he has the right to remain silent?

I'm about to rewrite history. History.

We have ways of making you talk. What we really need is a way to make you shut up.

My therapist said I have multiple personalities and rage issues. So we hit him.

I've just bought a hive, but it's not producing any honey. It's as if the occupants don't have a clue what to do. Bloody new bees.

I have an on-again off-again relationship with clothing.

If you want to understand politics, you have to read between the lies.

I just invited all the guys at my Arsonists Anonymous group to a house-warming party.

I wish I could remember that joke I heard about Alzheimer's.

Did you hear about the Christmas-themed porn? Jesus gets nailed.

I like long walks, especially when they're taken by people who annoy me.

A bit of advice: never read a pop-up book about giraffes.

I was pulled over by the police... 'Have we been drinking, sir?' 'No,' I replied. 'I don't remember you buying me a pint.'

My wife just phoned me and said, 'I've got water in the carburettor.' I said, 'Where's the car?' 'In the river,' she said.

I was at the beach the other day and loads of meat floated past. It was a bit choppy.

I'd be much happier about my test results coming back negative if it hadn't been a personality test.

As tales go, my life is more cautionary than fairy.

Breaking news: '£10,000 Jewellery Snatch.' Wow, these vajazzles are really getting out of hand.

If you were twelve when 'Red Red Wine' was released then this year UB40.

'Doctor! Doctor! How long can a man live without a brain?' 'I don't know. How old are you?'

Diplomacy is the art of letting someone else have your way.

I went to the chemist and said, 'I've got a really bad headache. Can you make me something up?' He said, 'Frank Sinatra was in here earlier.'

The missus said, 'I'm fed up with you being so lazy: pack your bags and leave.' I said, 'You pack them.'

Be a minimalist. It's the least you can do.

I recently joined my local gym. So far, I've lost ninety pounds... But no weight.

Life is like a penis: simple, soft, straight, relaxed and hanging freely. Then women make it hard.

I'll be tweeting telepathically today, so if you think of something funny, that's me.

I understand, you love interfering. What do you want, a meddle?

Warm milky drinks do not cure insomnia... Twelve pints of beer and half a bottle of Jack Daniels will, though.

How does Bob Marley like his doughnuts? Wi' jam in!

If I were an accountant, I'd call myself The Thought. My slogan would be, 'It's the Thought that Counts.'

The only yoga stretch I've perfected is the yawn.

I'm going to take a hot shower. It's the same as a normal shower, but with me in it.

It's easy to distract fat people. Piece of cake.

One day I would like to hit the refresh button and actually feel refreshed.

Yesterday I set my Wi-Fi name to 'Hack this if you can'. When I checked it today, it was called 'Challenge accepted'.

The last time my body was swimsuit ready I was wearing armbands.

My wife still has an hourglass figure. Just with a few extra minutes.

It's time to take stock. Go home with some office supplies.

I was talking to the butcher last night and he had blood all down his shirt. I wonder how he got that nickname working in an office, though.

My children won't even eat chips because some know-all bastard at school told them a potato was a vegetable.

I shaved my commute time in half by changing my car's horn to sound like gunfire.

I killed a wasp with my shoe. I don't care how big the wasp is – it's not stealing my shoe.

You see, my next-door neighbour worships exhaust pipes. He's a catholic converter.

Nothing beats the love of a really good woman. Except the love of a really bad woman.

My friend says she suffers from water retention. It looks more like cake retention to me.

To all of those people who said that I would never amount to anything, I can now truly say, 'How did you know?'

Why was six afraid of seven? Because seven eight nine.

Some advice: keep your eyes wide open before marriage and half shut afterwards.

I'd love to make money at home in my spare time. But counterfeiting is harder than you'd think.

Ironically, game hens aren't much fun.

The hardest part about going to Hypochondriacs Anonymous is admitting that you don't have a problem.

Last night, hot words flew between us. She threw alphabet soup in my face.

The dog: 'OK, I messed up. But you don't have to rub my nose in it.'

The first rule of Thesaurus Club is, you don't talk about, mention, speak of, discuss or chat about Thesaurus Club.

If you sign up for *Pig Breeders Weekly*, you get a free pen.

My doctor said that my heavy drinking was making me paranoid. 'So when did you have your last drink?' he asked. I said, 'What do you mean, "last"?'

Poodles aren't as absorbent as they look.

I never run with scissors. Actually, those last two words were unnecessary.

Sometimes a majority just means all the fools are on the same side.

Is there any dance more positive than the can-can?

Last night my girlfriend and I watched three DVDs back-to-back. Luckily, I was the one facing the telly.

'I kicked a football as hard as I could at my girlfriend yesterday.' 'Why did you do that?' 'I had to see if she was a keeper.'

Wine improves with age. The older I get, the more I like it.

Nothing really prepares you for when your phone rings while you're fake talking on it.

In the Tantric Sex Olympics, the loser comes first.

I looked up 'lazy' in a business thesaurus and now I can add 'delegator' to my list of strengths.

Wife and dog missing. Reward for dog.

Another twelve-step programme and I still can't dance.

An ice-cream seller was found today on the floor of his van covered in hundreds and thousands. Police said he topped himself.

My girlfriend texted me earlier: 'Why don't you ever put an x at the end of your texts?' I replied, 'Sorry babe. Michelle.'

Procrastinators of the world, UNITE! Tomorrow.

My dad was behind bars for twenty years. He was a hell of a bartender.

My brother's in prison for something he didn't do. He didn't run fast enough.

If you keep your feet firmly on the ground, you'll have trouble putting on your trousers.

My dogs are excellent guard dogs. As long as the burglars remember to ring the doorbell.

Give a man a fish and he will eat for a day. Teach him how to fish, and he will sit in a boat and drink beer all day.

Two years ago I married a lovely young virgin, and if that doesn't change soon, I'm going to divorce her.

If at first you don't succeed, skydiving is not for you.

I've been teaching hobbits how to play cricket. Bilbo's really good at catching. He can't really Frodo.

When I get younger I'm going to be a time traveller.

If there's one thing I can't stand, it's up.

At every party there are two kinds of people: those who want to go home and those who don't. The trouble is, they're usually married to each other.

I may be middle-class, but I'm hard. Al dente, you might say.

An intellectual thought doesn't last long in my head. It can't stand the solitary confinement.

Each day is like a gift. A gift from someone who doesn't know your size and doesn't bother to include the receipt.

My mate's been really depressed and confused ever since he couldn't find the notes he did for his book. I think he's lost the plot.

My wife moans at me to say 'I did' instead of 'I done' because it's not proper grammar. Easier said than did.

I watered my houseplants with Smart Water and now they're doing my taxes.

The secret to a welcome opinion is keeping it to yourself.

Be careful when it comes to reincarnation... One time I asked to be a singer and I spent thirty years as a sewing machine.

People like crowds. The bigger the crowd, the more people show up. Small crowd, hardly anyone shows up.

My intellectual property is in foreclosure.

Some drink at the fountain of knowledge. Others just gargle.

'Doctor! Doctor! My husband makes me boiling mad!' 'Now, just simmer down.'

I schedule conference calls just so I can cancel them at the last minute. Because everybody loves that guy.

They say it's National Margarita Day, but I'd take that with a grain of salt if I were you.

Give a man a job and you have an employee. Teach a man how to shift blame and you have a manager.

My wife's on her way back from the shrink. I can't wait to find out what I need to work on.

I really need a diet plan that will take my breadth away.

Does the name Pavlov ring a bell?

I'm so broke, I can't even pay attention.

I have costraphobia: fear of high prices.

I know I'm paranoid, but am I paranoid enough?

I have a drinking problem. The bar closes at 2 a.m.

I may only be a branch manager for now, but one day I hope to control the whole tree.

I've always been prone to car sickness... Usually when the monthly payment is due.

Not to boast, but before something can be labelled 'idiot proof', they have to run it by me.

At last I've managed to find my girlfriend's G-spot! Who would have thought her sister had it all the time?

I didn't pay my syntax, and got a poorly constructed prison sentence.

My wife always has a headache so I've started taking a tablet to bed with me. It's got all of the porn I need on it.

I can't go to spelling competitions. I'm allergic to bees.

The postal service has got so slow that last month my flower seeds arrived as a bouquet.

Facing your fears builds strength, but running away from them makes for an excellent cardio workout.

I slept like a log last night. Woke up in the fireplace.

I was thinking about how people seem to read the Bible a lot more as they get older, and then it dawned on me – they're cramming for their final exam.

When I was younger, my brother's suicide attempt hit me hard. He landed on me when he jumped out of the window.

I put the o in illiterate.

If someday we all go to jail for downloading music, I just hope they split us by music genre.

The three dimensions of a credit card are length, width and debt.

Speech therapists: they have ways of making you talk.

I think the Discovery Channel should be on a different channel every day.

I miss my bus every morning. I never realised how attached we'd become until I bought my car.

Fault finding is like window washing. All the dirt seems to be on the other side.

Children are a great comfort in your old age. And they help you get there faster, too.

Be nice to your kids: they'll choose your nursing home.

Do infants enjoy infancy as much as adults enjoy adultery?

They say you are what you eat. So I'm going to start eating skinny people.

I always cry after sex. £500 is a lot of money.

Whenever someone asks, 'Can I be perfectly honest with you?' The answer should always be, 'No.'

I got in a fight one time with a really big guy, and he said, 'I'm going to mop the floor with your face.' I said, 'You'll be sorry.' He said, 'Oh, yeah? Why?' I said, 'Well, you won't be able to get into the corners very well.'

My mate phoned me earlier and said, 'Do you fancy moving abroad?' 'Is she dead like the last one?' I replied.

Whatever you do, try not to sneeze during sex. Most couples don't like to discover that they're being watched.

Funny new trend at the office: people have started naming the food in the company fridge. Today I had a tuna sandwich named Bob.

I hate clichés. They're a dime a dozen.

If I want something done right, the last thing I would do is do it myself.

Men are a bit like spiders... They're bound to have sticky hands after being on the web.

I do ten sit-ups every morning. It might not sound like much, but there are only so many times you can hit the snooze button.

My wife got good news from the doctor today. He said she wasn't going to die if she didn't get that new designer handbag.

The difference between a baby and a boyfriend is you can leave a baby alone with the babysitter.

I'm not myself today. Maybe I'm you.

I've always wanted to get into a cab and yell, 'Follow that car!'

Before you criticise someone, you should walk a mile in their shoes. That way, when you criticise them, you're a mile away and you have their shoes.

I took a physics course that was so hard I couldn't find the classroom.

I used to think never forgetting a face was a good thing until I saw yours.

Somebody should tell actresses over forty that they're all buying the same face.

How hard can it be to proof red?

Talk about others and you're a gossip. Talk about yourself and you're a bore.

The difference between divorce and legal separation is that a legal separation gives a husband time to hide his money.

Recipe calls for a quarter cup of thyme. That's fifteen minutes, right?

I half intend almost half of what I think I mean to say.

The closest I've ever got to murder is holding cookies under the milk until the bubbles stopped.

What if the light we see at the end of the tunnel when we die is really just us being pushed out of a vagina into our next life?

I understand the concept of cooking and cleaning but not how it applies to me.

We're living in a Golden Age. All you need is gold.

I always duck down in the seat when I see a police officer, so he can't see me texting while driving.

My morning-after pill is ibuprofen.

Apparently everyone in my town thinks the saying is, 'Don't think and drive.'

Common sense: so rare it's a goddamn superpower.

Shooting for the stars really is a waste of bullets.

If winning isn't everything why do they keep score?

How do you get a sweet little old lady to say the F word? Get another sweet little old lady to yell 'Bingo!'

I'm not a doctor, but I play one in the emergency room until security turns up.

After screaming and crying at 3 o'clock this morning due to a terrible nightmare, my son came into my bedroom. 'Dad, are you OK?'

I bet in prison everyone's Facebook relationship status is set to 'it's complicated'.

It's too bad that it's easier to get older than it is to get wiser.

Twitter is kind of like putting the voices in your head on speakerphone.

Does court-ordered community service count as work experience?

I'm really tired from all of this metamorphosising from a single cell.

What is it with chimpanzees and that middle parting? Stuck in the '20s, aren't they?

I thought having my wife gone was going to be all kinds of fun. Turns out I'm not as much fun as I thought I was.

Please don't interrupt me while I'm ignoring you.

In this year's Valentine's card I wrote: 'I still love you. See last year's card for full details.'

I drew pupils on my eyelids in case I want to take a nap at work.

Why is there an expiration date on sour cream?

Just ignore me. That's what I do.

Buy a parrot and teach him how to say this one thing: 'Help, they turned me into a parrot!'

After ninety minutes of waiting in line I finally have COD. I couldn't believe the line at the fish counter.

Ever notice that a drunk woman in high heels looks like a baby giraffe trying to walk?

The North Korea/South Korea debacle at the Olympics wasn't a great start to things. But they got the Swiss flag right, which is a big plus.

A sandwich walks into a bar and the bartender says, 'Sorry buddy, white breads only.'

Dog heaven is full of tennis balls. Dog hell is full of cats.

I like work. It fascinates me. I can sit and look at it for hours.

Tragically I was an only twin.

Love wouldn't be so blind if the Braille weren't so great.

Well, what day will you have time for my shenanigans?

I consider the word Dodge on the front of my truck fair warning to jaywalkers.

Dating tip: sometimes the sparks are flying because you're scraping rock bottom.

Looking back on the UK riots of August 2011, I really wish I had taken a stand. I got a lovely new TV for Christmas, but it looks silly on the floor.

Pants: not the best thing on earth, but next to it.

Warning: the consumption of alcohol may cause you to think you can sing.

The best way to get a man's attention is to mute the TV.

Sometimes I miss being in a relationship, but then I look at my wallet and I feel all right again.

In class: 2 + 2 = 4. Homework: 2 + 4 + 2 = 8. Exam: John had 4 apples. He eats one and gives one to a friend. Calculate the sun's mass.

Crack, heroin and meth ought to be manufactured by the pharmaceutical companies. That way, nobody would be able to afford them.

I will not tell anyone you said, 'Hi.'

Lifestyle tip: the best way to avoid parking tickets is to remove your windshield wipers.

Hey, you know that compound that freezes off warts? How much would you need to make an entire co-worker disappear?

There may be no excuse for laziness, but I'm still looking.

The worst thing about growing old is having to listen to a lot of advice from one's children.

What if April Fools' Day doesn't exist and it's been the longest prank in history?

Make sure your goals are unattainable so you'll feel better when you give up on them.

People who make medicine clearly have no idea what fruit tastes like.

Me: 'I'd like to report a disturbance.' Police dispatcher: 'OK, where, sir?' Me: 'In the force, I can feel it.'

What do you call a lawyer who's gone bad? Politician.

All I really want is to be understood. That's why I'm yelling.

I don't know why I even bother having a smartphone any more. It spends so much time on charge, you might as well call it a landline.

'Nuclear option' is not a button on this microwave. But it should be.

All bread is flatbread if you sit on it.

My mate texted me earlier, 'Go outside... Hail stones!' I replied, 'What weird religion are you trying to get me to join?'

I never know whether to screw up my taxes myself or hire a professional to do it.

Mornings probably wouldn't be so bad if they didn't always catch me in the middle of a dead sleep.

You can fool some of the people all of the time. Mostly, those people are in Management.

I wonder how police on bikes arrest people. 'All right, get in the basket.'

The best advice that I can give you is to not listen to anything that I say.

I chose the road less travelled. Now where the hell am I?

I hate when I'm at someone's house and they keep asking stupid questions like, 'Who are you?' And, 'Is that a gun?'

When I want to hide money from my wife, I put it with her keys.

'Hello, 999? I think my husband is trying to bore me to death.'

I'm pretty sure I could win the Olympic gold for going downhill.

I'm proof that God has a sense of humour.

Never pick a fight with an ugly person; they've got nothing to lose.

I picked a bad week to get out of bed.

The bigger they are, the harder I fall.

If you think nobody cares if you're alive, try missing a couple of bill payments.

The only yoga stretch I've perfected is the yawn.

If you want a man's heart, go through his stomach. If you want his money, go through his pockets.

When my choice is to be kind or to be right, I choose to be kinda right.

Farmers never know exactly how many sheep they have. They fall asleep every time they try to count them.

We will continue having meetings every day until I find out why no work is getting done.

Well, that was awkward. I was just about to hug someone extremely attractive and I walked right into the mirror.

I understand good things come to those who wait. Might I enquire, how long is the line?

Don't worry about biting off more than you can chew. Your mouth is probably a lot bigger than you think.

Out to dinner sounds much more stable than out to lunch.

In a restaurant window: 'Eat now – Pay waiter.'

Doesn't expecting the unexpected make the unexpected become the expected?

Watching porn at night is so inconvenient. I mean how can the difference between mute and one volume bar be so much?

If you're not using social media to spout your uninformed opinions then you're totally missing the point of the Internet.

If money talks, why won't it have a conversation with me?

No one would listen to you talk if they didn't know it was their turn next.

'Measure once, cut twice.' I don't think this dyslexic carpenter is going to work out.

Life is proving to be much more challenging than TV made it out to be.

It's a small world, but I wouldn't want to have to paint it.

There should be a children's song called 'If you're happy and you know it, keep it to yourself and let your parents sleep'.

My thoughts ought to be ashamed of themselves.

So many women, so little time to disappoint them all.

I hate it when I key someone's car, then realise it's my own car.

Men look at a woman's behind and go 'Oh! What an ass!' Women look at a man's face and go 'Oh! What an ass!'

A bargain is something you don't need at a price you can't resist.

There's an old proverb that says pretty much whatever you want it to.

I took a lie detector test. No, I didn't.

I wish people had a brightness setting.

Not even my skin is skintight.

Some very sweaty geniuses are actually 100 per cent perspiration.

I'd go to the gym more often, but I can never find a parking space near the front door.

Shouldn't the air and space museum be empty?

What did the vampire say to the teacher? See you next period.

When I say 'word to the wise', what I really mean is 'word to the stupid'.

Accidentally quoting lyrics may be funny or embarrassing, but in the end, it doesn't even matter.

Sunny today with a slight chance of participation.

Smartphone users need to get their head out of their apps.

I fish, therefore I lie.

The man who smiles when things go wrong has thought of someone to blame it on.

I feel for footballers. I know what it's like to try to score for ninety minutes and get nowhere.

As tales go, my life is more cautionary than fairy.

I'm just going to delete a few dumb tweets, I'll be right back. Oh, can I have your password?

'My spirits are up.' – Me, checking the prices at the off-licence.

Tablet computers are hard to swallow.

Blackpool is just like Las Vegas – you can pay for nookie with chips.

Their plan for a paperless office looked good, on paper...

I ignored my doctor's advice and ended up in hospital. Maybe I should have stopped shagging his wife.

Just remember, if the world didn't suck, we'd all fall off.

The only time I laugh out loud at jokes is when my boss is telling them.

Why do they use sterilised needles for death by lethal injection?

My wife would be a great success on the parole board. She never lets anyone finish a sentence.

Good girls are bad girls that never get caught.

Guys like you don't grow on trees. They swing from them.

All my friends can see right through me – Casper the Ghost.

If you're not part of the solution, you're part of this meeting.

I'm surprised my alarm clock hasn't hit me back yet.

Life is like a dick: sometimes it gets hard for no reason at all.

We are all connected and we are all one. Except for you.

I don't understand you. You don't understand me. What else do we have in common?

Weekend's coming up. What do you say we surf the real world?

If it weren't for the fact that the TV and the fridge are so far apart, some of us wouldn't get any exercise at all.

It might look like I'm doing nothing, but at the cellular level I'm really quite busy.

Yes, I had camouflage parachute pants in the '80s, but in my defence, I was in the army's elite breakdancing unit.

Love is blind. Hate is deaf. You'd think Stupid would be mute, but I just keep on talking.

Ides of March fact: after Brutus murdered Caesar, he went on to become Popeye's nemesis.

No matter how many times I watch my wedding video I always say 'I do'.

I'm on that diet where you eat everything you want and pray for a miracle.

Who remembers when a journey of a thousand miles began with Dad saying, 'I know a shortcut'?

Clearly your mouth was intended for a much larger person.

Bank robbers give a bad name to people who just want to deposit their cheque with a mask on.

I just found my life remote control. This changes everything.

Today I saw a baby with a bib that said, 'This dumbass put my cape on backwards.'

I broke a light bulb today. Seven years of bad ideas?

I'm not sure which pants to wear today – smarty or fancy?

Google: helping drinking buddies determine who is right and wrong since 1997.

I took a walk on the wild side... I got arrested for trespassing.

It's been years since I went out of my mind. I doubt I'll ever go back.

Carrier pigeons were the original form of text message.

Some day you'll go far. And with any luck, you'll stay there.

How many men does it take to change a roll of toilet paper? We don't know; it's never happened before.

My fan has three speeds: useless, useless and wind tunnel.

It's really easy to lose your train of thought when the tracks don't lead to the station.

Of course I've been flossing. I've also been pulling over to make phone calls and reporting my eBay income.

Why is the place in a stadium where people sit called a stand?

Broken glass tastes just like blood.

Real blondes don't drive smart cars.

March came in like a lion. Oh wait ... that was my wife. Never mind.

I don't trust anything that could kill me, like wild animals or angry women.

Brain freeze: legitimate issue or zombie treat?

Rome did not create a great empire by having meetings – they did it by killing all those who opposed them.

Some people are only alive because it's illegal to shoot them.

Fun fact: the Mamas & Papas song 'Monday, Monday' was inspired by the Beatles song 'Eight Days A Week'.

You don't have to lie to me. That's what the government's for.

A hard thing about a business is minding your own.

I'm hoping this holiday will go into overtime.

Twitter feels a lot like group therapy ... only everyone is talking at once and no one wants to be cured.

Babies: people who wield disproportionate power, considering they can't even speak the language.

Take your troubles like a man. Blame them on your wife.

Exorcism is nothing but the removal of a beast implant.

I got my tax refund yesterday. Now, I'm just trying to decide which vending machine to spend it at.

Therapy has taught me that it is all your fault.

I'm 72 per cent water anyway – this vodka doesn't need a mixer.

God's last name is not 'Dammit'.

A woman told me that I take the 'e' out of 'dude'. She digs me, right?

And God created light, and saw that it was good. Then God created man, and saw that it was hilarious.

Before they invented drawing boards, what did they go back to?

I don't know what I'd do without Twitter. Probably my work.

'Hello, is that 555555?' 'Yes.' 'Can you call an ambulance for me? I've glued my finger to the phone.'

You leaving the office for two weeks is all the holiday time I need.

Don't confuse my personality with my attitude. My personality is who I am, and my attitude depends on who you are.

I love the way garages leave black buckets outside for your dead flowers.

The blue whale ejaculates over 40 gallons of sperm when mating, but only 10 per cent enters the female. And you always wondered why the sea tasted salty.

My ex-wife believed marriage should be between a man, a woman, her mother, her sisters and the neighbours across the street.

Why does the sound of the newspaper opening always remind my wife that the rubbish needs taking out?

I used to get lost in the shuffle. Now I shuffle along with the lost.

If it wasn't for dumb luck, most people would just be dumb.

Don't think of it as getting older, think of it as a greycation.

I'm living the dream! I sleep all the time.

If we're all God's children, what's so special about Jesus?

The best place to miss a train is at a crossing.

I'm as confused as a baby in a topless bar.

I'm out of my mind, but feel free to leave a message.

I just looked at the price of pushchairs. I think we're going to have an indoor baby.

My dog is taking a cat nap.

Hippopotomonstrosesquippedaliophobia: fear of long words.

Not only do I not know what's going on, I wouldn't know what to do about it if I did.

What is a social life and where can I download one?

If you can't say something constructive to me, just give me a shallow compliment.

Let's pretend to get together soon.

When things get me down, I take a deep breath and go to my happy place. The fridge.

I believe that every person has a story to tell ... which is why I stay at home.

She was the flabbiest stripper I've ever seen. When she ran off the stage she started her own applause.

Downhill: that's how I roll.

Look, I don't want to say I'm better than you. So I'll just write it down. Better ... than ... you...

I just gave my new girlfriend a high five. Or, as I like to call it, the clap.

I wonder if football tables look like shish kebab buffets to a cannibal.

My local supermarket uses four checkouts. Unless it's really busy: then they use one.

A human cannonball can't quit before he's fired.

The trouble with jogging is that, by the time you realise you're not in shape, it's too far to walk back.

I got a dig bick. You this read wrong. You read that wrong too.

Did Styx and the Stones ever perform together?

Trainspotters: how sad are they? I counted thirty-five the other day.

Everything you eat and anything you do will end up killing you. Have a great week.

You and I are best friends. Always remember that I will pick you up if you fall. Right after I stop laughing.

It's far easier to be flexible when you're spineless.

I'm a mover and shaker. When I move, I shake.

Women, not all blokes are talking to you because they want to get in your pants... Sometimes they want to get in your friends' pants.

I'm not saying my wife is fat, but the other day I found a copy of *Playboy* in her centre fold.

Men, chocolate and coffee are all better rich.

I reject your reality and substitute my own.

Good mothers let you lick the beaters when they're making a cake. Great mothers turn the mixer off first.

Frankly, I don't know why so many people go looking for trouble. It's usually right behind them and gaining ground.

Did I just hear that New York has legalised some-sex marriage?

Women are like police. They have all the evidence in the world against you but they still ask for your confession.

Plane crashes are caused when they develop a bad altitude.

I had no idea time zones were so far apart... I just landed in China and it's New Year, apparently.

Life was much simpler when Apple and Blackberry were just fruits.

If I had more skill in what I'm attempting, I wouldn't need so much courage.

Feel like you're sleeping with a woman by shaving just one leg.

Of the world's many superheroes, my favourite's The Ice-Cream Man.

Nobody notices what I do until I don't do it.

I go from stool to stool in singles bars hoping to get lucky, but there's never any gum under any of them.

I'm generally known as the 'who brought that guy?' of parties.

I'm just a few crows short of a murder.

My face is becoming a made-for-TV plot line, where a new wrinkle emerges every day.

Philosophy graduates ask. '*Why* do you want fries with that?'

My girlfriend got me a £20 cinema voucher for my birthday, which was really sweet of her. It meant I could buy a small Coke.

Chocoholics Anonymous doesn't exist, because no one wants to quit.

A man says to his wife, 'I had a wet dream about you last night. I dreamt you got run over by a bus and I pissed myself laughing.'

Following gorgeous lady who lives down the road from me on Twitter. Sorry, did I say Twitter? I meant my bike.

I believe in taking the bull by the horns. Then I believe in steering it in the direction of whoever's annoying me.

No one makes a bigger fuss about driving to work than fire engines.

Yawn: an honest opinion openly expressed.

Waking the Dead: One letter away from being the most controversial TV show ever made.

Wally must owe a lot of people money.

I bet lawyers love to eat trial mix.

I always find something I've lost when I do my spring cleaning. This year it was my mind.

Don't let depression ruin your future. That's what relationships are for.

Why doesn't Santa visit naughty kids any more? Have you seen the price of coal?

Why aren't lawyers sworn to tell the truth along with everyone else at the proceedings?

Let's go somewhere that we can be alone without each other.

I wish I was the person I've always wanted to be. He's rich.

I try not to be as hard on myself as I am on other people.

The problem with people who have no vices is that you can pretty much guarantee they're going to have some very annoying virtues.

I always add 'capers' to my shopping list because I love madcap hijinks and fun.

My new sports car is just like my 11-inch penis. I don't have a new sports car.

I'm not much of a cook, but I don't need a recipe for disaster. I can make one with pretty much any ingredients.

Dear Fork, I thought you should know, you have a son. His name is Spork. Love, Spoon. P.S. He has your hair.

Did you know that it takes forty-three muscles to frown? That's why I try to help my fat friends to burn calories by insulting them all the time.

When tempted to fight fire with fire, remember that the fire brigade normally use water.

I taught myself how to read minds recently. But around here all the pages seem to be blank.

'I let a fly into the house.' 'Not to worry, I'll swat it.' 'It was a dragonfly.' 'Then I'll slay it.'